Committed
Couples

Committed Couples

*God's Plan for Marriage
and the Family*

Jimmy Ray Lee

Baker Books

A Division of Baker Book House Co.
Grand Rapids, Michigan 49516

© 1995 by Jimmy Ray Lee

Published by Baker Books
a division of Baker Book House Company
P.O. Box 6287, Grand Rapids, MI 49516-6287

Second printing, July 1997

Printed in the United States of America

ISBN 0-8010-5693-4

For current information about all releases from Baker Book House, visit our web site:
http://www.bakerbooks.com

To my wife, Louise, who is a godly example of a wife and mother. "A wife of noble character . . . is worth far more than rubies" (Prov. 31:10).

Contents

Part 3   Resources

Part One
A Personal Guide

Introduction

Committed Couples is for married couples or engaged-to-be-married couples who are committed to God's plan for marriage and family relationships. The various aspects of God's design for marriage and the principles that support this sacred institution are highlighted.

The purpose of *Committed Couples* is to help each married couple grow spiritually and emotionally in their relationship to each other through an awareness and application of biblical principles. It is important that each participant enter *Committed Couples* with *the purpose of wanting to be all God would have him/her to be in his/her marriage rather than trying to change his/her partner.* If you have not received Christ as your Savior, we invite you to make this important decision. Please see page 163.

Committed Couples is not a substitute for psychological care. We never advise anyone to stop taking medication or discontinue a doctor's care.

There is a page at the end of each session for you to write down your thoughts.

May the Lord bless you and keep his hand on you.

Session One

In the Beginning — Marriage

1. Introduction

Take thirty minutes each day to be alone with God for the purpose of meditation and prayer. Read Genesis 1–3. What do these chapters mean to you, and how do they apply to your life?

2. Self-Awareness

The goal of *Committed Couples* is to help each married couple grow spiritually and emotionally in their relationship to each other through an awareness and application of biblical principles. It is important for each participant to enter this group wanting to be all God would have him/her to be in his/her marriage rather than trying to change his/her partner.

In each of the sessions it is also important for one to speak for oneself—not for one's spouse. In your own words describe what *you* want to receive from *Committed Couples*.

3. Spiritual Awareness

Read Genesis 2:22–24. Marriage is an institution of God. God's design for marriage is presented in the first marriage relationship.

Check box when read	
☐ Genesis 2:22–24	God is the creator of the marriage relationship.
☐ Genesis 3:20; Leviticus 18:22	Heterosexuality is God's design for marriage. Adam was male; Eve, female.
☐ Genesis 4:1; Hebrews 13:4	Monogamy is God's design for marriage. God gave Adam one wife.
☐ Matthew 19:4–5	God's design for marriage is for physical and spiritual unity.
☐ Matthew 19:6	God's design for marriage is permanency.

☐ Genesis 5:1–2	☐ Romans 1:18–32	☐ Romans 5:14
☐ 1 Corinthians 15:22	☐ 1 Corinthians 15:45	☐ 2 Corinthians 11:3
☐ 1 Timothy 2:13		

4. Spiritual Application

At the very dawn of history God said, "It is not good for the man to be alone. I will make a helper suitable for him" (Gen. 2:18). Husband and wife companionship is important to God's design for marriage. Describe your own personal need for your husband's or wife's companionship.

Notes

Diary

The Example: Christ and the Church

1. Introduction

Take thirty minutes each day to be alone with God for the purpose of meditation and prayer. Read Ephesians 5 and Colossians 1 and 2. What do these chapters mean to you, and how do they apply to your life?

2. Self-Awareness

The union between Christ and the church serves as a great example for the marriage relationship. For successful living it is important to follow biblical examples and principles rather than human doctrine. In what ways does the world tend to ignore the principles of God's design for marriage? Give examples.

Name and describe a biblical character that has been an example for you.

Establishing a strong marriage is a process with a plan. How do you feel about taking a look at your personal marital responsibility in light of the example of Christ and the church?

3. Spiritual Awareness

Read Ephesians 5:22–33. The apostle Paul shows how the union between Christ and the church is the perfect example for the ideal Christian family. (Christ illustrates the husband; the church illustrates the wife.)

Check box when read	
☐ Ephesians 5:23	"Christ is the head of the church."
☐ Ephesians 5:24	The church submits to Christ.
☐ Ephesians 5:25	"Christ loved the church and gave himself up for her."
☐ Ephesians 5:29	Christ feeds and cares for the church.
☐ Ephesians 5:32	Paul describes Christ and the church as "a profound mystery."
☐ Matthew 16:18 ☐ 1 Corinthians 11:3 ☐ 1 Corinthians 12:21–31	
☐ Ephesians 1:22–23 ☐ Ephesians 4:1–4 ☐ Revelation 19:6–9	

4. Spiritual Application

Having talked about the supremacy of Christ and "Christ in you, the hope of glory" in Colossians 1:15–27, Paul writes in verses 28–29, "We proclaim him, admonishing and teaching everyone with all wisdom, so that we may present everyone perfect in Christ. To this end I labor, struggling with all his energy, which so powerfully works in me." Paul was interested in helping believers become more like Christ ("that we may present everyone perfect in Christ"). Working toward a Christ-centered marriage will include struggles. What encouragement does verse 29 ("his energy, which so powerfully works in me") give to you? Describe in your own words. In what ways does God's strength help you in times of weariness?

Notes

Diary

God's Plan for the Husband

1. Introduction

Take thirty minutes each day to be alone with God for the purpose of meditation and prayer. Read 1 Corinthians 13 and 1 Peter 3 and 4. What do these chapters mean to you, and how do they apply to your life?

2. Self-Awareness

In God's design for the family, each family member has a role to fulfill. The analogy of Christ and the church helps us understand God's plan for the husband in the marriage and family relationship. Christ's role as head of the church is the guideline for the husband's role and responsibility to his wife. The husband's primary responsibility to his wife is love, not dictatorship. How do you see the husband's role of love? How does this differ from dictatorship?

In what ways do you see the husband's role of love and leadership building the framework of the family?

3. Spiritual Awareness

Read Ephesians 5:22–33. The apostle Paul shows the analogy of Christ and the church as it relates to the role of the husband to his wife and family.

Check box when read	
☐ Ephesians 5:23	"For the husband is the head of the wife as Christ is the head of the church."
☐ Ephesians 5:25	"Husbands, love your wives, just as Christ loved the church."
☐ Ephesians 5:28	Husbands are to love their wives as their own bodies.
☐ 1 Peter 3:7	Husbands are to be considerate and respectful of their wives.
☐ Ephesians 6:4	Fathers (or parents) are not to exasperate their children.

☐ Romans 7:2	☐ 1 Corinthians 7:2–4	☐ 1 Corinthians 7:10–11
☐ 1 Corinthians 7:39	☐ Colossians 3:19	☐ 1 Timothy 3:2
☐ 1 Timothy 3:12	☐ Titus 1:6	

4. Spiritual Application

Paul writes, "However, each one of you also must love his wife as he loves himself" (Eph. 5:33). In view of this entire passage (5:22–33), how do you summarize a husband's responsibility to his wife and family?

Notes

Diary

God's Plan for the Wife

1. Introduction

Take thirty minutes each day to be alone with God for the purpose of meditation and prayer. Read Ruth 1–4 and Proverbs 31:10–31. What do these chapters mean to you, and how do they apply to your life?

2. Self-Awareness

As we continue our study of God's design for each family member, we now turn to the wife. The analogy of Christ and the church helps us understand God's plan for the wife in the marriage and family relationship. The role of the church in submission to Christ is the guideline for the wife's role and responsibility to her husband. The wife's primary responsibility is to submit voluntarily to her husband's leadership role as the spiritual leader of the family. What is the difference between voluntary and forced submission?

How do you picture the wife's submission to her husband?

In what ways do you see the wife's role of voluntary submission as building the framework of the family?

3. Spiritual Awareness

Read Ephesians 5:22–33. The apostle Paul shows the analogy of Christ and the church as it relates to the role of the wife to her husband and family.

Check box when read	
☐ Ephesians 5:22	"Wives, submit to your husbands as to the Lord."
☐ Ephesians 5:24	"Now as the church submits to Christ, so also wives should submit to their husbands in everything."
☐ Ephesians 5:33	"The wife must respect her husband."
☐ Proverbs 31:10	"A wife of noble character . . . is worth far more than rubies."
☐ Ephesians 6:4	Fathers (or parents) are not to exasperate their children.

☐ Genesis 3:16	☐ Deuteronomy 24:5	☐ Proverbs 5:18
☐ Proverbs 18:22	☐ Proverbs 19:13	☐ Proverbs 19:14
☐ Matthew 1:20	☐ Matthew 19:3–9	☐ 1 Peter 3:1–6

4. Spiritual Application

Paul writes in Ephesians 5:22, "Wives, submit to your husbands." In verse 25 he says, "Husbands, love your wives." How do you picture the scriptural balance of "wives, submit . . . husbands, love"? How does this provide a check and balance?

Notes

Diary

Session Five

God's Plan for the Children

1. Introduction

Take thirty minutes each day to be alone with God for the purpose of meditation and prayer. Read Ephesians 6 and Colossians 3 and 4. What do these chapters mean to you, and how do they apply to your life?

2. Self-Awareness

Having studied God's plan for the husband and wife, we now focus on God's plan for the children (including any age child that is still living at home). It is important to remember that God's plan is for the ideal Christian family. Although many of us may fall short of God's ideal family, we must never lose sight of our goal or become complacent with anything less than God's best for the home. It is important to teach children God's plan for them as it pertains to parental oversight and authority. How do you view the parental role of authority over children?

In what ways can parental authority be abused?

Describe in your own words how parents can be both parent and friend to their children.

3. Spiritual Awareness

Read Ephesians 6:1–2 and Colossians 3:20. The apostle Paul shows the child's responsibility in God's plan for the family and the parents' responsibility to teach the children their role.

Check box when read	
☐ Ephesians 6:1	"Children, obey your parents in the Lord, for this is right."
☐ Ephesians 6:2–3	"Honor your father and mother."
☐ Colossians 3:20	"Children, obey your parents in everything, for this pleases the Lord."
☐ Proverbs 1:8–9	Children are encouraged to listen and not to forsake their parents' instruction.

☐ Deuteronomy 4:9	☐ Deuteronomy 11:19	☐ Psalm 127:3
☐ Proverbs 2:1–5	☐ Proverbs 4:1–4	☐ Proverbs 5:7
☐ Proverbs 13:24	☐ Proverbs 22:6	☐ Proverbs 23:22
☐ Proverbs 29:15	☐ Proverbs 29:17	☐ Proverbs 30:17
☐ Matthew 19:14	☐ Mark 10:16	☐ 1 Timothy 3:4
☐ 1 Timothy 3:12		

4. Spiritual Application

Paul instructs parents to bring their children up "in the training and instruction of the Lord" (Eph. 6:4). Moses writes, "Impress them [God's commandments] on your children. Talk about them when you sit at home and when you walk along the road, when you lie down and when you get up" (Deut. 6:7). In light of the above verses, how do you view the responsibility of a parent in regard to training and instruction?

What is the difference between punishment and discipline?

Why is consistency of instruction and discipline important?

Notes

Diary

Session Six

Submitting to One Another

1. Introduction

Take thirty minutes each day to be alone with God for the purpose of meditation and prayer. Read Galatians 1–6. What do these chapters mean to you, and how do they apply to your life?

2. Self-Awareness

In God's plan for the family, each family member has a role to fulfill. God's divine revelation for the family is mutual submission. Each family member submits to and respects the other family members' God-given roles.

Important lessons about marriage are taught by the parents to the children through verbal and nonverbal communication. These lessons can have a tremendous influence—good or bad—on children. For example, if a husband loves and respects his wife, his son will probably love and respect his wife. When a family member repeatedly crosses the boundaries of his/her role and this develops into a pattern, unhealthy relationships will likely develop. For example, a marriage partner may take on the role of a parent or child to the other partner, or a child may assume the role of a parent. However, flexibility in roles is good when not taken to extremes and when boundary lines remain clear. For example, parents can be playful and childlike with children, and children can support and foster their parents in certain areas.

How do you view mutual submission?

Describe in your own words how role flexibility in the family can be fun and even healthy. In what ways can it be abused?

3. Spiritual Awareness

Read Ephesians 5:21. The apostle Paul shows the importance of submitting to one another and how submission relates to marriage and family relationships.

Check box when read		
☐ Ephesians 5:21a	"Submit to one another."	
☐ Ephesians 5:21	"Submit to one another out of reverence for Christ."	
☐ Ephesians 5:18–6:4	Verse 21 is a bridge between being "filled with the Spirit" and practical relationships.	
☐ Galatians 5:13	We are encouraged to "serve one another in love."	
☐ Romans 13:1–10	☐ Colossians 3:18–4:1	☐ Hebrews 12:2
☐ Hebrews 13:17	☐ James 4:7	☐ 1 Peter 2:13–3:12

4. Spiritual Application

In light of Paul's instruction to "submit to one another out of reverence for Christ" (Eph. 5:21), mutual submission is an acknowledgment of the lordship of Jesus Christ. How can you apply the principle of this verse to your marriage and family relationship?

How does being under the lordship of Jesus Christ make you feel?

Notes

Diary

Session Seven

Becoming One in Christ

1. Introduction

Take thirty minutes each day to be alone with God for the purpose of meditation and prayer. Read John 15–17. What do these chapters mean to you, and how do they apply to your life?

2. Self-Awareness

Becoming one in Christ is God's plan for husbands and wives. This spiritual and physical union is a special miracle of God. Each partner has a responsibility to the other in commitment, love, acceptance, and respect toward this miracle of God.

Although each partner has ministry responsibility to the other, only Christ can provide each individual with true security and significance. Becoming one in marriage does not imply a loss of one's personal identity.

Children benefit from parents who exhibit oneness in Christ. A genuine loving relationship between husbands and wives is important for the children's personal development. Giving attention and focus of affection to children is good; however, it should not interfere with the loving relationship between the parents. A demonstration of this love and affection between parents (doing things together, for example) will contribute to the children's sense of security and self-worth.

In your own words describe the "specialness" of the spiritual and physical union in the marriage relationship.

In what ways can parents demonstrate a loving relationship to their children?

Leaving home or former life to join your husband or wife in marriage is like leaving your former life to follow Jesus Christ as Savior. In your own words describe this likeness.

3. Spiritual Awareness

Read Ephesians 5:31–32. The apostle Paul shows the analogy of Christ and the church as it relates to "oneness" in the husband and wife relationship. This union can be described as a "miracle of relationship."

Check box when read	
☐ Ephesians 5:31a	"For this reason a man will leave his father and mother."
☐ Ephesians 5:31a	"For this reason a man will leave his father and mother and be united to his wife."
☐ Ephesians 5:31	"For this reason a man will leave his father and mother and be united to his wife, and the two will become one flesh."
☐ Ephesians 5:32	Paul describes becoming one in Christ as a "profound mystery."

☐ Genesis 2:24	☐ Ecclesiastes 4:9–12	☐ Malachi 2:15–16
☐ Matthew 19:5–6	☐ Mark 10:7–9	☐ 1 Corinthians 6:16–17
☐ Ephesians 1:9	☐ Ephesians 3:3–6	☐ Colossians 1:26–27
☐ Colossians 2:2	☐ Colossians 4:3	

4. Spiritual Application

Paul writes, "For this reason a man will leave his father and mother and be united to his wife, and the two will become one flesh" (Eph. 5:31). The "leaving behind" is often difficult when it comes to "baggage" (unhealthy behavior patterns, neglect, abuse, lack of role models, and so on). Some suffer from unmet childhood needs. Demanding that those unmet needs be fulfilled by a partner may cause more harm. Paul writes, "When I was a child, I talked like a child. . . . When I became a man, I put childish ways behind me" (1 Cor. 13:11). What are some areas of baggage that you need to allow God to help you with in the process of "becoming one"? What about if and when the baggage resurfaces?

Notes

Diary

Session Eight

Forgiving

1. Introduction

Take thirty minutes each day to be alone with God for the purpose of meditation and prayer. Read Matthew 18 and 19 and Genesis 50. What do these chapters mean to you, and how do they apply to your life?

2. Self-Awareness

Having built on God's plan for the marriage and family relationship in sessions 1–7, we now begin to focus on principles that contribute to the success of this special relationship. Forgiving one another is vital to the success of marriage and family relationships.

In this session we will focus on God's plan for forgiving one another in the marriage and family relationship. Forgiveness means that family members do not permit anger to grow, hold grudges, or keep a record of misdeeds. The forgiver receives the greatest benefit from forgiveness. Forgiveness means we forgive ourselves as well as others.

In what ways can unforgiveness lead to emotional and spiritual problems?

Describe the benefits of forgiving one another.

3. Spiritual Awareness

Read Colossians 3:13. The apostle Paul shows Christ's example of forgiveness, which relates to forgiving one another in the husband and wife relationship.

Check box when read	
☐ Colossians 3:13	Paul emphasizes the believer's personal responsibility to forgive one another.
☐ Colossians 2:13–14	Believers have received forgiveness through Christ.
☐ Ephesians 4:32	Forgiveness of sin can be viewed as a gift from God "forgiving each other, just as in Christ God forgave you."
☐ Matthew 18:21–35	Jesus stresses the importance of forgiveness in the parable of the unmerciful servant.
☐ Ephesians 4:26–27	Anger should not last longer than a day.

☐ 2 Chronicles 7:14	☐ Psalm 19:12	☐ Matthew 5:23–24
☐ Matthew 6:12	☐ Mark 11:25	☐ Luke 11:4
☐ Luke 23:34	☐ Ephesians 1:7	☐ 1 John 1:9

4. Spiritual Application

In Matthew 6:14–15, Jesus shows the divine significance of forgiveness: "For if you forgive men when they sin against you, your heavenly Father will also forgive you. But if you do not forgive men their sins, your Father will not forgive your sins." In light of these verses, why is it important that each marriage partner be quick to extend the gift of forgiveness to each other?

Discuss this passage in light of Proverbs 8:34–36 (Example: One who does not forgive harms himself or herself).

Notes

Diary

Session Nine

Communicating with One Another (Part 1)

1. Introduction

Take thirty minutes each day to be alone with God for the purpose of meditation and prayer. Read Ephesians 1–4. What do these chapters mean to you, and how do they apply to your life?

2. Self-Awareness

Proper communication plays a significant role in the relationship between husbands and wives. Faulty communication is a common problem that can cause marital conflict. Most marriages experience miscommunications (the message sent is not in accord with the message received). When miscommunication becomes the norm, the marriage is likely to experience difficulty.

According to H. Norman Wright, "Our messages consist of three components: Content composes 7 percent of the message;

tone of voice, 38 percent; nonverbal (or 'body language'), 55 percent" (*Marital Counseling,* 308). It is important that these three components be consistent. Eye contact, "I" statements, and active listening also contribute to good communication.

Read "Communicating with I-Messages," pages 53–54. Describe ways I-messages can be used with your marriage partner.

Read "Active Listening," pages 55–56. How can the "Examples of Active Listening" be used with your marriage partner?

3. Spiritual Awareness

Read Colossians 4:6. The apostle Paul gives instructions on wholesome communication skills that are applicable to the husband and wife relationship.

Check box when read	
☐ Colossians 4:6	Paul emphasizes wholesome conversation.
☐ Ephesians 4:29	Paul warns against unwholesome talk.
☐ 2 Corinthians 10:8	Paul emphasizes that his authority in the Lord is to build up rather than to pull down.
☐ Proverbs 18:13	It is foolish and shameful to answer before listening.
☐ James 1:19–20	James notes the importance of being "quick to listen."

☐ 1 Kings 4:34	☐ Proverbs 1:5	☐ Proverbs 10:19
☐ Proverbs 12:15	☐ Proverbs 12:25	☐ Proverbs 16:24
☐ Ecclesiastes 5:1	☐ 1 Thessalonians 5:15	☐ 2 Timothy 2:24

4. Spiritual Application

The Bible is a book that communicates a special and clear message from God to mankind—"I love you." There are many ways you can express these three special words to your marriage partner such as by purchasing a gift for him or her or planning a special dinner or trip. One sure way not to miscommunicate is to often say the three words "I love you" to your partner.

In your own words what feelings are conveyed by the phrase "I love you"?

Can you remember the first time your marriage partner said these three words to you? Describe. (This is for your own personal reflection.)

Communicating with I-Messages

An I-message is a tool to be used when the other person has strong feelings or a problem. It is important to use non-judgmental messages when dealing with conflictive conversations. Some of these inner feelings that may cause conflict include frustration, annoyance, and resentment.

You-Messages

You-messages tend to increase conflict by triggering the other person's defense mechanisms. These messages may cause the other person to feel put down, rejected, resistant, or unimportant.

Examples of you-messages:

- You just don't care.
- You are a problem.
- Can't you . . . ?
- You are so . . .

I-Messages

I-messages are more effective than you-messages. I-messages tell what you feel or how the other person's behavior is making you feel. This type of message helps to communicate your feelings without strengthening the defenses of the other person.

I-messages deal with facts rather than evaluation. They communicate honesty and openness. I-messages are less likely to cause harm to the relationship since the self-esteem of the other person is not attacked. An I-message is different from a you-message in that the speaker takes responsibility for his or her own feelings.

Examples of I-messages:

- I feel very angry because . . .
- I feel rejected because . . .
- I feel hurt because . . .

Let your conversation be always full of grace, seasoned with salt, so that you may know how to answer everyone.

Colossians 4:6

Active Listening

Active listening is perhaps the most important communication tool in helping people. It helps communicate that you are a caring person. It shows that you accept the other person and have respect for him/her. It is a display of empathetic understanding.

Examples of active listening:

- **Restatement:** Repeats the content of what the other person said. This conveys that the person talking is being heard and that you are "with" him or her.
- **Clarifying:** Helps to clear up aspects of the other person's conversation that were unclear.
- **Summarizing:** Pulls together the other person's message and draws it to a concluding point based on what you have seen and heard in the conversation.

Active listening is effective because

- It helps build new relationships.
- It helps you better understand what the other person is saying.
- It helps build the trust level.
- It helps the other person get in touch with his/her feelings.
- It helps the other person when he/she is angry or frustrated.
- It helps the other person gain more understanding of himself/herself.
- It is a way to encourage and build up the other person.
- It shows the other person he/she is being accepted.

Active listening is not effective when

- The other person is out of control (intoxicated, severely depressed).
- The other person needs immediate action.
- The other person requests you to betray your own biblical values.

He who answers before listening—that is his folly and his shame.

Proverbs 18:13

Everyone should be quick to listen, slow to speak and slow to become angry.

James 1:19

Notes

Diary

Session Ten

Communicating with One Another (Part 2)

1. Introduction

Take thirty minutes each day to be alone with God for the purpose of meditation and prayer. Read John 3, 4, and 8. What do these chapters mean to you, and how do they apply to your life?

2. Self-Awareness

This session is a continuation of session 9. Positive communication is very important to the husband and wife relationship. However, conflicts do occur in relationships and can cause disastrous results if not managed properly.

Author David Augsburger offers a creative way through conflict called "care-fronting." He describes caring as a good word and confronting as a bad word. He says, "Together they provide the balance of love and power which lead to effective human relationships" (*Caring Enough to Confront*, 9). Care-fronting is a creative way to work through marital misunderstanding and miscommunication. It is important to practice nonjudgmental communication rather than "put-downs" and "cut-downs."

Read "Five Options for Dealing with Conflict," pages 62–63. Which of the five options have you used more frequently? Explain.

Read "Ways of Care-Fronting without Being Judgmental," pages 63–65. In what ways do you see yourself using this information with your marriage partner?

3. Spiritual Awareness

Read Ephesians 4:14–15. The apostle Paul emphasizes the need to speak "the truth in love," which is applicable to the husband and wife relationship. Speaking the truth in love implies a real, noncounterfeit expression and reality of love while holding on to the truth. It also suggests spiritual growth.

Check box when read	
☐ Ephesians 4:14	Paul describes immature Christians.
☐ Ephesians 4:15	In contrast to immaturity, Paul notes the value of "speaking the truth in love."
☐ John 8:1–11	Jesus spoke the truth in love to a woman caught in adultery.
☐ Proverbs 15:28; 29:20	Speaking the truth in love implies weighing one's answers before speaking.
☐ 1 Peter 2:17	Speaking the truth in love suggests respect.

☐ Proverbs 12:25 ☐ Proverbs 25:11 ☐ Proverbs 26:4–6

☐ Galatians 5:14–15 ☐ Romans 12:9–10 ☐ Ephesians 4:2

☐ Ephesians 4:16 ☐ 1 Corinthians 13:4–7

4. Spiritual Application

A concern about a misunderstanding or disagreement between husband and wife may cause a partner to react in a condemning manner. In light of John 3:17, describe God's reason for sending his Son.

John 16:8 describes conviction as a work of the Holy Spirit. What differences do you see between condemnation and the Holy Spirit's work of conviction?

Have you ever tried to change the behavior or attitude of your marriage partner or another loved one through condemnation? If so, how did that make you feel? (This is for your own personal reflection.)

In what ways do you see yourself relying on the Holy Spirit to bring about change?

Communication by Care-Fronting

Definitions

Caring—a good word.

Confronting—a word with bad connotations because it is often done when angry.

Care-fronting—a good word because it is confronting in a caring way. Caring is the first word. Therefore, the caring must be genuine. The confronting is not negative because it is done out of love.

Care-fronting is a way to communicate with both impact and respect, with truth and love.

Five Options for Dealing with Conflict

I'll get him. "I win and you lose because I am right and you're wrong." This is all power and little or no love.

I'll get out. "I'm uncomfortable, so I'll withdraw from the conflict." "The situation is hopeless because people cannot be changed." This way of avoiding conflict can be advantageous for instant safety. There is no risk of power and no trusting love.

I'll give in. "I'll yield to be nice since I need your friendship." "I will be nice and submit to your demands so that we can be friends." You become a doormat who is frustrated and smiling.

I'll meet you halfway. "I have only half of the truth, and I need your half." This is the attitude of creative compromise. Compromise is a gift to human relationships, and conflict is natural. Also, compromise is the willingness to give a little to work out a satisfactory solution for everyone. The danger of compromise is the risk that my half-truth and your half-truth may not give the total truth. You may have two half-truths, or it may produce a whole untruth. You must care enough to tussle with truth so it can be tested, retested, and refined. Perhaps you will find more of it through working together.

I care enough to confront. "I want a relationship, and I also want honest integrity." Conflict is viewed as neutral (neither good nor bad) and natural (neither to be avoided nor short-circuited). This is an "I care" and "I want" position saying, "I want to stay in a respectful relationship with you, and I want you to know where I stand and what I am feeling, needing, valuing, and wanting."

Caring		Confronting
I care about our relationship		I feel deeply about this issue.
I want to hear your view	**and**	I want to express my view clearly.
I want to respect your insights		I want respect for mine.
I give you my loving, honest respect		I want your caring-confronting response.

Care-fronting invites another to change but does not demand it.

Ways of Care-Fronting without Being Judgmental

Focus your feedback on the action, not on the actor. This gives the person the freedom to change the behavior without feeling personal rejection. *Example:* "When someone criticizes people who are not present, as you were doing a moment ago, I get uptight. I'd encourage you to say what you have to say to the person."

Focus your feedback on your observations, not on your conclusions. Comment not on what you think, imagine, or infer, but rather on what you have actually seen or heard. Conclusions will evoke immediate defensiveness. *Example:* "You are not looking at me and not answering when I speak. Please give me both attention and answer."

Focus your feedback on descriptions, not on judgments. Do not comment on another's behavior as nice or rude, right or wrong. Use a clear, accurate description in neutral language. When a value judgment is received, there is a momentary breaking contact. *Example:* "I am aware that your reply to my request for information was silence. Please tell me what this means."

Focus feedback on quantity, not on quality. Comment not on character, traits, or classification (qualities) of the other person, but rather on the amount of feeling, expression, or action (quantity). Use adverbs (which tell how much) rather than adjectives (which tell what kind of). Use terms denoting more or less (quantity) rather than either/or categories (quality). *Example:* "You talked considerably more than others," not "You were a loudmouth." "You have asked for and received more of my time than any other student," not "You are clinging, dependent, and always demanding my time."

Focus feedback on ideas, information, and alternatives, not on advice and answers. Comment not with instructions on what to do, but rather with the facts and the additional options. The more options available, the less likely is a premature solution. *Example:* "I've several other options that you may have thought about, but let me run them by you again."

Focus feedback not on why, but on what and how. "Why" critiques values, motives, and intents. "Why" is judgmental;

"what" and "how" relate to observable actions, behaviors, words, and tone of voice. *Example:* "Here is where we are; let's examine it."

Care-fronting focuses on action, observations, descriptions, quantity, information, alternatives, and the reality of the here and now. It does not focus on actor, conclusions, judgments, qualities, advice, or why.

Care-fronting should be done caringly, gently, constructively, and clearly. Never care-front with any possible interpretations of blaming, shaming, or punishing.

Notes

Diary

Session Eleven

Family Finances

1. Introduction

Take thirty minutes each day to be alone with God for the purpose of meditation and prayer. Read 1 Timothy 1–6. What do these chapters mean to you, and how do they apply to your life?

2. Self-Awareness

Financial stewardship is important to the family because money problems can contribute greatly to difficulty in the marriage relationship. Financial stress can usually be traced to poor management and/or distorted attitudes toward family finances.

Unwise family financial management (impulsive buying, lack of a budget, slavery to credit buying) can develop into a trap. Marriages can also become trapped in distorted financial attitudes (centering the marriage on money, get-rich-quick schemes, the pursuit of money for happiness, and greed).

Read "Unwise Family Financial Management," page 71.

Which area causes you most concern? Describe steps you can take to avoid this trap.

Read "Distorted Financial Attitudes," page 72. Which area causes you most concern? Describe steps you can take to avoid this trap.

Read "The Five Most Common Mistakes in Handling Family Finances," page 73. Write a brief summary describing how to reverse these common mistakes.

3. Spiritual Awareness

Read 1 Timothy 6:6–10. The apostle Paul gives instructions on financial matters that are applicable in the marriage and family relationship. He shows ways that the trap of the love of money can be avoided.

Check box when read	
☐ 1 Timothy 6:6–7	Paul emphasizes godliness with contentment.
☐ 1 Timothy 6:8	Paul associates food and clothing with contentment.
☐ 1 Timothy 6:9–10	Paul describes the trap of the love of money.
☐ 1 Timothy 6:10	"The love of money is a root of all kinds of evil."
☐ Proverbs 22:7	"The borrower is servant to the lender."

☐ Luke 6:38; Acts 20:35	God blesses those who give.
☐ Malachi 3:10–11	We are to give back to the Lord his portion.
☐ 1 Corinthians 16:2	Paul provides instruction regarding the principle of giving.

☐ Deuteronomy 8:17–18	☐ Ecclesiastes 5:10	☐ Isaiah 55:1–2
☐ Matthew 6:24	☐ Luke 12:15	☐ 2 Corinthians 8:12
☐ 2 Timothy 3:2	☐ Hebrews 13:5	☐ 1 Peter 5:2

4. Spiritual Application

Having discussed the guidelines of financial stewardship and possible financial pitfalls, we now focus on God's blessings for his people. First, God owns everything (Ps. 24:1). Second, God has promised to supply our needs (Matt. 6:33; Phil. 4:19). Third, God promises to bless those who sow generously. Paul writes, "Whoever sows sparingly will also reap sparingly, and whoever sows generously will also reap generously. Each man should give what he has decided in his heart to give, not reluctantly nor under compulsion, for God loves a cheerful giver. And God is able to make all grace abound to you, so that in all things at all times, having all that you need, you will abound in every good work" (2 Cor. 9:6–8).

How can you apply verses 6 and 7 to your marriage and family relationship?

What encouragement does verse 8 provide for a generous, cheerful giver? How does this differ from greed?

Unwise Family Financial Management

Impulsive Buying

- Buying without regard for need
- Buying without regard for the quality of the purchase
- Buying without regard for the price
- Buying to feel good

Lack of Budget

- No plan for family money management
- No plan to limit spending
- No guidelines or controls

Slavery to Credit Buying

- Buying on impulse is encouraged through convenience
- Buying becomes a credit merry-go-round
- Buying more than we need or can afford is a constant temptation

Laziness

- Too lazy to work
- Too lazy to manage money

Distorted Financial Attitudes

Keeping Up with the Joneses

- Coveting what others have
- Living beyond our means
- Wanting the latest fashion, toy, car, etc.

Centering Marriage on Money

- Centering self-worth on materialism
- Pursuing money instead of God
- Gaining financially at the expense of others

Get-Rich-Quick Schemes

- Trying to earn money quickly without much work
- Taking shortcuts
- Investing in financial programs that lack substance and integrity

Greed

- Never being satisfied
- Being overly tight with finances
- Always being starved for more money

Unrealistic Expectations

- Fantasizing about wealth
- Not counting the cost

The Five Most Common Mistakes in Handling Family Finances

1. Failure to give back to the Lord his portion
2. Lack of discipline
3. Lack of financial goals
4. Lack of plan to reach those goals
5. Spending more than you earn

Monthly Household Budget

Month _____

Category	Budget	Actual
Revenue		
Salary (Take Home)	_____	_____
Interest	_____	_____
Dividends	_____	_____
Pension	_____	_____
Other	_____	_____
Total Revenue	_____	_____
Expenses		
Church (10%)	_____	_____
Savings	_____	_____
House Payment	_____	_____
Electric Bill	_____	_____
Water Bill	_____	_____
Phone Bill	_____	_____
Food	_____	_____
Car Payment	_____	_____
Gas for Cars	_____	_____
Car Insurance	_____	_____
Car Maintenance	_____	_____
Insurance		
Life	_____	_____
Disability	_____	_____
Health	_____	_____
Entertainment	_____	_____
Pest Control	_____	_____
Cable TV	_____	_____
Lunch	_____	_____
Newspaper	_____	_____

Doctor
    Family Member #1   _____   _____
    Family Member #2   _____   _____
Dentist
    Family Member #1   _____   _____
    Family Member #2   _____   _____
Vacation   _____   _____
Home Maintenance   _____   _____
Other Contributions   _____   _____
Laundry   _____   _____
Haircuts/Hair Care   _____   _____
Gifts   _____   _____
Day Care   _____   _____
Miscellaneous   _____   _____
Total Expenses   _____   _____

Net Revenue/Expenses   _____   _____

Notes

Diary

Session Twelve

Watch for the Little Foxes

1. Introduction

Take thirty minutes each day to be alone with God for the purpose of meditation and prayer. Read the Song of Songs (Song of Solomon) 1–8. What do these chapters mean to you, and how do they apply to your life?

2. Self-Awareness

It is important to be alert and safe from those little things that turn into big things and subsequently cause harm to the marriage and family relationship. The Song of Songs 2:15 points to this principle, "Catch for us the foxes, the little foxes that ruin the vineyards, our vineyards that are in bloom."

Little things (like the "little foxes") may go unnoticed because they are often cunning, cute, deceitful, or sneaky. Being so small, the little foxes may seem unimportant, but they may eventually knock a marriage and family relationship off its feet.

Always being alert to the little things will benefit your home. The little foxes are attracted to a marriage when it is in its prime ("vineyards that are in bloom"). It is important that each marriage partner take a personal look at the little foxes as they relate to his or her own responsibility in the marriage and family relationship.

There are certain little foxes that are common:

- unkindness
- preoccupation
- forgetting special days (anniversary, birthdays, etc.)
- nagging
- criticism
- neglecting the Lord's house
- unthankfulness

Name other "little foxes" that come to your mind. Describe.

3. Spiritual Awareness

Read 2 Corinthians 2:11. The apostle Paul's emphasis on the need for alertness to Satan's schemes is applicable to the husband and wife relationship.

Check box when read	
☐ 2 Corinthians 2:11	Paul highlights the importance of having an awareness of Satan's schemes.
☐ 1 Peter 5:8–9	"Be self-controlled and alert."
☐ 2 Corinthians 11:14	Satan "masquerades as an angel of light."
☐ Genesis 3:1–7	Satan showed his deceitfulness in the fall of humanity.

☐ Job 1:6–12	☐ Matthew 4:1–11	☐ Mark 4:15
☐ John 8:44–45	☐ Ephesians 4:27	☐ Ephesians 6:12
☐ 2 Timothy 2:26	☐ Revelation 12:9–11	☐ Revelation 20:2, 7

4. Spiritual Application

Destroying the tracks of the little foxes is important to all husband and wife relationships. With God's help, how can each partner go about identifying the little things before they become big things?

The little fox of unkindness.
    With God's help, I will:

The little fox of preoccupation.
    With God's help, I will:

The little fox of forgetting special days.
    With God's help, I will:

The little fox of nagging.
    With God's help, I will:

The little fox of criticism.
    With God's help, I will:

The little fox of neglecting the Lord's house.
    With God's help, I will:

The little fox of unthankfulness.
    With God's help, I will:

"Little Fox" Termination Prayer

Dear Lord,

Notes

Diary

The Family Altar

1. Introduction

Take thirty minutes each day to be alone with God for the purpose of meditation and prayer. Read Matthew 5–7. What do these chapters mean to you, and how do they apply to your life?

2. Self-Awareness

This session brings us to a point of completion; however, the growth of our marriage and family relationships should continue. Although we have discussed very needful and pertinent spiritual growth aspects in the family relationship during the previous twelve sessions, all will fall short if the marriage and family relationship is not built on prayer. Prayer is the very fabric that will hold our marriage and family in the loving hands of our Lord.

The first altar recorded in the Bible is the altar built by Noah after leaving the ark (Gen. 8:20). Today we refer to the altar as a place where we express our total dependence on God through intercession, request, praise, and confession.

The family altar will greatly contribute to the spiritual well-being of any family. It may be advisable for husbands and wives to designate a certain room or piece of furniture as a place where the family assembles to pray at a certain time every day. Although prayer is not limited to certain rooms or places, there is sacredness about a designated family altar that will leave a lasting impression on family members.

Many factors (television, interruptions from various sources, fatigue, overworked schedule, and meetings) will fight against the establishment of the family altar. Disciplining ourselves to make prayer a top priority will reap eternal dividends.

In what ways has the "altar of TV" been given priority over the family altar? How does this affect the family?

Describe the rewards of the family altar.

3. Spiritual Awareness

Read Matthew 7:7–12. The value of prayer as presented is applicable to the husband and wife relationship.

Check box when read	
☐ Matthew 7:7–12	Jesus encourages us to pray.
☐ Psalm 55:17; 119:164; Daniel 6:10; Acts 3:1	The Bible urges us to pray and worship God regularly.
☐ Psalm 66:18; Proverbs 28:13; 1 Peter 3:1–7	Prayers can be hindered when family relationships are not right.

☐ Ephesians 6:11–12	Christian families are in spiritual warfare for the preservation of their homes.	
☐ Ephesians 6:17–18	The Word of God and prayer play a vital part in spiritual warfare.	
☐ Deuteronomy 4:7	☐ 1 Samuel 12:23	☐ 2 Chronicles 7:14
☐ Psalm 6:9	☐ Psalm 86:6	☐ Proverbs 15:8
☐ Mark 11:24	☐ Luke 18:1	☐ Acts 16:25–34
☐ Philippians 4:6	☐ 1 Thessalonians 5:16–18	

4. Spiritual Application

During the past few weeks, you have had the opportunity to study and have been encouraged to apply certain biblical principles to marriage and family relationships. Having a personal responsibility to both God and your marriage partner, it is important to follow through with commitment. With God's help, you can publicly commit yourself as Joshua did: "But as for me and my household, we will serve the LORD" (Josh. 24:15).

How do you plan to fulfill this commitment?

What role will the family altar play?

Notes

Diary

Part Two
A Facilitator's Group Guide

Suggested Group Format

Getting Started

We suggest that the group have two group leaders (facilitators) and a maximum of twelve group participants. Having more than twelve may prevent some from being a part of the much-needed discussion.

The facilitators should meet prior to each group session to pray and make final plans for the session. They should also meet after each session to discuss what happened during the meeting and whether any follow-up is needed.

Since there is homework for the first session, *Committed Couples* should be distributed to each group member prior to the start of session 1.

Facilitators should have a thorough understanding of this book before distributing it to group participants. Encourage group members to complete the appropriate learning assignment prior to each group meeting. This prepares them for the upcoming session. Follow this format for each session.

The facilitators should study the format suggested on the following pages since this is the pattern in which the curriculum is to be presented. After reviewing the format, please note that in the "Spiritual Awareness" part of each session there are statements and questions regarding certain biblical passages and sometimes general questions concerning the subject being presented. These same statements are listed in the group member's personal guide. The questions are not in the group member's guide in order to enhance the spontaneity of the group process.

The small group format for each session consists of four phases: Introduction, Self-Awareness, Spiritual Awareness, and Spiritual Application. There is a reason for each phase. The facilitators should always plan each session with this format in mind.

1. Introduction (10–15 minutes)

Begin with prayer. The facilitator may ask one of the group members to lead in prayer. After the prayer, use a go-around (sharing question) to help get the group at ease and more comfortable in being a part of the discussion. (Suggested go-arounds are listed in the Resources section.) The lead facilitator should respond to the go-around first, followed by the co-facilitator to help group members feel safer in participating in the exercise. After the facilitators have shared, the group members will share one after another around the circle. Always remind group members that they are not expected to share if they do not wish to share. The rule is that everyone works within his/her comfort level.

The go-arounds are not for detailed conversation. Ask the group to keep their comments brief. If a person is obviously in pain during the go-around, the facilitator should interrupt the go-around and have prayer for the person in pain. After prayer, the go-arounds may resume.

2. Self-Awareness (20–25 minutes)

After the introduction phase (go-arounds) is completed, the facilitator will lead the group into the self-awareness phase. The facilitator may say, "Now it is time for our self-awareness. Tonight we are going to discuss . . ."

Self-awareness is a time to practice James 5:16. "Therefore confess your sins to each other and pray for each other so that you may be healed. The prayer of a righteous man is powerful and effective." It is important to stay on the subject matter. This is a time to focus on needs and healing, not to have a "martyr session" or "pity party."

It is suggested that the facilitators ask the group members to share as they wish, unlike the go-around segment referred to in the introduction phase. Because people are at various comfort levels, they should not feel pressured to self-disclose if they are uncomfortable. As the group continues to meet, members will feel more and more comfortable in being a part of the discussion.

Remember, prayer is *always* in order. If during this phase a group member is hurting, stop and pray. One of the facilitators may lead in prayer or ask another group member to lead the prayer. This says two things to the group member: that each member is important, and that you care about each individual.

3. Spiritual Awareness (20–25 minutes)

After the self-awareness phase, the facilitator will lead the group into the Bible study time. The facilitator may say, "Turn in your Bibles to . . . Our discussion will be on . . ."

Having briefly explained the topic, the facilitator should assign Scriptures listed in this guide to group members. When each Scripture is called by the facilitator, the group member should read the verse(s). After all the verses are read, give time for discussion.

4. Spiritual Application (25 minutes)

This phase is actually a continuation of phase 3. Use the question for the appropriate session listed in this guide. The facilitator may say, "For our application of the Scripture passage, I would like the group to discuss this question. . . ." Ask for volunteers to share their reflections on the question. The facilitators should emphasize the importance of the group members' applying biblical principles to their lives. Help for marriage and family rela-tionships begins with *right thinking*. "But be transformed by the renewing of your mind" (Rom. 12:2). Obedience to the Word should follow with *right behavior. Right feelings* will follow right thinking and right behavior.

Session One

In the Beginning — Marriage

1. Introduction (10–15 minutes)

Opening Prayer

Ask the group members to introduce themselves. This should be done as a go-around.

2. Self-Awareness (20–25 minutes)

In this first session, review with group members what will be expected of them regarding attendance, absence, confidentiality, and so on. Encourage group members to call or notify one of the facilitators if they cannot attend a session. Also, discuss the format that will be used for each group session and elaborate on the goals of the marriage group.

Explain that the goal is to help each married couple grow spiritually and emotionally in their relationship to each other through an awareness and application of biblical principles. Give each person an opportunity to share why he/she is in this group. To be effective, each group member should enter this group wanting to be all God would have him/her to be in his/her marriage rather than trying to change his/her partner.

Specific goals for the session are:

- To emphasize that the marriage group is a nonthreatening environment. Everyone works within his/her own "comfort level."
- To stress the importance of each group member's *speaking for himself/herself—not for his/her spouse.*
- To stress the importance of each group member's *being open to God's working in his/her personal life rather than trying to change his/her spouse.*
- To stress the importance of attending each group session.
- To have group members report why they are in the group.
- To stress the need for personal devotion time.
- To stress the need for confidentiality.
- To distribute the books to participants who have not received one.
- To explain the group format that will be used for each session (Introduction, Self-Awareness, Spiritual Awareness, and Spiritual Application).

Spiritual awareness lead-in question: In each session our spiritual awareness will be based on biblical principles that emphasize healthy marriage relationships. Genesis 2:22–24 presents to us the beginning of marriage. Let's read the text together. What does this text say to you about the first marriage?

> Then the LORD God made a woman from the rib he had taken out of the man, and he brought her to the man.
> The man said,
> > "This is now bone of my bones
> > and flesh of my flesh;
> > she shall be called 'woman,'
> > for she was taken out of man."
> For this reason a man will leave his father and mother and be united to his wife, and they will become one flesh.
> > Genesis 2:22–24

3. Spiritual Awareness (20–25 minutes)

The main objective of this session is to help group members understand the following aspects of God's design for the first marriage relationship.

Genesis 2:22–24

- *God is the creator of the marriage relationship (vv. 22–24).*
  How did God create the woman (vv. 21–22)? Why did he create Eve for Adam (v. 18)?

- *Heterosexuality is God's design for marriage. Adam was male; Eve female. (v. 23; Gen. 3:20; Lev. 18:22).*
  In what ways do you think homosexuality defiles God's law for marriage and family relationships?

- *Monogamy is God's design for marriage. God gave Adam one wife (Gen. 2:22–24; 4:1; Heb. 13:4).*
  In what ways does sex outside of marriage cause physical, emotional, and spiritual problems?

- *God's design for marriage is for physical and spiritual unity (Gen. 2:24; Matt. 19:4–5).*
  How does love and respect for each other contribute to a couple's being "one flesh"?

- *God's design for marriage is permanency (Gen. 2:24; Matt. 19:6).*
  How does marital unity contribute to permanency?

Help group members understand the significance of the lessons we learn from the creation of Adam and Eve and the marriage relationship.

Assign Scripture references in the spiritual awareness section to group members. The Scriptures should be read and discussed as time permits. Caution: Stay on the subject.

4. Spiritual Application (25 minutes)

Group Discussion: At the very dawn of history God said, "It is not good for the man to be alone. I will make a helper suitable for him" (Gen. 2:18). In view of this verse, why is husband and wife companionship so important to God's design for marriage?

Additional Scripture References		
Genesis 5:1–2	Romans 1:18–32	Romans 5:14
1 Corinthians 15:22, 45	2 Corinthians 11:3	1 Timothy 2:13

Session Two

The Example:
Christ and the Church

1. Introduction (10–15 minutes)

Opening Prayer
Use a "Past Tense Go-Around." See pages 155–56.

2. Self-Awareness (20–25 minutes)

The general goal of this session is to help group members understand the significance of the example of Christ and the church to the marriage relationship. Emphasize the importance of biblical examples and principles rather than human doctrine for successful living.

Specific goals for the session are:

- To discuss a married couple that has been a good example.
- To discuss a biblical character who has been a good example.
- To discuss ways the world tends to ignore the principles of God's design for marriage.

Spiritual awareness lead-in question: Establishing a strong marriage is a process with a plan. How do you feel about taking a look

at your personal marital responsibility in light of the example of
Christ and the church?

3. Spiritual Awareness (20–25 minutes)

*The main objective of this session is to learn the aspects of how
Christ and the church are the perfect example for the ideal Christian
family.* (Christ illustrates the husband; the church illustrates the
wife.)

Ephesians 5:22–23

- *"Christ is the head of the church" (v. 23).*
  To whom is the church compared in this verse?

- *The church submits to Christ (v. 24).*
  Is this forced or voluntary submission?

- *"Christ loved the church and gave himself up for her" (v. 25).*
  In view of verses 26 and 27, why did he give himself up for
  the church?

- *Christ feeds and cares for the church (v. 29).*
  In view of verses 29 and 30, how does the apostle Paul relate
  the physical body to the body of Christ?

- *Paul describes Christ and the church as "a profound mystery" (v. 32).*
  In view of verses 31 and 32, describe the closeness between Christ and his church.

Help group members understand the great illustration of Christ and the church to the marriage relationship.

Assign Scripture references in the spiritual awareness section to group members. The Scriptures should be read and discussed as time permits. Caution: Stay on the subject.

4. Spiritual Application (25 minutes)

Group Discussion: Having talked about the supremacy of Christ and "Christ in you, the hope of glory," Paul writes: "We proclaim him, admonishing and teaching everyone with all wisdom, so that we may present everyone perfect in Christ. To this end I labor, struggling with all his energy, which so powerfully works in me" (Col. 1:28–29). Paul was interested in helping believers become more like Christ ("that we may present everyone perfect in Christ.") Working toward a Christ-centered marriage will include struggles. As we enter the weeks to come in *Committed Couples,* what encouragement does verse 29 ("his energy, which so powerfully works in me") give to you?

Additional Scripture References		
Matthew 16:18	1 Corinthians 11:3	1 Corinthians 12:12–31
Ephesians 1:22–23	Ephesians 4:1–6	Colossians 1:18–27
Revelation 19:6–9		

God's Plan for the Husband

1. Introduction (10–15 minutes)

Opening Prayer
Use a "Past Tense Go-Around." See pages 155–56.

2. Self-Awareness (20–25 minutes)

The general goal of this session is to help group members understand the significance of the analogy of Christ and the church as it relates to God's role for the husband in the marriage and family relationship. Christ's role as head of the church is the guideline for the husband's role and responsibility to his wife. Emphasize that the husband's primary responsibility to his wife is love, not dictatorship.

Specific goals for the sessions are:

- To discuss the role of love versus dictatorship.
- To discuss the role of the husband as the head of the household.
- To discuss the role of the husband as the primary provider.
- To discuss the role of the husband as friend and lover.

Spiritual awareness lead-in question: In what ways do you see the husband's role of love and leadership building the framework of the family?

3. Spiritual Awareness (20–25 minutes)

The main objective of this session is to learn the aspects of the analogy of Christ and the church as it relates to the role of the husband to his wife and family.

Ephesians 5:22–33

- *"For the husband is the head of the wife as Christ is head of the church"* (v. 23).

  Why is it important to consider this verse in light of "as to the Lord" in verse 22? What protection does this provide against unscriptural demands?

- *"Husbands, love your wives, just as Christ loved the church"* (v. 25).

  In view of this verse, what does this say to you about the expression of Christ's love for the church? How does this kind of love prevent a husband's abuse of his God-given role?

- *"Husbands ought to love their wives as their own bodies"* (v. 28).

  For a husband to mistreat his wife is to mistreat himself. Explain in your own words.

- *Husbands are to be considerate and respectful of their wives (1 Peter 3:7).*
  In light of this verse, how can a husband's lack of respect or consideration for his partner affect his relationship with God?

- *Fathers (or parents) are not to exasperate their children (Eph. 6:4).*
  How might unreasonable expectations cause a child to feel helpless? In view of this verse (6:4), describe in your own words Paul's answer for raising children.

Help group members understand the analogy between Christ and the church and the husband's relationship to the wife and family.

Assign Scripture references in the spiritual awareness section to group members. The Scriptures should be read and discussed as time permits. Caution: Stay on the subject.

4. Spiritual Application (25 minutes)

Group Discussion: Paul writes, "However, each one of you also must love his wife as he loves himself" (Eph. 5:33). In view of this entire passage (5:22–33), how do you summarize a husband's responsibility to his wife and family?

Additional Scripture References		
Romans 7:2	1 Corinthians 7:2–4, 10–11, 39	Colossians 3:19
1 Timothy 3:2, 12	Titus 1:6	

Session Four

God's Plan for the Wife

1. Introduction (10–15 minutes)

Opening Prayer
Use a "Present Tense Go-Around." See pages 156–57.

2. Self-Awareness (20–25 minutes)

The general goal of this session is to help group members understand the significance of the analogy of Christ and the church as it relates to God's role for the wife in the marriage and family relationship. The role of the church in submission to Christ is the guideline for the wife's role and responsibility to her husband. Emphasize that the wife's primary responsibility is to submit voluntarily to her husband as the spiritual leader of the family.

Specific goals for the session are:

- To understand the difference between voluntary and forced submission.
- To discuss the role of the wife's submission to her husband.
- To recognize ways submission can be abused.
- To discuss the role of the wife as friend and lover.

Spiritual awareness lead-in question: In what ways do you see the wife's role of voluntary submission as building the framework of the family?

3. Spiritual Awareness (20–25 minutes)

The main objective of this session is to learn the aspects of the analogy of Christ and the church as it relates to the role of the wife to her husband and family.

Ephesians 5:22–23

- *"Wives, submit to your husbands as to the Lord"* (v. 22).

  The apostle Paul uses the term obey in Ephesians 6:1 as it relates to a child's relationship to his or her parents. In what ways are the terms *submit* and *obey* different?

- *"Now as the church submits to Christ, so also wives should submit to their husbands in everything"* (v. 24).

  Why is it important to consider the term "everything" in light of the expression "as to the Lord" in verse 22?

- *"The wife must respect her husband"* (v. 33).

  In what ways can a wife show respect and honor for her husband?

- *"A wife of noble character . . . is worth far more than rubies"* (Prov. 31:10–31).

  In light of verses 11 and 12, what kind of effect does she have on her husband?

In light of verses 13–19, discuss her industrious virtues.

In light of verse 20, discuss her concern for the poor and needy.

According to verses 28–31, the wife is deserving of honor and praise. In what ways can the husband and children praise and reward her?

Help group members understand the analogy between Christ and the church and the wife's relationship to her husband and family.

Assign Scripture references in the spiritual awareness section to group members. The Scriptures should be read and discussed as time permits. Caution: Stay on the subject.

4. Spiritual Application (25 minutes)

Group Discussion: Paul writes in Ephesians 5:22, "Wives, submit to your husbands." In verse 25 he says, "Husbands, love your wives." How do you picture the scriptural balance of "wives, submit . . . husbands, love?" How does this provide a check and balance?

Additional Scripture References		
Genesis 3:16	Deuteronomy 24:5	Ruth 4:13
Proverbs 5:18	Proverbs 18:22	Proverbs 19:13–14
Matthew 1:20	Matthew 19:3	1 Peter 3:1–6

Session Five

God's Plan for the Children

1. Introduction (10–15 minutes)

Opening Prayer
Use a "Present Tense Go-Around." See pages 156–57.

2. Self-Awareness (20–25 minutes)

Having discussed God's plan for the husband and wife, we now focus on God's plan for the children (including any age child that is still living at home). Emphasize that God's plan is for the ideal Christian family. Although many of us may fall short of God's ideal family, we must never lose sight of our goal or become complacent with anything less than God's best for the home. Also emphasize the importance of teaching children God's plan for them as it pertains to parental authority.

Specific goals for the session are:

- To discuss the parental role of authority over children.
- To discover ways they can teach their children God's plan for the children.
- To discuss ways parental authority can be abused.
- To find ways they can be both parents and friends to their children.

Spiritual awareness lead-in question: God is the creator of life. How do you feel about being a partner in the marital union that works with God in creation of another life?

3. Spiritual Awareness (20–25 minutes)

The main objective of this session is to learn the aspects of the child's responsibility in God's plan for the family and the parents' responsibility to teach the children their role.

Ephesians 6:1–2; Colossians 3:20

- *"Children, obey your parents in the Lord, for this is right"* *(Eph. 6:1).*

  How do you picture the term "in the Lord" as being the qualifier to prevent children from being abused, neglected, or commanded to do things that are wrong?

  In view of the phrase "for this is right," how can you express to your children that obedience to their parents is the right thing for them to do?

- *"Honor your father and mother" (Eph. 6:2–3)*

  In what ways can children who have already left home and started their own careers continue to honor their parents?

  Verse 3, quoted from Exodus 20:12, is the promise of God's blessings for those who obey God's commands. What are some of the ways parents can teach this basic philosophy of longevity of life to their children?

- *"Children, obey your parents in everything, for this pleases the Lord" (Col. 3:20).*
  How can children be taught to please God?

- *Children are encouraged to listen and not forsake their parents' instruction (Prov. 1:8–9).*
  In light of verse 9, what will be the result?

Help group members understand the significance of teaching their children God's plan for each child in the Christian family.

Assign Scripture references in the spiritual awareness section to group members. The Scriptures should be read and discussed as time permits. Caution: Stay on the subject.

4. Spiritual Application (25 minutes)

Group Discussion: Paul instructs parents to bring their children up "in the training and instruction of the Lord" (Eph. 6:4). Moses writes, "Impress them [God's commandments] on your children. Talk about them when you sit at home and when you walk along the road, when you lie down and when you get up" (Deut. 6:7). In light of the above verses, how do you view the responsibility of a parent in regard to training and instruction? What is the difference between punishment and discipline? Why is consistency of instruction and discipline important?

Additional Scripture References		
Deuteronomy 4:9	Deuteronomy 11:19	Psalm 127:3
Proverbs 2:1–5	Proverbs 4:1–4	Proverbs 5:7
Proverbs 13:24	Proverbs 22:6	Proverbs 23:22
Proverbs 29:15	Proverbs 29:17	Proverbs 30:17
Matthew 19:14	Mark 10:16	1 Timothy 3:4
1 Timothy 3:12		

Session Six

Submitting to One Another

1. Introduction (10–15 minutes)

Opening Prayer
Use a "Present Tense Go-Around." See pages 156–57.

2. Self-Awareness (20–25 minutes)

The general goal of this session is to help group members understand the significance of the role God has for each family member. God's divine revelation for the family is mutual submission. Each family member submits to and respects the other family members' God-given roles.

Emphasize that lessons about marriage are taught by the parents to the children through verbal and nonverbal communication. These lessons can have a tremendous influence on children—good or bad. For example, if a husband loves and respects his wife, his son will probably love and respect his wife. Also emphasize that when a family member repeatedly crosses the boundaries of his/her role and this develops into a pattern, unhealthy relationships will likely develop. For example, a marriage partner may take on the role of a parent or child to the other partner, or a child may assume the role of a parent. However, flexibility in roles is good when not taken to extremes and when boundary lines remain clear. Parents can be playful and childlike with children, for example, and children can support and foster their parents in certain areas.

Specific goals for the session are:

- To discuss verbal and nonverbal lessons taught by parental role.
- To understand "mutual submission."
- To understand role flexibility.
- To discuss ways role flexibility can be abused.

Spiritual awareness lead-in question: Submitting to one's role in God's plan for the family does not imply slavery, inferiority, or dominance. Paul writes, "There is neither Jew nor Greek, slave nor free, male nor female, for you are all one in Christ Jesus" (Gal. 3:28).

Discuss why submission to authority does not interfere with God's view of equality.

3. Spiritual Awareness (20–25 minutes)

The main objective of this session is to learn the aspects of Christians submitting to one another as it relates to marriage and family relationships.

Ephesians 5:21

- *"Submit to one another" (Eph. 5:21a).*

  In what ways does "mutual submission" foster peaceful relationships in the home? In what ways can authority submit? How did Christ submit his authority to God's will?

- *"Submit to one another out of reverence for Christ" (Eph. 5:21).*
  In view of this verse, how do you picture "mutual submission" as respect and glory for Christ?

- *Verse 21 is a bridge between being "filled with the Spirit" and practical relationships (5:18–6:4).*
  In your own words, describe the association of "be filled with the Spirit" (or be controlled by the Spirit) and the manifestation that follows with "mutual submission" in marriage and family relationships.

- *We are encouraged to "serve one another in love" (Gal. 5:13).*
  In light of verse 13, what are ways we can use our freedom in Christ to serve one another in love versus indulgence in the sinful nature? Discuss the difference between serving "one another in love" versus serving because of duty.

Help group members understand the significance of "mutual submission" as being divine revelation rather than human understanding.

Assign Scripture references in the spiritual awareness section to group members. The Scriptures should be read and discussed as time permits. Caution: Stay on the subject.

4. Spiritual Application (25 minutes)

Group Discussion: Mutual submission is an acknowledgment of the lordship of Jesus Christ. In light of Paul's instruction to "submit to one another out of reverence for Christ" (Eph. 5:21), how can you apply the principle of this verse to your marriage and family relationship?

Additional Scripture References		
Romans 13:1–10	Colossians 3:18–4:1	Hebrews 12:2
Hebrews 13:17	James 4:7	1 Peter 2:13–3:12

Session Seven

Becoming One in Christ

1. Introduction (10–15 minutes)

Opening Prayer
Use a "Future Tense Go-Around." See page 157.

2. Self-Awareness (20–25 minutes)

The general goal of this session is to help group members understand God's plan for husbands and wives becoming one in Christ. Emphasize that this spiritual and physical union is a special miracle of God. Also emphasize that each partner has a responsibility to the other in commitment, love, acceptance, and respect toward this miracle of God.

Although each partner has ministry responsibility to the other, only Christ can provide each individual with true security and significance. Becoming one in marriage does not imply a loss of one's personal identity.

Children benefit from parents who exhibit oneness in Christ. A genuine loving relationship between husbands and wives is important for the children's personal development. Giving attention and focus of affection to children is good; however, it should not interfere with the loving relationship between the parents. A demonstration of the love and affection between parents (doing things together, for example) will contribute to the children's sense of security and self-worth.

Specific goals for the session are:

- To recognize the "specialness" of spiritual and physical union in the marriage relationship.
- To discuss the responsibility of commitment, love, acceptance, and respect toward "oneness" in the marriage relationship.
- To recognize one's true significance and security in light of Jesus Christ.
- To discuss ways parents can demonstrate a loving relationship to their children.

Spiritual awareness lead-in question: Leaving home or former life to join your husband or wife in marriage is like leaving your former life to follow Jesus Christ as Savior. In your own words describe this likeness.

3. Spiritual Awareness (20–25 minutes)

The main objective of this session is to learn the aspects of the analogy of Christ and the church as it relates to "oneness" in the husband and wife relationship.

Ephesians 5:31–32

- *"For this reason a man will leave his father and mother" (Eph. 5:31a).*

  In light of verses 28–30, describe the meaning of the phrase "For this reason."

- *"For this reason a man will leave his father and mother and be united to his wife" (v. 31a).*

  Paul described the leaving of the former childhood family unit. Why is it usually better for newly married couples not to live with their childhood family or be dominated by them?

In light of the term "be united to his wife," in what ways can couples accept each other in the process of "oneness" instead of trying to change their partners?

- *"For this reason a man will leave his father and mother and be united to his wife, and the two will become one flesh" (v. 31).* Marriage can be compared to salvation. It is both a position (legally united) and a process (experientially united). As we allow God to work in this process, we become one flesh. Describe this weaving process in your own words. What is Christ's part? What is your part?

- *Paul describes becoming one in Christ as a "profound mystery" (v. 32).* This secret is also viewed as a symbol of the husband/wife relationship—an intimate relationship. Describe the difficulty marriage partners will have explaining this revealed secret without a personal relationship with Christ.

Help group members understand the significance of "oneness" being divine revelation rather than human understanding.

Assign Scripture references in the spiritual awareness section to group members. The Scriptures should be read and discussed as time permits. Caution: Stay on the subject.

4. Spiritual Application (25 minutes)

Group Discussion: Paul writes, "For this reason a man will leave his father and mother and be united to his wife, and the two will become one flesh" (Eph. 5:31). The "leaving behind" is often difficult when it comes to baggage like unhealthy behavior patterns, neglect, abuse, and lack of role models. Some people suffer from unmet childhood needs. Demanding that those unmet needs be fulfilled by a partner may cause more harm. Paul writes, "When I was a child, I talked like a child, I thought like a child, I reasoned like a child. When I became a man, I put childish ways behind me" (1 Cor. 13:11).

What are some areas of baggage that you need to allow God to help you with in the process of "becoming one"? What about if and when the baggage resurfaces?

Additional Scripture References		
Genesis 2:24	Ecclesiastes 4:9–12	Malachi 2:15–16
Matthew 19:5–6	Mark 10:7–9	1 Corinthians 6:16–17
Ephesians 3:3–6	Colossians 1:26–27	Colossians 2:2
Colossians 4:3		

Session Eight

Forgiving

1. Introduction (10–15 minutes)

Opening Prayer
Use a "Future Tense Go-Around." See page 157.

2. Self-Awareness (20–25 minutes)

Having built on God's plan for the marriage and family relationship in Sessions 1–7, we now begin to focus on principles that contribute to the success of this special relationship. Forgiving one another is vital to the success of marriage and family relationships.

In this session we will focus on God's plan for forgiving one another in the marriage and family relationship. Emphasize that forgiveness means that family members do not permit anger to grow, hold grudges, or keep a record of misdeeds. Also, emphasize that the forgiver receives the greatest benefit from forgiveness. It is important for group members to understand that forgiveness means we forgive ourselves as well as others.

Specific goals for the session are:

- To explore definitions of forgiveness.

- To discuss ways unforgiveness can lead to emotional and spiritual problems.
- To discuss ways to handle misunderstandings.
- To discover the benefits of forgiving one another.

Spiritual awareness lead-in question: Jesus is our perfect example of forgiveness. On the cross Jesus said, "Father, forgive them, for they do not know what they are doing" (Luke 23:34).

Describe in your own words this ultimate expression of love.

3. Spiritual Awareness (20–25 minutes)

The main objective of this session is to learn the aspects of Christ's example of forgiveness as it relates to forgiving one another in the husband and wife relationship.

Colossians 3:13

- *Paul emphasizes the believer's personal responsibility to forgive one another (Col. 3:13).*

  How do you view this verse? How might you relate Paul's command to your personal responsibility to your husband or wife?

- *According to Colossians 2:13 and 14, believers have received forgiveness through Christ.*

  In light of these verses, discuss Christ's example of forgiving our sins as the ultimate incentive to forgive one another.

- *Forgiveness of sin can be viewed as a gift from God: "forgiving each other, just as in Christ God forgave you" (Eph. 4:32).*
  In light of this verse (and John 3:16), how do you picture forgiveness as a gift to give or receive?

- *Jesus stresses the importance of forgiveness in the parable of the unmerciful servant (Matt. 18:21–35).*
  In light of verses 34 and 35, what are the consequences for a person who is unwilling to forgive?

- *Anger should not last longer than a day (Eph. 4:26–27).*
  How do you view these verses in light of preventing anger buildup?

  In what ways do you see "unresolved anger" as providing Satan with a foothold or advantage?

Help group members understand that forgiving one another results from divine revelation rather than human understanding.

Assign Scripture references in the spiritual awareness section to group members. The Scriptures should be read and discussed as time permits. Caution: Stay on the subject.

4. Spiritual Application (25 minutes)

Group Discussion: In Matthew 6:14–15, Jesus shows the divine significance of forgiveness: "For if you forgive men when they sin against you, your heavenly father will also forgive you. But if you do not forgive men their sins, your Father will not forgive your sins." In light of these verses, why is it important that each marriage partner be quick to extend the gift of forgiveness to each other? Discuss this passage in light of Proverbs 8:34–36 (Example: One who does not forgive harms himself or herself).

Additional Scripture References		
2 Chronicles 7:14	Psalm 19:12	Matthew 5:23–24
Matthew 6:12	Mark 11:25	Luke 11:4
Luke 23:34	Ephesians 1:7	1 John 1:9

Session Nine

Communicating with One Another (Part 1)

1. Introduction (10–15 minutes)

Opening Prayer
Use a "Future Tense Go-Around." See page 157.

2. Self-Awareness (20–25 minutes)

The general goal of this session is to help group members understand the significance of proper communications between husbands and wives. Faulty communication is a common problem that can cause marital conflict. Most marriages experience miscommunications (the message sent is not in accord with the message received). When miscommunication rather than clear communication becomes the norm, the marriage is likely to experience difficulty.

According to H. Norman Wright, "Our messages consist of three components: content composes 7 percent of the message; tone of voice, 38 percent; nonverbal (or 'body language'), 55 percent" (*Marital Counseling,* 308). Emphasize the importance of these three components being consistent. Also emphasize the need for eye contact, "I" statements, and active listening.

Specific goals for the session are:

- To understand "Communicating with I-Messages." (See pages 53–54.)
- To understand "Active Listening." (See pages 55–56.)
- To discuss ways to be consistent with the three components of our messages (content, tone of voice, and nonverbal).

Spiritual awareness lead-in question: Being consistent with the three components of our messages helps to create warm affection in the relationship. Paul writes, "Let us have real warm affection for one another as between brothers, and a willingness to let the other man have the credit" (Rom. 12:10, *Phillips*). How do you see "warm affection" as a contribution to communication skills?

3. Spiritual Awareness (20–25 minutes)

The main objective of this session is to learn the aspects of wholesome communication skills as they relate to the husband and wife relationship.

Colossians 4:6

- *Paul emphasizes wholesome conversation (Col. 4:6).*
  According to this verse, there are two ways in which to answer everyone. What are they?

  Describe the meaning of "full of grace" and "seasoned with salt" in your own words.

- *Paul warns against unwholesome talk (Eph. 4:29).*
  In this verse a parallel is presented to unwholesome talk. What is it?

- *Paul emphasizes that his authority in the Lord is to build up rather than to pull down (2 Cor. 10:8).*
  How does this verse relate to the use of authority in the family?

  How does it relate to communication skills as well?

- *It is foolish and shameful to answer one before listening (Prov. 18:13).*
  How does the phrase "jumping to conclusions" relate to this verse?

- *James notes the importance of being "quick to listen" (James 1:19–20).*
  How can slowness to speak and slowness to anger contribute to one's righteousness?

Help group members understand the value of wholesome communications in the marriage and family relationship.

Assign Scripture references in the spiritual awareness section to group members. The Scriptures should be read and discussed as time permits. Caution: Stay on the subject.

4. Spiritual Application (25 minutes)

Group Discussion: The Bible is a book that communicates a special and clear message from God to mankind—"I love you." There are many ways you can express these three special words to your marriage partner such as by purchasing a gift for him or her, or planning a special dinner or trip. One sure way not to miscommunicate is to often say the three words "I love you" to your partner. In your own words what feelings are conveyed by the phrase "I love you?"

Additional Scripture References		
1 Kings 4:34	Proverbs 1:5	Proverbs 10:19
Proverbs 12:15, 25	Proverbs 16:24	Ecclesiastes 5:1
1 Thessalonians 5:15	2 Timothy 2:24	

Session Ten

Communicating with One Another (Part 2)

1. Introduction (10–15 minutes)

Opening Prayer
Use an "Affirmation Go-Around." See page 158.

2. Self-Awareness (20–25 minutes)

This session is a continuation of session 9. Positive communication is very important to the husband and wife relationship. However, conflicts do occur in relationships and can cause disastrous results if not managed properly.

Author David Augsburger offers a creative way through conflict called "care-fronting." He describes caring as a good word and confronting as a bad word. He says, "Together they provide the balance of love and power which lead to effective human relationships" (*Caring Enough to Confront,* 9). The general goal of this session is to help group members understand the significance of care-fronting as a creative way to work through marital misunderstanding and miscommunication. Emphasize the importance of nonjudgmental communication as opposed to "put-downs" and "cut-downs."

Specific goals for the session are:

- To discuss "Five Options for Dealing with Conflict." (See pages 62–63.)
- To discuss "Ways of Care-Fronting without Being Judgmental." (See pages 63–65.)

Spiritual awareness lead-in question: Truth and love are necessary ground for growth in the husband and wife relationship. How do you picture the balance of truth and love in the marriage relationship? How does this balance build trust? Integrity? Spiritual growth?

3. Spiritual Awareness (20–25 minutes)

The main objective of this session is to learn the aspects of truth spoken in love as it relates to the husband and wife relationship.

Ephesians 4:14–15

- *Paul describes immature Christians (v. 14).*
  What are the characteristics of immaturity listed in verse 14?

  How can these same characteristics relate to the husband and wife relationship?

- *In contrast to immaturity, Paul notes the value of "speaking the truth in love" (v. 15).*
  How do you relate the phrase "speaking the truth in love" as a manner of life which is pleasing to our Lord?

- *"Speaking the truth in love" implies a real, noncounterfeit expression and reality of love while holding on to the truth.*
  Why is this so important in communications between husbands and wives?

- *"Speaking the truth in love" suggests spiritual growth (v. 15).*
  Who is the source of our growth?

- *Jesus spoke the truth in love to a woman caught in adultery (John 8:1–11).*
  In verse 11 Jesus communicated truth in love, "Then neither do I condemn you [caring]," Jesus declared. "Go now and leave your life of sin [confronting]."
  Describe care-fronting as it relates to this verse.

- *"Speaking the truth in love" implies weighing one's answers before speaking (Prov. 15:28; 29:20).*
  Describe "weighing one's answers before speaking" as it relates to these verses.

- *"Speaking the truth in love" suggests respect (1 Peter 2:17).*
  Why is it important not to answer seriously intended remarks with "put-downs"?

Why is it important not to answer seriously intended remarks with "cut-downs"?

Describe "cut-downs" as they relate to Proverbs 26:18–19.

Help group members understand the value of wholesome communications in the marriage and family relationship.

Assign Scripture references in the spiritual awareness section to group members. The Scriptures should be read and discussed as time permits. Caution: Stay on the subject.

4. Spiritual Application (25 minutes)

Group Discussion: A concern about a misunderstanding or disagreement between husband and wife may cause a partner to react in a condemning manner. In light of John 3:17, describe God's reason for sending his Son.

John 16:8 describes conviction as a work of the Holy Spirit. What differences do you see between condemnation (punishment) and the Holy Spirit's work of conviction? (The Holy Spirit guides one into all truth.)

Additional Scripture References		
Proverbs 12:25	Proverbs 25:11	Proverbs 26:4–6
Romans 12:9–10	1 Corinthians 13:4–7	Galatians 5:14–15
Ephesians 4:2, 16		

Session Eleven

Family Finances

1. Introduction (10–15 minutes)

Opening Prayer
Use an "Affirmation Go-Around." See page 158.

2. Self-Awareness (20–25 minutes)

The general goal of this session is to help group members understand the importance of financial stewardship in the marriage and family relationship. Money problems can contribute greatly to difficulty in the marriage relationship. Financial stress can usually be traced to poor management and/or distorted attitudes toward family finances.

Emphasize the trap of unwise family financial management. (Examples are impulsive buying, lack of a budget, slavery to credit buying.) Also emphasize the trap of distorted financial attitudes (centering the marriage on money, get-rich-quick schemes, the pursuit of money for happiness, and greed).

Specific goals for the session are:

- To discuss the trap of unwise family financial management. (See page 71.)

- To discuss the trap of distorted financial attitudes. (See page 72.)
- To discuss "The Five Most Common Mistakes in Handling Family Finances." (See page 73.)

Spiritual awareness lead-in question: Placing an emphasis on materialism causes a husband and wife to lose touch with their spiritual needs. Jesus warns, "Be on your guard against all kinds of greed; a man's life does not consist in the abundance of his possessions" (Luke 12:15).

How can greed turn into a trap? As Christians we may say, "I want to earn more so I can give more." Although this may be a good intention, is it also possible to use this phrase as a cover-up for materialism?

3. Spiritual Awareness (20–25 minutes)

The main objective of this session is to learn the aspects of certain biblical principles as they relate to stewardship in the marriage and family relationship.

1 Timothy 6:6–10

- *Paul emphasizes godliness with contentment (vv. 6–7).*
  Paul describes a contrast to "godliness with contentment" in verse 5. What is it?

How do you picture the inward quality of contentment (trust in God's provisions) as a guard against greed?

In your own words, describe the phrase "great gain" as it relates to prosperity. Does it mean more than material wealth?

In light of verse 7, why can materialism be considered as brief and of secondary importance?

- *Paul associates food and clothing with contentment (v. 8).*
  Why is it important to focus our contentment on the real basics of life, as related in Matthew 6:25–34?

- *Paul describes the trap of the love of money (vv. 9–10).*
  According to verse 9, certain people are vulnerable to this trap. Who are they?

- *"The love of money is a root of all kinds of evil" (v. 10).*
  This verse describes the results of greed. What are they? How do you relate heartbreak to this verse?

- *The borrower is servant to the lender" (Prov. 22:7).*
  How do you relate this verse to financial slavery?

- *God blesses those who give (Luke 6:38; Acts 20:35).*
  According to these verses, there are benefits for those who give. What are they?

- *We are to give back to the Lord his portion (Mal. 3:10–11).*
  How do you relate the blessings of God to these verses?

- *Paul provides instruction regarding the principle of giving (1 Cor. 16:2).*
  What does this verse say about systematic giving?

Help group members understand the value of applying biblical principles to stewardship in the marriage and family relationship.

Assign Scripture references in the spiritual awareness section to group members. The Scriptures should be read and discussed as time permits. Caution: Stay on the subject.

4. Spiritual Application (25 minutes)

Group Discussion: Having discussed the guidelines of financial stewardship and possible financial pitfalls, we now focus on God's blessings for his people. First, God owns everything (Ps. 24:1). Second, God has promised to supply our needs (Matt. 6:33; Phil. 4:19). Third, God promises to bless those who sow generously. Paul writes, "Whoever sows sparingly will also reap sparingly, and whoever sows generously will also reap generously. Each man should give what he has decided in his heart to give, not reluctantly nor under compulsion, for God loves a cheerful giver. And God is able to make all grace abound to you, so that in all things at all times, having all that you need, you will abound in every good work" (2 Cor. 9:6–8). How can you apply verses 6 and 7 to your marriage and family relationship? What encouragement does verse 8 provide for a generous, cheerful giver? How does this differ from greed?

Additional Scripture References		
Deuteronomy 8:17–18	Ecclesiastes 5:10	Isaiah 55:1–2
Matthew 6:24	2 Corinthians 8:12	2 Timothy 3:2
Hebrews 13:5	1 Peter 5:2	

Session Twelve

Watch for the Little Foxes

1. Introduction (10–15 minutes)

Opening Prayer
Use an "Accountability Go-Around." See pages 158–59.

2. Self-Awareness (20–25 minutes)

The general goal of this session is to help group members be alert and safe from those little things that turn into big things and subsequently cause harm to the marriage and family relationship. The Song of Songs 2:15 points to this principle, "Catch for us the foxes, the little foxes that ruin the vineyards, our vineyards that are in bloom."

Little things (like the "little foxes") may go unnoticed because they are often cunning, cute, deceitful, sneaky. Being so small, the little foxes may seem unimportant, but they may eventually knock a marriage and family relationship off its feet.

Emphasize the importance of being alert and safe from the little things. Also emphasize that the little foxes are attracted to a marriage when it is in its prime ("vineyards that are in bloom"). It is important that each group member take a personal look at the little foxes as they relate to his or her own responsibility in the marriage and family relationship.

Specific goals for the session are:

- To have each person consider safety from the little foxes as it relates to personal responsibility to his or her partner.
- To have group members discuss:
  - * The little fox of unkindness
  - * The little fox of preoccupation
  - * The little fox of forgetting special days (anniversary, birthdays, etc.)
  - * The little fox of nagging
  - * The little fox of criticism
  - * The little fox of neglecting the Lord's house
  - * The little fox of unthankfulness

Spiritual awareness lead-in question: Learning what the little foxes may be and bringing their progress to a halt is important to our homes. This prevents Satan from getting an advantage or foothold. How do you feel about going on a little fox hunt?

3. Spiritual Awareness (20–25 minutes)

The main objective of this session is to become alert to Satan's schemes as they relate to the husband and wife relationship.

2 Corinthians 2:11

- *Paul highlights the importance of having an awareness of Satan's schemes (2 Cor. 2:5–11).*

  According to verses 5–11, Paul and the Corinthians were aware of a certain danger that could cause Satan to outwit them. What was it?

Paul was aware of the need to forgive and comfort the brother lest Satan outwit them. How can you relate verse 11 to little foxes?

* *"Be self-controlled and alert"* *(1 Peter 5:8–9).*
  In verse 8, Peter gives the reason for self-control and alertness. What is it?

  In what ways can you relate the little foxes to verse 8?

  In light of verse 9, how do we counter Satan's attempt to devour a marriage relationship?

* *"Satan himself masquerades as an angel of light"* *(2 Cor. 11:14).*
  Being the father of lies, Satan regularly presents himself "as an angel of light." In what ways can Satan disguise the little foxes and make them appear to be unimportant? (Examples: "Everybody's doing it," "We're doing it for the kids," "It must be OK; God is blessing us.")

* *Satan showed his deceitfulness in the fall of humanity (Gen. 3:1–7).*
  How did Satan use the power of suggestion?

Help group members understand the significance of watching for the little foxes that can wreck a marriage and family relationship.

Assign Scripture references in the spiritual awareness section to group members. The Scriptures should be read and discussed as time permits. Caution: Stay on the subject.

4. Spiritual Application (25 minutes)

Group Discussion: Destroying the tracks of the little foxes is important to all husband and wife relationships. With God's help, how can each partner go about identifying the *little things* before they become *big things?*

> The little fox of unkindness.
> With God's help, I will:
>
> The little fox of preoccupation.
> With God's help, I will:
>
> The little fox of forgetting special days.
> With God's help, I will:
>
> The little fox of nagging.
> With God's help, I will:
>
> The little fox of criticism.
> With God's help, I will:
>
> The little fox of neglecting the Lord's house.
> With God's help, I will:
>
> The little fox of unthankfulness.
> With God's help, I will:

Additional Scripture References		
Job 1:6–12	Matthew 4:1–11	Mark 4:15
John 8:44–45	Ephesians 4:27	Ephesians 6:12
2 Timothy 2:26	Revelation 12:9–11	Revelation 20:2, 7

Session Thirteen

The Family Altar

1. Introduction (10–15 minutes)

Opening Prayer
Use an "Accountability Go-Around." See pages 158–59.

2. Self-Awareness (20–25 minutes)

This session brings us to a point of completion; however, the growth of our marriage and family relationships should continue. Although we have discussed very needful and pertinent spiritual growth aspects in the family relationship during the previous twelve sessions, all will fall short if the marriage and family relationship is not built on prayer. Prayer is the very fabric that will hold our marriage and family in the loving hands of our Lord.

The first altar recorded in the Bible is the altar built by Noah after leaving the ark (Gen. 8:20). Today we refer to the altar as a place where we express our total dependence upon God through intercession, request, praise, and confession.

Emphasize that the family altar will greatly contribute to the spiritual well-being of any family. It may be advisable for husbands and wives to designate a certain room or piece of furniture as a place where the family assembles to pray at a certain time every day. Although prayer is not limited to certain rooms or places, there is sacredness about a designated family altar that will leave a lasting impression on family members.

Also emphasize that many things will compete against the establishment of the family altar (television, interruptions from various sources, fatigue, overworked schedules, and meetings). Disciplining ourselves to make prayer a top priority will reap eternal dividends.

Specific goals for the sessions are:

- To have group members find a place in their home that could be designated as the family altar.
- To discuss the rewards of the family altar.
- To compare and contrast the value of the family altar to the altar of TV.
- To discuss ways marriage partners can discipline themselves against those things that rival the family altar.

Spiritual awareness lead-in question: Prayer is the way we express our total dependence upon God for our marriage and family. Paul writes, "For from him [creator] and through him [sustainer] and to him [our aim] are all things. To him [object of our praise] be the glory forever! Amen" (Rom. 11:36). How do you picture total dependence on God for your marriage in light of this verse?

3. Spiritual Awareness (20–25 minutes)

The main objective of this session is to learn the aspects of prayer as they relate to the husband and wife relationship.

Matthew 7:7–12

- *Jesus encourages us to pray (Matt. 7:7–12).*

  There is a tremendous promise to those who ask (keep asking), seek (keep seeking), and knock (keep knocking). How can you relate this promise in verses 8–12 to your marriage and family?

  Although we should not set our hearts on material things (see Ps. 62:10), the Lord does not deprive us of material things or doors of opportunity. As parents, we want what is best for our children. In light of verses 9–12, what similarities and contrasts do you see between earthly fathers and our heavenly Father?

- *The Bible urges us to pray and worship God regularly (Pss. 55:17; 119:164; Dan. 6:10; Acts 3:1).*

  In what ways do you see systematic prayer and worship in these verses? How can you relate this to your family altar?

- *Prayers can be hindered when family relationships are not right (Ps. 66:18; Prov. 28:13; 1 Peter 3:1–7).*

  In light of these verses, how can each marriage partner prevent these obstacles to answered prayers?

- *Christian families are in spiritual warfare for the preservation of their homes (Eph. 6:11–12).*

  In this battle for our home, whom does Paul present as the enemy in verse 12?

Why should the husband and wife stand together in this fight for their home?

*   *The Word of God and prayer play a vital part in spiritual warfare (Eph. 6:17–18).*
    In your own words, describe these verses and how they can apply to the family altar.

Help group members understand the value of setting aside a time each day for family prayer and worship.

Assign Scripture references in the spiritual awareness section to group members. The Scriptures should be read and discussed as time permits. Caution: Stay on the subject.

4. Spiritual Application (25 minutes)

Group Discussion: During the past few weeks, we have had the opportunity to study and have been encouraged to apply certain biblical principles to marriage and family relationships. Having a personal responsibility to both God and our marriage partner, it is important to follow through with our commitment. With God's help, we can publicly commit ourselves as Joshua did, "But as for me and my household, we will serve the LORD" (Josh. 24:15).

How do you plan to fulfill this commitment? What role will the family altar play?

Additional Scripture References		
Deuteronomy 4:7	1 Samuel 12:23	2 Chronicles 7:14
Psalm 6:9	Psalm 86:6	Proverbs 15:8
Mark 11:24	Luke 18:1	Acts 16:25–34
Philippians 4:6	1 Thessalonians 5:16–18	

Part Three
Resources

Selected Scriptures

Anger	Prov. 14:29; 15:18; 16:32; 17:27; 19:11; 29:11; Matt. 5:22–26; James 1:19–21; Eph. 4:26–27; Eccles. 7:9
Anxiety/Worry	Ps. 43:5; Matt. 6:31–32; Luke 12:29–31; 1 Peter 5:7
Bereavement/Loss	Deut. 31:8; Pss. 27:10; 119:50; Lam. 3:32–33; 2 Cor. 6:10; Phil. 3:8
Fatherless	Ps. 68:5
Bitterness (General)	Eph. 4:31–32; Heb. 12:15; 1 John 2:11
Won't Listen	Prov. 15:32
Malice	Col. 3:8; Eph. 4:31; 1 Peter 2:1
Resentments	1 Peter 2:1–3; 1 John 2:11; Prov. 26:23–26
Revenge	Rom. 12:19
Slander	Eph. 4:31; 1 Peter 2:1; Ps. 69
Unforgiveness	Matt. 6:14–15; Mark 11:25–26; Eph. 4:32; 2 Cor. 2:10–11; Matt. 18:21–22
Comfort	Rom. 8:26–28;15:4; 2 Cor. 1:3–5; 2 Thess. 2:16–17; Heb. 13:5–6
Complaining	Phil. 2:14; 1 Cor. 10:10; 1 Peter 4:9
Condemnation	Ezek. 18:20; Ps. 34:22; Rom. 4:5; 8:1; 1 John 1:7; 3:19–21
Confidence (in God)	Gen. 18:25; Jer. 9:24; 32:17–19, 27; Isa. 30:15; Ps. 138:3; Prov. 3:26; 14:26; Rom. 8:26–28; 2 Cor. 2:14; Eph. 3:11–12; Phil. 4:13; Heb. 10:35
Contentment	Phil. 4:11–12; 1 Tim. 6:6–10; Heb. 13:5–6
Danger	Ps. 34:17, 19; Isa. 43:2; Rom. 14:8; James 4:7
Depression	Isa. 60:1; Ps. 27:14; John 16:33; 2 Cor. 4:1–17; Gal. 6:9–10; Phil. 4:8–13; 2 Thess. 3:11–13; Heb. 12:4–7

Disappointment in God	Pss. 43:5; 55:22; 126:6; Gen. 18:25; Jer. 9:24
Discouragement in Ministry	1 Sam. 30:6; Ps. 27:14; John 14:27; 16:33; Acts 14:22; Rom. 5:5; 15:13; 2 Cor. 10:5; Eph. 6:16; 1 Thess. 5:11; Heb. 2:3–13; 10:24–25; Gal. 6:9; 1 Cor. 15:58
Divorce	Mal. 2:14–16; Matt. 5:31–32; 19:4–6; Mark 10:11–12; Luke 16:18; 1 Cor. 7:10–11, 27
Drunkenness	Rom. 14:21; 1 Cor. 6:9–11; 10:31–32; Eph. 5:18; 1 Tim. 3:8; 1 Peter 4:3
Envy/Jealousy	Prov. 23:17; James 3:14–16; 1 Cor. 13:4; Heb. 13:5; Gal. 5:26
Faith	Rom. 4:3–5; 10:11, 17; Gal. 2:16; Phil. 4:13, 19; Heb. 12:2; James 1:3; 1 Peter 1:7; Acts 13:39; 15:8–11
Fear	Pss. 27:1; 34:4; 56:3, 11; John 14:27; Rom. 8:15; Rom. 8:31; 2 Tim. 1:7; James 4:7; 1 John 4:18
Forgiveness	Pss. 32:5; 103:3; Prov. 28:13; Isa. 55:7; John 5:24; 6:47; Acts 10:43; 13:39; 26:18; Heb. 8:12; James 5:15–16; 1 John 1:9
Forgiving	Matt. 6:14–15; Mark 11:25; Eph. 4:32; Col. 3:13
Freedom	Rev. 1:5; Rom. 6:6–7; 11–14
Friendships	Prov. 14:7; 17:7; 18:24; 22:24–25; 2 Cor. 6:14; Rom. 12:16; 1 Cor. 15:33; James 4:4
Gospel	1 Cor. 15:3–4; Acts 2:22–24; 10:38–43; 13:30–39; 1 Peter 2:22–24; Titus 3:5
Greed	Prov. 28:22; Eph. 5:5; Matt. 6:19–24; Col. 3:5; 1 Tim. 6:5–10
Guidance	Ps. 32:8; Isa. 30:21; 58:11; Rom. 8:14; John 16:7, 13
Hatred	1 John 2:9–11; 4:19–21
Help	Pss. 34:7; 37:5, 24; 55:22; Jer. 29:11–13; 2 Cor. 2:14; 9:8; 1 Peter 5:7; Heb. 4:16; Isa. 54:17
Homosexuality	1 Cor. 6:9–11; Rom. 1:24, 27, 32; Lev. 18:22; 20:13
Inspiration of Word	1 Thess. 2:13; 2 Tim. 3:16–17; Matt. 5:17–18; 22:43; 2 Peter 1:19–21; 3:16; Heb. 4:12; Jer. 8:9
Intolerance	
Bigotry	Gal. 3:28; Col. 3:11; Rom. 15:7
Criticism	Num. 11:1; James 5:9
Gossip	1 Tim. 5:13

Hatred	1 John 4:19–21
Jealousy	1 Cor. 13:4; James 3:14–16; 1 Cor. 3:3; Gal. 5:19–21; Rom. 13:13
Judgmental Spirit	Matt. 7:1–2; Rom. 14:10
Rebellion	Num. 16:1–11
Revenge	Rom. 12:19
Snobbery	Rom. 12:16; 15:7; Phil. 2:3
Judging	James 5:9; Matt. 7:1; 1 Cor. 4:3–5; Rom. 14:10
Laziness	Col. 3:23; 2 Thess. 3:10–12; Rom. 12:11; Eph. 4:28; 1 Thess. 4:11–12; Prov. 15:19; Titus 1:12
Love (God's)	John 3:16; 15:9; Rom. 5:8; 8:38–39; 1 John 3:1; 4:10–11; Jer. 31:3
Masturbation	Rom. 13:14; 1 Thess. 4:3–5; Matt. 5:28; 2 Cor. 10:5
Moral Impurity	Eph. 5:5; 1 Cor. 6:9–11; Col. 3:5–6; Rom. 13:13–14; 1 Thess. 4:3–8; 2 Tim. 2:22; Titus 2:12–15; Heb. 13:4
Perseverance	1 Cor. 13:7; Heb. 10:35–12:1; Phil. 1:6; 1 Thess. 5:24; 2 Tim. 1:12; 2:12–13; James 5:11; Heb. 4:16
Pride	Jer. 9:23–24; 1 Cor. 1:26–29; Rom. 12:16; Prov. 16:18; Gal. 6:3, 14; 5:26
Procrastination	Eph. 5:15–16; Rom. 12:11
Quarrelsome	2 Tim. 2:24–25; Heb. 12:14; Rom. 14:19; James 4:1–2; Gal. 5:15
Rebellion	1 Tim. 1:9; Titus 1:6; Heb. 13:17; Rom. 13:2, 5; 1 Peter 2:13–15; 1 Sam. 15:22–23
Rejection	Isa. 53:3–4; Luke 6:22; Heb. 13:5
Repentance	2 Cor. 7:9–10; 2 Tim. 2:25; Acts 3:19–21; 26:18–20
Righteousness	Phil. 3:9–10; Jer. 23:5–6; Rom. 3:21–26; 4:3, 13, 22; Gal. 2:21; 3:6; 1 Tim. 6:11; 1 John 3:10; Titus 2:11–12
Self-Ambition	James 3:16; Rom. 2:8; Phil. 1:17
Self-Control	Gal. 5:22–24; Ps. 119:11; Prov. 25:28; Luke 22:40; Rom. 12:2; 2 Cor. 10:5; Phil. 4:8–9; 2 Thess. 3:10–12; 1 Thess. 4:11–12
Self-Dignity (in Christ)	Eph. 5:8; Gal. 2:19–20; 3:26, 29; 1 John 2:12–14; 3:2, 19; 1 Peter 2:5, 9
Self-Indulgence	Titus 1:6; Prov. 21:17; Matt. 23:25
Self-Willed	Titus 1:7; 2 Peter 2:10; 1 Cor. 10:33
Selfishness	Phil. 2:3; 1 Cor. 10:33–11:1; Rom. 13:8–10

Sickness	Matt. 8:17; Isa. 53:4; Ps. 103:3; 1 Peter 2:24; James 5:15–16
Sin Cycle	Judges 2:10–23; Ps. 106:6–48; Neh. 9:26–31; 1 Cor. 10:1–13
Spiritual Growth	Gal. 5:24–25; 6:1–2; 2 Cor. 1:12; Eph. 3:17–19; 6:10–18; Col. 1:9–12; 3:16; 2 Tim. 2:15; 2 Peter 1:5–8; 3:18
Strength	Pss. 27:14; 28:7; 138:3; Isa. 41:10; 2 Cor. 9:8; 12:9; Phil. 4:13; 1 Thess. 3:2–3; 1 Peter 5:10
Suffering (Sin) (for God)	Jer. 2:19; 5:25; 1 Peter 2:11; Gal. 6:7 1 Peter 2:20–23; 1 Thess. 3:3; Phil. 3:8–10; 2 Tim. 1:12; 1 Peter 4:12–13, 16, 19; 5:9–10; Acts 14:22; Ps. 34:19; John 16:33; Rom. 8:18
Testing/Trial	1 Peter 1:6–7; 4:12–13; 5:9–10; James 1:2–4, 12; Prov. 17:3; 1 Cor. 10:12–13; Jude 24
Thankfulness	Eph. 5:20; Phil. 4:6; Col. 3:17; 1 Thess. 5:18
Trust	Pss. 5:11; 18:2; 37; 118:8–9

Choosing to Love

by Jerry and Barbara Cook

If I am the object of your love
and you are the object of my love,
then we are each free
to be ourselves.

When secure in your love
I need not control you,
manipulate you,
compete with you
or remake you in my image.

I admire you,
accept you totally,
respect and trust you.

But I do not feel I must apologize
for not being like you,
for thinking different thoughts,
feeling different emotions,
enjoying something you don't
or being excited about something
that bores you.

If I deny who I am,
I have nothing to give you
but a mindless china doll;
an empty shell who is not a
real woman,
but a toy you've outgrown.

When I share what I think
It is not to coerce—or
demand that you agree.

I offer myself
to persuade—
encourage—
But—
not to dominate.

Whatever I share is a gift of my love,
an act of trust that you'll accept me
and understand that
I'm making an offer,
an honest disclosure;
not a power play.

Love is not possible between superiors and inferiors
since the superior can only condescend
and the inferior only admire.

Mutual respect means I do not exploit
either your strengths
or your weaknesses,
but enjoy you
as a unique friend.

To believe we can have a marriage of
sustained mutual respect
can only mean
we believe in forgiveness!

So when I ask, in the pattern of Jesus,
"What do you want?"
"What are your needs?"

I am not being subservient
nor am I giving my will to you
(handing over the lordship of my life . . .
even God will not take over my will).

I am rather
making a choice,
a decision to love,
to truly give—for the joy of it
because of your value to me.

Used by permission

"One Another" Scriptures

Be devoted to *one another* . . . Romans 12:10

Love *one another* . . . Romans 13:8; 1 Peter 1:22; 1 John 3:11, 23; 4:7, 11–12; 2 John 5

Accept *one another* . . . Romans 15:7

Instruct *one another* . . . Romans 15:14

Concern for *each other* . . . 1 Corinthians 12:25

Serve *one another* . . . Galatians 5:13

Carry *each other's* burdens . . . Galatians 6:2

Be kind and compassionate to *one another* . . . Ephesians 4:32

Bear with *each other* . . . Colossians 3:13

Forgive *one another* . . . Colossians 3:13

Comfort *one another* . . . 1 Thessalonians 4:18 KJV

Encourage *one another* . . . Hebrews 3:13

Confess your sins to *each other* . . . James 5:16

Pray for *each other* . . . James 5:16

Spur *one another* on toward love . . . Hebrews 10:24

Jesus replied: "'Love the Lord your God with all your heart and with all your soul and with all your mind.' This is the first and greatest commandment. And the second is like it: 'Love your neighbor as yourself'" (Matt. 22:37–39).

Sharing Questions

Go-arounds (Sharing Questions) are an effective way to start each group meeting. This helps group participants talk about themselves in a structured context, setting the stage for the self-awareness or spiritual awareness and application phases of the small group format. Go-arounds are not designed for in-depth sharing but to prepare each participant for meaningful group interaction.

Past Tense Go-Arounds

These questions are effective in the early stages of group life. They serve to acquaint participants with each other, which helps to build friendship and trust.

Past Tense Questions (Examples)

- When was the first time you realized that you were in love with your husband/wife?
- What was the best vacation you ever took with your family?
- Where did you meet your husband/wife?
- Where did you live and what were you doing when you were in the sixth grade?
- What do you remember most about your wedding or marriage ceremony?
- As a child, who had the most influence on your life?
- When and where was the first time you remember your husband/wife telling you that he/she loved you?

- As a child, how was your relationship with your family?
- As a child, what kind of relationship did you have with the church?
- As a child, what was your favorite holiday? Why?
- What do you remember most about your grandparents?
- What do you remember most about your first date with your husband/wife?
- What is your first remembrance of God?
- What was your most embarrassing experience in school?
- What is your first remembrance of your husband/wife?

Present Tense Go-Arounds

These questions invite participants to discuss experiences in daily living.

Present Tense Questions (Examples)

- What is your favorite Bible verse? Why?
- What is your husband's/wife's favorite restaurant? Why?
- What is your favorite place in your home? Why?
- What favorite nickname does your husband/wife call you?
- In your free time, what do you like to do most?
- What is one thing you are proud of about yourself?
- What Bible character does your husband/wife remind you of? Why?
- If you could pick one person in the Bible or church history that you would prefer to be like, who would that be? Why?
- What is one thing you are proud of about your husband/wife?
- How has the "weather" been in your life since we last met? Has it been sunny, cloudy, rainy, stormy, etc.?
- What is the most significant thing that happened to you this week?
- What social activity do you enjoy most with your husband/wife?

- What were the high and low spots of your week?
- What is one area where you would like to grow in your Christian faith? What kind of help do you need to do it?
- What does freedom in Christ mean to you?
- What is your current relationship with God?
- How do you feel when you think about God as your heavenly Father?
- If you could receive one unexpected present, what would it be? Why?
- What do you do on a typical Monday evening?
- What are two things that you like about yourself? Why?

Future Tense Go-Arounds

These questions invite people to focus on the future aspects of their lives, their expectations, hopes, and dreams. These questions are usually more effective after the group has been together for a few weeks.

Future Tense Questions (Examples)

- What career do you picture for yourself in ten years?
- If you suddenly received a million dollars, how would you spend it?
- What would be a dream home for you?
- If you could predict your relationship with God in ten years, what would it be?
- What kind of a person do you want to be remembered as?
- What kind of a husband/wife do you want to be remembered as?
- What one question would you like to ask God when you meet him?
- How would you like for your children to remember you?
- What one Bible character from the Old Testament would you most like to meet? Why?
- What one Bible character from the New Testament, in addition to Jesus, would you most like to meet? Why?

Affirmation Go-Arounds

These questions invite people to say encouraging and positive things to each other. Affirmation questions are particularly effective during the later stages of group life.

Affirmation Questions (Examples)

- What has been said by a group member that has been most meaningful to you?
- What spiritual insight have you received in this group?
- What do you value most about this group?
- What kind of help have you received from this group?
- What will you miss most at the conclusion of this group?
- How would you describe the qualities of this group?
- How would you describe the qualities of your husband/wife?
- If you could present a gift of encouragement to each member in this group, what would it be?
  Examples:
  To John—A set of weights to remind him of spiritual discipline.
  To Sue—An eagle to remind her that she can fly above the clouds with God's help.
  To Pam—A piece of expensive pottery to remind her of the beauty in her that has resulted from the test of fire.
  To Joe—A pair of shoes to remind him that Christ is walking with him.
- What are two things that you like most about your husband/wife?

Accountability Go-Arounds

These questions invite people to deeper commitment. They are designed to help group members stand with each other (not dominate) in their faith. Such questions should be reserved for group members who have agreed to be accountable to one another.

Accountability Questions (Examples)

- What one relationship needs your atte
  steps can you take to strengthen it?
- What is the weak link in your relationship w
  plans do you have to correct it?
- Who will help you remain accountable to you   ⌐l
  goals? How?
- How do you remain accountable to your commitments?
- In what one area do you struggle most with accountability?
  What steps are you taking to correct it?
- What one decision are you making, or thinking about, that
  will require you to remain accountable to someone? Who
  will you look to for help?
- What kind of devotional time (prayer and Bible study) will
  you observe this week?
- What area of commitment do you need to renew with your
  husband/wife?

Friend Search

Each of us comes in contact daily with others who share similar interests. Put a checkmark in each box that tells about you, and fill in the bottom row with things that tell about you (like, "has a sister" or "speaks French"). To find out what you and others may have in common, ask group members to sign the boxes that tell something about them.

When you see what you have in common, share these mutual interests with a new friend.

has a record collection	can swim	likes to jog	likes to sing	likes to travel
likes to fish	drives a car	likes to shop	visited a foreign country	likes to read
likes to cook	likes movies	plays an instrument	has a computer	has a part-time job
collects something	is a class or club officer	likes to paint	has a hero	has a pet
likes sports	plays tennis	won an award	likes to draw	writes poetry
_____	_____	_____	_____	_____

Phases of Life-Controlling Problems

Phase 1 Experimentation	Phase 2 Social
FEELINGS High _____ Normal ⟋⟍⟋⟍⟋⟍ Pain _____	FEELINGS High _____ Normal ⋀⋀ ⋀⋀ Pain _____
Learns that experimenting with the allurement makes one feel good Does not generally recognize any serious negative consequences Learns to trust the allurement Learns how much to use (substance) or practice (behavior) to feel great	More regular use or practice Makes "this" a part of social life Use or practice at appropriate times and places Makes "safe" rules for self regarding use or practice Trust becomes locked on the compulsive behavior Turns into problem without warning
Phase 3 **Daily Preoccupation**	**Phase 4** **Using/Practicing to Feel Normal**
FEELINGS High _____ Normal ⋀⋀⋀⋀⋁⋁⋁⋁ Pain _____	FEELINGS High _____ Normal _____ Pain ⋀⋀⋀⋀
Becomes a harmful dependency Begins to lose control over use/practice Violates value system Cannot block out the emotional pain Unresolved problems produce more stress and pain Lifestyle centers on compulsive behavior Self-imposed rules broken regularly Deteriorating health, spirituality, relationships, etc.	Paranoid thinking—delusion Geographic escapes No desire to live Spiritual bankruptcy Loss of control and dignity Problems have "snowball effect" Broken family relationships

How to Receive Christ

1. Admit your need (that you are a sinner).
2. Be willing to turn from your sins (repent).
3. Believe that Jesus Christ died for you on the cross and rose from the grave.
4. Through prayer, invite Jesus Christ to come in and control your life through the Holy Spirit. (Receive him as Savior and Lord.)

What to pray . . .

Dear God,

I know that I am a sinner and need your forgiveness.

I believe that Jesus Christ died for my sins.

I am willing to turn from my sins.

I now invite Jesus Christ to come into my heart and life as my personal Savior.

I am willing, by God's strength, to follow and obey Jesus Christ as the Lord of my life.

Date _____

Signature _____

The Bible says

Everyone who calls on the name of the Lord will be saved.

Romans 10:13

To all who received him, to those who believed in his name, he gave the right to become children of God.

John 1:12

Therefore, since we have been justified through faith, we have peace with God through our Lord Jesus Christ.

Romans 5:1

When we receive Christ, we are born into the family of God through the supernatural work of the Holy Spirit who lives within every believer. This process is called regeneration or the new birth.

Share your decision to receive Christ with another person.

Suggested Reading

Augsburger, David. *Caring Enough to Confront*. Glendale: Regal Books, 1980.

Balswick, Jack O., and Judith K. Balswick. *The Family—A Christian Perspective on the Contemporary Home*. Grand Rapids: Baker Book House, 1991.

Crabb, Lawrence J. *Effective Biblical Counseling*. Grand Rapids: Zondervan Publishing House, 1977.

———. *The Marriage Builder*. Grand Rapids: Zondervan Publishing House, 1982.

———. *Men and Women*. Grand Rapids: Zondervan Publishing House, 1991.

Harley, William. *His Needs, Her Needs*. Grand Rapids: Fleming H. Revell, 1986, 1994.

———. *Love Busters*. Grand Rapids: Fleming H. Revell, 1992.

Harvey, Donald. *The Drifting Marriage*. Grand Rapids: Fleming H. Revell, 1988.

Hestenes, Roberta. *Using the Bible in Groups*. Philadelphia: The Westminster Press, 1983.

Lee, Jimmy Ray. *Behind Our Sunday Smiles*. Grand Rapids: Baker Book House, 1991.

Leman, Kevin. *Keeping Your Family Together When the World is Falling Apart*. New York: Delacorte Press, 1992.

———. *The Birth Order Book*. Grand Rapids: Fleming H. Revell, 1985.

Meier, Paul, Donald Ratcliff, and Frederick Rowe. *Child-Rearing*. Grand Rapids: Baker Book House, 1993.

Parrott III, Les. *Helping the Struggling Adolescent*. Grand Rapids: Zondervan Publishing House, 1993.

Smalley, Gary. *For Better or Best*. Grand Rapids: Zondervan Publishing House, 1988.

Stanley, Charles F. *Handle with Prayer*. Wheaton: Victor Books, 1988.

Wright, H. Norman. *Marital Counseling*. San Francisco: Harper and Row, 1983.

Turning Point is a training program designed to help your church reach out to people at various phases of life-controlling problems. This is accomplished through a systematic program which gives training, support, and a framework to a group of lay people in your church.

With practical curricula based solidly on Scripture, Turning Point materials will keep your small groups on track.

If you wish to have a Turning Point Seminar in your church or community, contact Jimmy Ray Lee, P.O. Box 22127, Chattanooga, TN 37422-2127.

Page 31 - Last line, change word "in" to "at"

Page 59 - Invert Fig. 4-10

Page 59 - 2nd line. Change 40-mm to 25-mm.

Page 71 - 22nd line. Change to read: a focal length 10 times smaller than that chosen for the carbon dioxide.

Page 72 - 21st line. Change word centimeters to centimeter.

Page 72 - (Equation at bottom of page) change to

$$P_s = \frac{P}{\pi (D_s/2)^2} = \frac{4P}{\pi (D_s)^2}$$

Page 107 - 6th line from bottom. Change word "aperature" to aperture

Page 162 - Insert the following discussion instead of that given for laser timer: A precision timing device, which is rugged, reliable, and unaffected by vibration and shock, with an accuracy of 0.1 percent is needed for underwater missile applications. Such a device should produce a fixed-frequency square wave on the order of a laser repeater-type diode logic circuitry. It would be a distint improvement over the mechanical timers, silver-wire bead timers, and electronic timers generally in use at present.

Page 177 - 17th line. Change to read "Fig. 16-1 shows the part of the laser beam that is absorbed by"

Laser Fundamentals
&
Applications

by

Hrand M. Muncheryan, B.Sc., M.Sc.

HOWARD W. SAMS & CO., INC.
THE BOBBS-MERRILL CO., INC.
INDIANAPOLIS · KANSAS CITY · NEW YORK

FIRST EDITION

FIRST PRINTING—1975

International Standard Book Number: 0-672-21130-0
Library of Congress Catalog Card Number: 74-15458

Preface

The discovery of lasers has created much interest both in the general public and among scientists. With this in view, this book is written for those who are making their first acquaintance with laser technology and for those who are now engaged in laser work. It is designed to expand their knowledge and stimulate their imagination so that new laser products can be developed by using the fundamental concepts presented here. The material in this text will help the reader understand the various underlying principles of laser technology. The material is organized so that the reader is progressively introduced to increasingly more complex systems. In this respect, the first chapter discusses the basic fundamentals that are applied in the use and application of lasers in industry and in the scientific laboratory. After the beginner has gained this preliminary knowledge, it is anticipated that he will readily understand the successive chapters covering varied technical and practical laser instrumentation.

The author has refrained from the use of highly mathematical expressions in the treatment of various subjects, but of necessity some exemplary problems have been presented and solutions worked out using a minimum of applicable mathematical relations and physical terms. What little mathematics that has been used is all that one will require in applied developmental work. These mathematical relations are merely introduced to verify and support the technical statements about any one subject treated in this book.

There are many who have wanted a practical, one-volume treatise on lasers that will be easy to understand and that will dispel the mystery of radiation, showing it to be a scientific tool, not a science-fiction implement or an ominous destructive weapon. This volume shows the many ways lasers can be used, such as to facilitate certain industrial operations and to enable surgeons to perform operations that would be difficult and at times impossible by conventional methods. In these respects, lasers have already played prominent roles in cutting, drilling, scribing, and trimming industrial materials. In the medical field, surgery on the brain and on bleeding organs in the body has been possible through the cauterizing action of the laser beam. In dentistry, the use of lasers for restorative dental work is being developed in many scientific and dental institutions. Last, but not least, is the upcoming use of lasers in the optical communication field to replace the bulky and expensive underground or above-ground transmission cables. Lasers are also gradually finding their way into private offices and homes for protection and security purposes. The application of lasers for making everyday life easier are just beginning to appear; their vast potentialities are still waiting to be exploited for the benefit of mankind. The successful application of a new discovery is not always a simple replacement operation but is often a matter of using the new discovery to complement an application presently in use. Initial approaches to such applications have been suggested in this volume.

The verification of the fundamental principles affecting the laser technology is unquestionably best understood by solving illustrative problems. And to this end, the author has selected a few practical problems and solved them using simple and basic mathematics. This text is developed primarily to be used by itself without supplementary information from other publications. The material contained in it is self-sufficient for practical, informational purposes.

The book has combined classical and quantum theories in the explanation of the laser-emission phenomenon. While it would be easy to compile well-known physical concepts and discuss topics already repeated in many publications, the author refrains from such schemes in order to advance his own method of treatment of the subjects discussed.

It is anticipated that the present treatise on the subject of lasers will fulfill a long-felt need for a complete presentation of practical laser technology and its present, as well as future, potentialities. It is not the intent of this book to be unduly extensive in the treatment of the subject matter. Those occupied in various phases of laser technology may wish to refer to other volumes specializing in a more-theoretical treatment. This book is for the practical solutions to everyday problems that may arise in routine and specialized work.

Appendix I lists a number of well-know manufacturers of laser and laser-oriented equipment. Appendix II contains equivalents of metric system units. Appendix III gives the definitions of some of the commonly used laser terminology, and Appendix IV contains a theoretical explanation of the concepts discussed in this book.

The author is grateful to those laser manufacturers who have permitted the inclusion of photographs of their equipment and some pertinent data.

HRAND M. MUNCHERYAN

Contents

CHAPTER 1

Applied Laser Principles

Laser has been defined as *L*ight *A*mplification by *S*timulated *E*mission of *R*adiation. The word *laser* is an acronym formed by the first letter of each word in its definition. However, to the uninitiated, this definition falls short of an explicit meaning. A simple definition for a laser would be "a light-emitting body with feedback for amplifying the emitted light." As an example, we may take an elementary light emitter or generator, such as a ruby rod of about 1 centimeter in diameter and 15 centimeters long. When this ruby rod is illuminated by a high-intensity light, such as that from a photoflash lamp, the rod fluoresces with a pink color. The fluorescence persists as long as the photoflash light persists. This effect is not a laser radiation, but just another optical characteristic of the emitter, the ruby rod, which is made of aluminum oxide (sapphire) containing 0.05% chromium which imparts to the rod the characteristic pink color.

In laser radiation, the ends of the ruby rod are highly polished so that light can pass through almost without absorption. Also, a mirror is placed at each end and aligned perpendicularly to the principal axis of the rod. When the rod is illuminated with an intense photoflash light, it emits a fluorescent light which reflects back and forth between the two mirrors, with an increase in intensity. This phenomenon, known as light amplification, is produced by the oscillation of the ruby light within an optically resonant cavity formed by the rod and the two reflecting surfaces of the mirrors. The light in the resonant cavity is known as a laser. If the flashlamp illumination (pumping) of the ruby rod continues for a few minutes, the energy accumulated within the ruby rod will be so great that the rod may crack or shatter into pieces. Accordingly, the laser energy must be removed as fast as it develops in the resonant cavity.

The removal of the laser energy, or radiation, from the resonant cavity is accomplished by making one mirror 100% reflective and the other mirror partially reflective. This allows some of the laser light generated within the resonant cavity to pass through as a laser beam of the same diameter as the ruby rod. Also, instead of having two mirrors aligned one at each end of the ruby rod, the highly polished ends can be mirrored or coated with a dielectric material, such as magnesium fluoride or cerium dioxide. One end is fully coated and the other end is partially coated so that the emitted laser light can pass through it. As this beam emerges from the ruby rod, it has a slight divergence, which will be taken up in a later section.

During the illumination (optical pumping) of the ruby rod by the flashlamp, some of the chromium atoms in the ruby rod become excited. This causes their electrons (negative charges) to move away from the atoms and position themselves at higher energy levels, from which they spontaneously fall back to their normal energy states. During this transition, each of these electrons produces a photon of light. These photons now oscillate by reflecting from one mirror surface to the other within the resonant cavity. On their way to the mirror, some of the photons encounter (collide with) one or more atoms, which are in an excited state due to the flashlamp pumping, and interact with them to produce a photon or photons identical in energy and frequency with the initial photon(s). The newly formed photons continue to interact with other excited atoms, producing more photons, and these (photons) continue interacting to produce more photons, and so on. When a threshold energy of the total photonic energy within the resonant cavity is attained, a pulse, consisting of a very intense laser beam formed by photon waves, bursts out of the partially reflective end of the ruby rod. This beam is known as the stimulated emission of laser radiation in which all projecting photon waves propagate in phase, resulting in a coherent laser beam— unlike white light which is not coherent because the light waves are not in phase with each other.

In this book, four types of lasers will be discussed in various laser system applications:

1. *Solid-state rod-type lasers,* which use materials such as ruby, neodymium-doped glass, and neodymium-YAG

(yttrium-aluminum-garnet) and in which stimulation for laser emission is the same for all.

2. *Semiconductor diode-type lasers* which use material such as gallium arsenide and which consist of a *pn junction* formed by a *p-type* material and an *n-type* material. In this type of laser, stimulation to laser emission occurs by passing a current through the pn junction.

3. *Gas-type lasers,* such as the helium-neon laser, the argon laser, the carbon dioxide laser, the nitrogen laser, and the xenon laser. In this type of laser, stimulation to laser emission occurs by passing a current through the gas. The current causes the gas to ionize and radiate. The radiation oscillates within a tube provided with mirrored ends and then discharges from the partially mirrored end of the tube.

4. *Liquid-type lasers* which consist of solutions such as coumarine, rhodamine red, a chelate, etc. In this type of laser, the liquid-laser materials are stimulated to emission by irradiating the lasing (laser-producing) liquid or dye solution with another laser beam, such as that from a ruby, neodymium-YAG, or carbon dioxide laser.

Most of the system applications to be described here will include solid-state lasers, semiconductor lasers, and gas lasers; all of them optically behave in the same characteristic manner as ordinary light.

Since laser radiation is the same as any electromagnetic radiation in the spectrum between ultraviolet and far infrared, the same optical principles that govern visible light apply to a laser beam. For instance, a laser beam can be reflected, refracted, polarized, and split by means of beam splitters, the same as a light beam can be. Also, the laser beam can be diverged and converged by means of lenses. Accordingly, whenever application of laser beams are discussed in the text, the reader should treat a laser beam optically the same as he would treat a light beam, with the exception that a laser beam is a coherent radiation and is said to be about one-million times more intense than the incident sun rays on the earth. Therefore, he should be aware that both physical and optical dangers exist when dealing with laser beams. For example, when operating a laser machine, looking directly into the rays or reflections of the rays should be avoided. Several brands of goggles suitable for wear while working with externally exposed laser beams are available on the market, and such goggles should be worn by the laser operator.

CONVERGENCE AND DIVERGENCE OF LASER BEAMS

A laser beam can be converged, or focused, to a point or diverged into a large solid angle by means of optical lenses. A converging lens is a convex lens and can concentrate the beam of a laser to a fine point (as small as 1 micron). A diverging lens is a concave lens, and it diverges the beam when the beam is transmitted through it. A converging lens may be biconvex or planoconvex, meaning one side is convex and the other side is plane. Similarly, a diverging lens may be either biconcave or planoconcave; (one side is concave and the other side is plane).

The illustrations in Figs. 1-1 through 1-4 demonstrate this. In Fig. 1-1, a light beam projects from an incandescent lamp

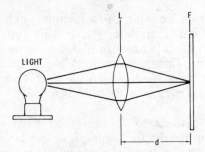

Fig. 1-1. Light beam.

through a biconvex lens, which converges the beam to a focus on a piece of cardboard. The distance between focal plane F and optical plane L of the lens is called the focal length, d, of the lens. The focal length of the lens must be well remembered because it will play an important role in laser applications to be discussed in the succeeding sections. As can be seen in Fig. 1-2, the laser beam behaves in the same manner, except that the laser-beam focus is sharper.

In Fig. 1-3, the lens is replaced by a biconcave lens which causes the light beam to diverge as it leaves the lens. Similarly,

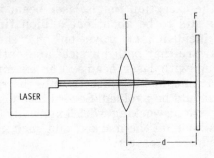

Fig. 1-2. Laser beam.

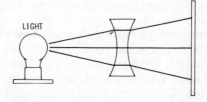

LIGHT

Fig. 1-3. Divergence of a light beam.

in Fig. 1-4 a laser beam is transmitted through a biconcave lens, which diverges the laser beam.

It will be noted from these illustrations that the incident light beam does not focus sharply because the light beam consists of many wavelengths which refract differently as they pass through the lens. The focal point of the laser beam has a sharper delineation because it is coherent and monochromatic and because the amount of refraction is practically the same for each ray as it passes through both thin and heavy sections of the lens.

The principal purpose of a focused laser beam is to increase the intensity of the beam by condensing it into a small area. For instance, a 1-joule (watt-second) laser energy emanating from a ruby rod of ¼-inch diameter can be projected on a thin sheet of metal without any effect on the metal. However, when the ¼-inch diameter laser beam is condensed by means of a convex lens to a focus of, for instance, 5-mil diameter, its intensity increases more than 2000 times. The beam is now capable of drilling a hole of 5-mil diameter through thin metal, for instance steel of 2 mils in thickness. Therefore, by using a convex lens, a laser beam can be used to cut, weld, drill, and remove metal from metallic objects placed at the beam focus. In the medical and dental fields, such a focused beam can be used for cauterizing, cutting, and sterilizing human tissue or glazing human teeth in restorative dentistry. Other dental applications are in glazing fillings for cosmetic purposes and welding dental bridgework.

A combination of a concave and a convex lens is used to collimate (make parallel) the laser beam at any beam diameter desired. Such a beam can then be used in holography, diffrac-

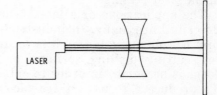

Fig. 1-4. Divergence of a laser beam.

LASER

tion, optical communication, beam splitting, and many other scientific experiments in the laboratory. Also, in range measurements, alignment, and surveying, a collimated laser beam can be projected to a greater distance than when it is not collimated. This is because the beam diverges ($\frac{1}{2}$ milliradian to several milliradians) as it leaves the laser emitter. Furthermore, a collimated laser beam can be focused to a much smaller area, as is necessary in medical surgery and semiconductor processing.

COLLIMATION OF A LASER BEAM

In order to collimate a laser beam, at least two lenses are required. One is preferably a biconcave lens and the other a biconvex lens. In Fig. 1-5, a demonstration setup is illustrated in which a beam of laser radiation projecting from laser generator LG becomes incident on biconcave lens L_1, preferably at its center area. As the beam leaves lens L_1, it diverges and becomes incident on lens L_2, which is a biconvex lens placed in register with and several inches from biconcave lens L_1. The laser beam emerging from lens L_2 becomes somewhat parallel.

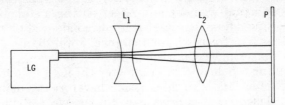

Fig. 1-5. Collimation of a laser beam.

True parallelism can be achieved by holding plane graphpaper P at right angles to the projecting laser beam. As lens L_2 is moved to and from lens L_1, the area covered on the graph paper by the collimated beam will become larger or smaller, or fuzzier or sharper. A sharp delineation of the beam on the graph paper will indicate that the distance between lens L_1 and lens L_2 is exactly right for producing a 100% collimation of the laser beam.

The applications of a laser beam collimated in the manner described are many. In industrial work, the laser beam must first be collimated before it is focused on any surface for welding, cutting, drilling, scribing, or resistor trimming. A sharp focus is necessary in order to obtain a desired focus diameter. To produce a focus, a third biconvex or planoconvex lens is

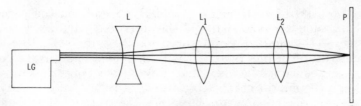

Fig. 1-6. Focus formation of a laser beam.

required. The third lens receives the collimated beam and focuses it to a point determined by its focal length, as illustrated in Fig. 1-6.

A collimated beam of pencil diameter or smaller is used in measuring distances, target ranging, surveying, and aligning large structural equipment parts, building sections, and pipe laying. In optical communication, a collimated laser beam will travel farther than a noncollimated beam; depending upon the weather conditions and the optical elements used, the laser beam can be projected as far as 50 miles in a line-of-sight situation. When the first collimated laser beam was projected to the moon, it diverged to an incident area of two miles due to the refraction of the beam during its travel through our contaminated atmosphere. Thus, 100% parallelism through atmosphere over long distances is not physically possible.

SPLITTING OF A LASER BEAM

A laser beam, collimated or uncollimated (although a collimated beam is preferred), can be split into two or more beams. One method is to project a laser beam through a partially mirrored, front-surface mirror. The beam partially passes through the mirror and partially reflects at an angle determined by the angular position of the mirror with respect to the projecting laser beam. Fig. 1-7 illustrates the splitting of a laser beam by front-surface mirror M positioned at 45° with respect to the laser beam. Part of the laser beam passes through the mirror as A and the other part is reflected as B.

Fig. 1-7. Laser beam-splitting with a mirror.

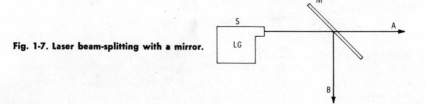

The intensity of each beam, A and B, depends on the percent transmission characteristic of the mirrored surface. For example, if the surface is mirrored to transmit 50%, then the intensities of beams A and B will be equal. The mirror coating can be controlled so that any degree of transmission through the mirror can be obtained. The reflection intensity of the beam will be equal to 100 minus the percent of transmission. The beam splitting can be continued any number of times until the laser-beam intensity is too weak to traverse the last partially mirrored surface.

A second method of beam splitting is accomplished by projecting a laser beam onto a cube formed by two 90° prisms with their bases cemented together with a balsam, as shown in Fig. 1-8. It will be noted that part A of the laser beam traverses the prism without transformation and part B reflects at 90° with respect to the beam propagation from laser source S. This type of beam splitting is preferable in some applications to mirror-type beam splitting because the balsam interface acts as a mirror and does not degrade as easily under certain laser wavelengths as the mirror type does.

A third type of beam-splitting arrangement is shown in Fig. 1-9, in which a laser beam from source S is collimated to expand the diameter of the laser beam. The collimated-expanded laser beam then is allowed to fall on reflecting body M_1 having three surfaces: one surface being a plain glass slide and positioned perpendicularly to the beam, and the other two surfaces, M_2 and M_3, being positioned at 45° angles with respect to the plane of the glass slide. The collimated laser beam is sufficiently expanded so that it covers equal perpendicular areas on the three surfaces. Beam A_1 passes through the perpendicular glass slide and becomes incident on biconvex lens L_1; beam B_1 reflects from mirror M_2 and falls on lens L_2; beam B_2 reflects from mirror M_3 and falls on lens L_3. Each of the lenses, L_1, L_2, and L_3, converge the respective beams to points F_1, F_2, and F_3, respectively, thus increasing the intensities at these points.

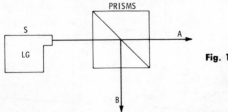

Fig. 1-8. Laser beam-splitting with a prism.

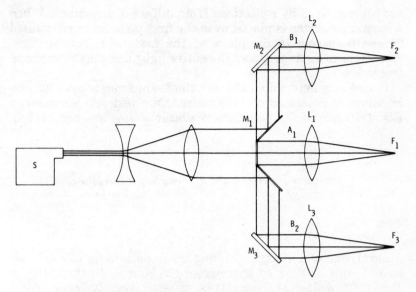

Fig. 1-9. Beam splitting by means of a slide and two mirrors.

If the laser beam from source S is, for instance, 6 joules and if the beams are split to propagate with equal energies, then the foci, F_1, F_2, and F_3, can be utilized to perform some work, such as drilling holes in metal, plastic, or rubber, and each focus will have an energy of 2 joules. The applications of such beam splitting are many and varied, and will be described in succeeding sections. A unique application of three-beam laser radiation is found in the manufacture of baby-nursing bottle nipples; the three-beam laser radiation allows three holes to be simultaneously drilled in the nipple—one in the center of the nipple through which the milk is fed to the infant, and the other two at the base of the nipple, one on each side, to permit air to pass into the bottle during nursing, thus preventing a vacuum condition from occurring in the bottle.

POLARIZATION OF A LASER BEAM

As a light ray propagates from its source, it vibrates in all directions. The ray can be made to vibrate in only one direction by using a polarizing element, such as a plastic-film polarizer, and the light is said to have become polarized. This effect is familiar to most people who wear Polaroid sunglasses on a sunny day at the beach. The sunglasses remove extraneous light reflections from the view of the wearer so that his eyes do not become tired by reflections from different directions. When a second polarizer is placed over the first polarizer and rotated 90° with respect to the plane of the first polarizer, all light vibrations are removed and the entire light becomes suppressed from view.

In order to determine whether the beam from a laser system is partially polarized or unpolarized, the test setup shown in Fig. 1-10 may be employed. Since laser beams are coherent in

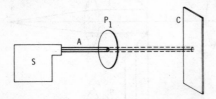

Fig. 1-10. Partial polarization of a laser beam.

general, one would expect to find some polarizing effect in all laser beams as they emanate from the source. In the setup in Fig. 1-10, white cardboard C is placed about 24 inches from laser-beam-source aperture A. When the laser beam is projected on the cardboard, a central, bright area surrounded by a pink halo, which constitutes the fluorescent rays scattered from the laser beam, appears on the cardboard. When polarizer disk P_1 is introduced between beam aperature A and cardboard C, a slight darkening of the projected laser-beam spot occurs; as disk P_1 is rotated on its axis, this effect becomes more predominant. When this effect is at its height, the polarization of the beam is at right angles to the plane of the polarizing crystals. This is due to the orientation of the polarizer at right angles to the polarized rays of the laser beam.

If a second (neutral) polarizer, P_2, is now introduced between the first polarizer, P_1, and cardboard C and is rotated gradually so that it is parallel to the plane of the first polarizer, an extinction of the laser beam will occur. The disappearance of the laser beam indicates that the laser beam has been totally polarized and that no beam is reaching cardboard C, as illustrated in Fig. 1-11. In these experiments, a low-energy laser

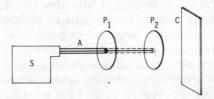

Fig. 1-11. Total polarization of a laser beam.

condition causes a 90° rotation of the polarization plane of the laser beam as the beam traverses it.

In operation, the high voltage is applied to the Kerr cell to activate it, and this action closes the optical switch. A fraction of a second later flashlamp F is triggered to pump lasing element L, and after about ½ millisecond, the voltage to the Kerr cell is turned off and the optical switch is opened. An avalanche of photons in the optical cavity of lasing element L begins to

Table 1-1. Laser Materials, Spectra, Wavelengths, Pumping Methods and Applications

Material	Spectrum	Wavelength A	Pumping Method	Application
Ne-YAG	Ultraviolet	2600	Flashlamp	Biomedical, chemical reactions, optical communication, military work
R6G		3600	Flashlamp*	
HeCd		3250	Electric	
N2		3371	Electric	
Kr		3507	Electric	
Xe		3645	Electric	
Dyes		2200 and up	Flashlamp	
Ar-N2		3577	Electric	*Argon laser used as flashlamp
SiC	Blue	4100	Electric	Biomedical, optical communications, industrial work
Ar		4100	Electric	
Kr		4500	Electric	
HeCd		4420	Electric	
Dyes	Green	4600	N2 laser	Biomedical, industrial work
Ar		5000 av	Electric	
Kr		5000 av	Electric	
Xe		5000 av	Electric	
Nd-YAG		5320	Flashlamp	Frequency-doubled
He-Ne	Red	6328	Electric	Industry, biomedical, metrology, communication, military work
Ruby		6943	Flashlamp	
GaAs		8525	Electric	
GaP		8300 av	Electric	
GaAlAs		8500	Electric	
R6G		6300	Flashlamp*	*Laser Pump, Kr
CO2	Infrared	106,000	Electric	Industrial, biomedical, military, optical communication
GaAs		9050	Electric	
Nd-YAG		10,600	Flashlamp	
Nd-Glass		10,600	Flashlamp	
InAs		35,000	Electric	

NOTE: Industrial applications cover: metalworking, heat treatment, erasers, monitors, tv sets, alarm systems, data processing, garment cutting, illumination, laser radar, sterilizers, credit-card identification, spectroscopy, holography, etc.
Biomedical applications cover: medical surgery, dental instrumentation, etc.
Metrological applications cover: range finders, alignment, lasergauges, surveying, etc.
Military applications cover: destructive lasers, soldier-training maneuvers, missile guidance, atomic fusion, etc.

beam (such as a 0.5 millijoule of laser energy from a helium-neon laser tube) may be used so that the polarizing film does not become damaged by the beam. Furthermore, in order to visually magnify the effect of the laser-beam polarization, the laser beam emanating from aperture A may be collimated subsequent to expansion by the usual method already explained previously.

Some of the most common applications of polarized laser beams are found in nondestructive testing of materials or parts that have been subjected to stresses or strains. Defective honeycomb joints of aircraft wings, welded junctions, areas around bolted structures that have cracked due to stresses, and surface anomalies of metallic materials can be examined by using polarized laser beams and then by analyzing the resultant effect with other polarizers. In some cases, vibrating the part by mechanical means or by ultrasonic waves will aid in the accurate localization of the defective area. This effect is somewhat different from stress analysis by use of photoelasticity.

SPATIAL FILTERING OF A LASER BEAM

When a laser beam emanating directly from the source is focused on a screen, a mottling effect will be noted around the central intense spot. This is due to an irregularity in the optical elements or to the presence of contaminants in them. This effect prevents the formation of a sharp focus on the screen. Thus, spatial filtering of the beam becomes essential to clarify the beam. A method for accomplishing this purpose is shown in the illustration given in Fig. 1-12.

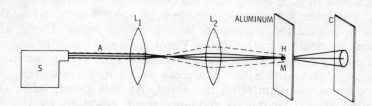

Fig. 1-12. Spatial filtering of a laser beam.

The method consists of arranging a 50-mm focal-length biconvex lens L₁ about 5 to 6 inches from laser-aperture A and centering it perpendicularly to the laser beam. A second lens, L₂, is positioned a few inches from lens L₁, with its principal axis placed in register with that of L₁. A hole of about 10 mils is drilled into a thin sheet of aluminum about 2 inches square, and the sheet is aligned so that the focus of the beam falls precisely in hole H. White cardboard screen C, about 5 inches square, is placed 6 inches from the aluminum sheet so that the laser beam emerging from hole H diverges and becomes perpendicularly incident on screen C. It will now be noted that the laser beam projected on the white cardboard screen has been "purified" and is exempt from the halo effects which remain at area M of the aluminum sheet. The divergent beam, becoming incident on the screen, appears without flaws or shadows on the screen.

Photographs taken with a laser beam that has been refined by the method just described are clear and blemishless, since all abnormal cluttering in the beam has been eliminated. Thus, prior to making holograms, the laser beam first must be filtered by the method explained above and then the filtered beam must be expanded (and collimated as necessary) to cover the entire object and the photographic plate. In microwelding, in drilling fine holes, and in scribing, the filtered laser beam can be focused to extremely small areas measured in microns.

Q-SWITCHING OF A LASER BEAM

A counteraction exists between the laser optical pumping source and the laser stimulation. That is, the laser pumping tends to increase the excited atoms and thus to increase the population inversion of the atoms in the Fabry-Perot cavity (resonant cavity). The laser action tends to decrease this effect, thus restricting the power level of the resonant oscillation. The process of Q-switching or Q-spoiling controls the resonance in such a way that the counteraction between pumping and laser action is eliminated. In Q-switching when the atomic population inversion is increasing cumulatively, the atomic excitation in the Fabry-Perot cavity is made nonresonant during pumping of the laser element. This action increases the population inversion in excess of normal resonance and maximizes the population inversion. At this point, when the excited atomic system is suddenly made resonant by the removal of the Q-switching mechanism, the stored energy in the excited levels of the ionized atoms (such as chromium ions in ruby rod) becomes suddenly stimulated to emission of laser radiation of high intensity. Because the conversion occurs in nanoseconds, the stored high energy will burst out of the lasing element in a giant pulse with power up to gigawatts per square centimeter, in certain types of Q-switching. Giant-pulse tech-

niques can be employed for ruby, neodymium-YAG, neod ium glass, and other solid-state lasing elements, with the ex tion of semiconductors that have pulse times too short Q-switching.

Several methods of Q-switching exist: the Kerr-cell te nique, the rotating-prism technique, the liquid-bleaching te nique, and the ultrasonic technique. Other techniques are a being developed, one of which utilizes the reflective proper of semiconductor surfaces—the reflectivity of the surface creases with intense irradiation that may be used for produ ing Q-switched giant pulses. One of the most common switching techniques is the Kerr-cell method illustrated Fig. 1-13; this method is also known as electro-optical tech nique.

In Fig. 1-13, the power-supply section energizes flashlam F so that it will pump lasing element L. One end, M_1, of th lasing element is coated to make it partially reflective, and th other end, T, is uncoated. Mirror M_2 is positioned with its re flecting surface parallel to the face of lasing element L. Kerr cell K, containing an optically active liquid, nitrobenzene, i positioned between mirror M_2 and lasing-element terminal T and is connected to direct-current source dc to receive a high voltage, such as 10 kV, from it. The cell is positioned so that when it is activated, the dc current field through it is at 45° with respect to the principal axis of lasing element L. This

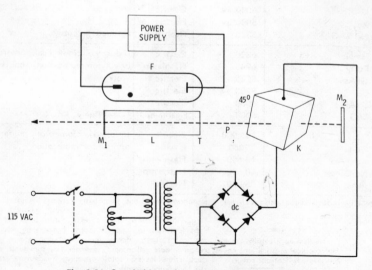

Fig. 1-13. Q-switching a laser beam with a Kerr cell.

oscillate between mirror M_2 and reflecting surface M_1 (a half mirror). The threshold excitation in the resonant cavity exceeds that which normally exists, and a giant pulse of laser bursts out through the end of lasing element L. The radiation is then known as Q-switched.

SPECTRAL RANGE AND APPLICATIONS OF LASER RADIATIONS

The spectra of laser radiations cover a range from ultraviolet to far infrared, with their wavelengths increasing from ultraviolet to infrared and their frequencies decreasing. The wavelengths are given in micrometers (microns), nanometers, or angstroms, the choice depending on the user. Table 1-1 lists the types of laser materials, spectra, pumping methods, and applications.

CHAPTER 2

Laser Holography

HOLOGRAPHIC PRINCIPLES

Holography is a photographic process in which split-beam laser radiations are expanded and used to produce three-dimensional images without the use of optical lenses. The holograms thus produced consist of wave patterns which possess both the amplitude and the phase variations of the object hologrammed. An ordinary photographic camera can sense only a two-dimensional view—the width and length or height, and the amplitude of the light received from the object. However, the human eye can receive both the amplitude (intensity) and the phase (direction) variations of light reflecting from the object; therefore, a sensation of depth as well as width and height is sensed by the eyes. In holography, the two split laser beams take the place of the eyes; one of the beams directly illuminates the photographic plate as a reference wavefront, while the other beam, after reflecting from the surface of the object, illuminates the photographic film or plate. The two beams interfere with each other in phase. The developed photographic film or plate forms an image pattern comprising a mixture of phase fronts and laser light intensity. It is a diffused image formed by the interference of the two split laser beams. In order to view the image of the object, the photographic plate is illuminated with a laser beam projected on the plate at the same angle of incidence as the original laser beam that was used to construct the image. The process of holographic image forming is illustrated in Fig. 2-1, and the process of image reconstruction is shown in Fig. 2-2.

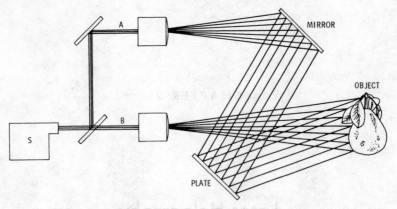

Fig. 2-1. Holographic image production by two laser beams.

It should be noted that photography utilizes only the intensity and the wavelength of the light from the subject, while holography uses the intensity, the wavelength, *and* the phase content of the laser light; the two laser beams replace the optical lenses of the camera. The hologram is an image of the interactions of these three attributes of the illuminating laser light in a pattern of interference. This pattern is formed by the two interference fringes of the laser waves advancing from two different directions at two different time relations. Accordingly, the wavefronts incident on the photographic plate are reflected at different time and space relations from different angles of the subject.

As mentioned previously, one of the split laser beams, such as beam A, provides the reference laser waves and the other beam, B, provides the illumination of the object. The wave-

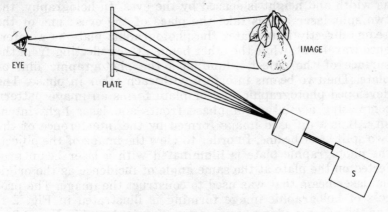

Fig. 2-2. Holographic image reconstruction.

fronts of both beams become superimposed on the photographic plate to impress on it a visually incoherent image. That is, the image appears to be a conglomeration of wavy lines and clusters of spots with no "picture" when viewed with a transmitted light. However, when the hologram is held against a spatially filtered and expanded beam of laser radiation at an angle equal to the original laser-illumination angle and is observed at right angles to the plane of the plate, as shown in Fig. 2-2, a three-dimensional image of the object can be observed. As the viewer moves his eyes sideways, he can see the sides of the object as if the object were suspended in air.

An interesting point is that if the photographic plate is cut into, for instance, four sections, each section will still be capable of producing the original hologram, with some sacrifice in resolution. Furthermore, either a photographic negative plate or a positive plate can be used to make the hologram. Of course, in either case the viewing angle should correspond to the angle of the holographic setup.

HOLOGRAPHIC APPLICATIONS

The holographic technique has numerous industrial and medical uses. In industry, defects in structural parts or materials, porosity of castings, and unbonded areas in the bonded-honeycomb wing structures of aircraft can be visualized. This application was detailed in 1966 to Lockheed Aircraft Company, Burbank, California, by the author and is illustrated in Fig. 2-3.

The system consists of a housing (1) having a coherent light, a polarizer, and a biconvex lens within a cylindrical extension (4) which illuminates the surface of a workpiece (5) with a polarized laser beam projecting into a chamber (3). An analyzer with a magnifying lens is located in a tube (2) through which the surface of the workpiece can be observed during operation of the system. A camera (6) provided with a wide-angle lens is located at the roof of the housing (1) to photograph the defect in the aircraft wing (workpiece). In order to visualize the defective area, the workpiece has to be vibrated, and this action is accomplished by means of an ultrasonic generating device (7) with a frequency that can be adjusted from 1000 Hz to 100,000 Hz.

In operation, the workpiece is fed into the system by means of a continuously moving belt (not shown) and is vibrated at a certain frequency until the defective area becomes visible through the analyzer in tube 2. The frequency, then, is kept

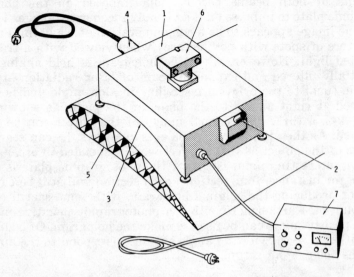

Fig. 2-3. Honeycomb defect inspection setup (simplified diagram).

constant for the entire operation, and photographs of the defect are made while the workpiece is gradually moving through housing 1. After inspecting or photographing one side, the workpiece is passed through the housing a second time for examination of the other side.

Other applications of holography include inspection of tires, bonded structures other than honeycombs, microcircuits, aerosols, cosmetics, foods, paints, fabrics, and rocket engines. The method given in Figs. 2-1 and 2-2 is used in some of these applications.

A versatile holographic system, manufactured by the Korad Division of Hadron, is shown in Fig. 2-4. This system is a completely self-contained unit weighing about 200 pounds. It can be used for reflective holography in nondestructive testing of materials and for transmission holography to produce three-dimensional records of stationary parts, moving particles, liquids and gases for particle sizing, flow visualization, etc. Because of its Q-switched operation, which uses 20-nanosecond exposure time, it "freezes" the moving particles on a permanent hologram. A conventional photographic camera can be mounted on it for producing holograms on photographic films. It operates from a 115-volt, 15- to 25-ampere, single-phase power source, and it produces a single-mode pulse of energy from 0.025 to 10 joules, with a pulse repetition rate of

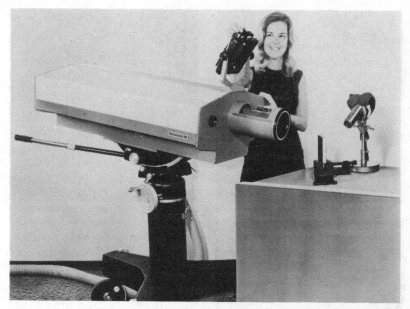

Fig. 2-4. KORAD holographic laser system Model KHC1.

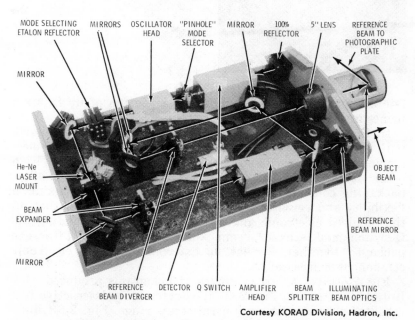

Fig. 2-5. KORAD Holocamera laser system with cover removed.

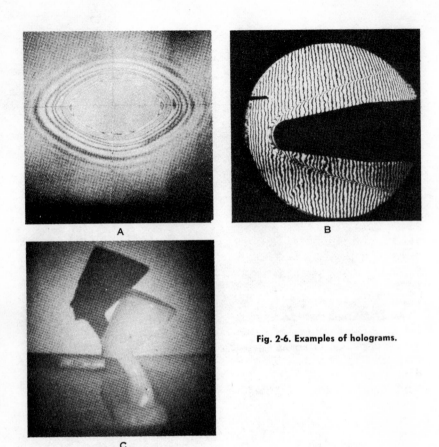

A

B

C

Fig. 2-6. Examples of holograms.

1 to 60 ppm (pulses per minute). A hologram of up to 4×5 inches in size can be obtained with this system.

In Fig. 2-5, the Korad Holocamera laser system is shown with its cover removed to show the various optical and electronic assemblies used and their positional relationship to each other. It should be noted that this system uses the smallest packaging construction possible in order to obtain maximum flexibility and versatility from the equipment. Notice that all the required electronic and optical components, including the Q-switch, mode selector, beam expander, and beam splitter, are packaged together so that no external optics or electronic component is necessary.

Fig. 2-6 gives a few examples of holograms produced by a Korad Holocamera. Fig. 2-6A illustrates a nondestructive test result of a bond with peripheral stress rings. Fig. 2-6B illustrates the air turbulence surrounding a bullet as it traverses air, and Fig. 2-6C shows an object of art that can be holographed to detect any surface anomalies as well as possible imitations or counterfeits. In the past, radiography was used to detect forgeries of old paintings until holography became a nondestructive industrial tool of inspection.

Holographic equipment and cameras are also available from other laser companies (see Appendix I). Many of these systems do not need heavy vibration-stabilized tables since they use Q-switched laser beams to increase the laser illumination power and to shorten the time of exposure. Several of these companies also sell holographic kits that can be assembled by hobbyists or by laboratory personnel.

A unique application of holography is found in the medical field. Using this method, three-dimensional views can be obtained of malignant growths and of diseased structures and tissues in the human skull, heart, lungs, liver, and body cavities. Externally to the body, a hologram can detect incipient breast cancer, dermal affections, ocular dislocations, superficial stress areas, etc.

Another possible application of holography is that of making three-dimensional television-image sets, employing blue, green, and red laser beams—preferably from dye lasers since they can be tuned to different spectral colors. Work in this direction is already underway by several laser companies in the United States and in Japan.

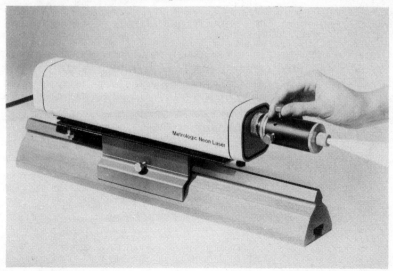

Courtesy Metrologic Instruments, Inc.

Fig. 2-7. Metrologic neon laser ML-680 with 60-618 spatial filter.

A sophisticated helium-neon laser system used for holographic work and optical bench experiments and manufactured by Metrologic Instruments, Inc. is shown in Fig. 2-7. The system has a laser output of 1.5-mW TEM_{00} (transverse electromagnetic), and the beam from it is collimated, spatially filtered, and then expanded to cover almost any practical size of holographic specimen. For general-purpose holographic work, the user will find that this system is very versatile and that the holograms made by means of this system are sharp and free from any optical blemishes. For superficial medical holography, such as cancer of the breast and subcutaneous growths, the laser beam from this system is unexcelled.

The spatial filter used with this system is Metrologic Model 60-618, which provides a clean, noise-free laser beam. Such a beam can be employed in experimental and metrological applications as well as in holography because the laser beam is rectified by eliminating intereference fringes and off-axis modes. The filter may be used on any other brand laser with a TEM_{00} mode of operation.

The field of holography is growing at a rapid pace as new techniques are devised for its application and as instruments are constructed to implement these techniques. In industry, besides its routine use for nondestructive tests conducted with specialized equipment, holography is invaluable in the design, development, and testing of high-performance fuel nozzles for gas turbines and carburetors, and of fuel injectors for combustion chambers and solid and liquid rocket engines. Wind-tunnel flow-visualization tests of projectiles passing through air can be conveniently made with a mobile holographic system having a mounted camera, such as the system shown in Fig. 2-4. This is because the holographic equipment is easily positioned at any angle with respect to the projectile. Also, holographs of objects of art can be made in three dimensions for authentication and restoration.

CHAPTER 3

Laser-Beam Capabilities
and Energies

With the discovery of the ruby laser, first announced in 1960 by Dr. Theodore H. Maiman who was working then at Hughes Research Laboratories, much interest was aroused in possible industrial applications of the laser beam. The thoughts of many companies, small and large, appeared to concentrate on one point—laser welding of sophisticated electronic devices, which were then being welded by the electronic-resistance welding method. Proper application of laser welding in the electronics industry would bring a lucrative financial return to the manufacturer who first built and marketed a laser welder. Soon after Dr. Maiman's announcement, commercial applications of laser-beam welding began to be demonstrated at technical meetings, conventions, and technical expositions.

Some of the newly started companies had high ambitions and hopes of flooding the market with laser welding equipment and becoming wealthy almost overnight. But these companies hardly reached the threshold of the market before they became extinct with considerable loss of investments in the form of loans or personal funds. During the first five or six years of the laser's infancy, much confusion developed as to whether laser welding was the ultimate in welding and fabrication of miniature devices. Some of the laser welders demonstrated in conventions stopped operating at a crucial time—when the prospective customer was eagerly waiting to see fantastic results with the laser. It was reported that one company's laser welder "exploded" during operation in an eastern electro-optical convention. Those few laser welders that were purchased by the manufacturers of microelectronic devices required frequent repairing by the manufacturer who sold the unit. The cost of repairing and maintaining the equipment, and the consultations between the vendor and the purchaser became costly to both the vendor and the purchaser. As a result, by approximately 1968 practically all the original laser-welder vendors had shifted their interest to other more-profitable and more rapidly constructed laser devices and systems, and the laser welding method was almost abandoned as being impractical.

Laser welding is *not* impractical; however, the technique used, imitated, and repeated was a failure from the beginning. For instance, it is a well-known fact that a laser beam is not a magical radiation but just a very intense heat radiation. This heat has to be controlled precisely in order to conduct the heat equally between the two or more surfaces being bonded or welded. It is also a well-known physical fact that in order to conduct heat between the elements to be bonded, their surfaces must be in intimate contact without any film of insulating material, such as air between them. The laser welding-equipment vendors unhappily refused to accept this fact. They continued to build their equipment so that it projected a laser beam on the upper layer of the material being welded without regard to how the heat would be transferred from the upper layer to the bottom layer of the workpiece, if an intimate contact was not established between them.

Paper after paper and article after article were written in trade magazines, technical journals, convention papers, and booklets. All stubbornly stated that a laser bean *can* weld without contacting the surface of the material being welded. Yet there was not a single laser welding machine in use in the electronic-joining field that could be called the workhorse of that field. To date, the concept still persists, and only a very few laser companies are building laser welding machines. And if they do, it is upon special customer request. One may now wonder whether it is worthwhile to have a laser welding process in a plant. Why should a laser be used as the welding means? Is it a better method? Does it produce welds that are superior to resistance welds? Is it less costly and less time consuming? In other words, what characteristics of a laser beam make it advantageous for industrial and electronic applications? It is anticipated that the following list of laser capabilities will convince the reader of the high degree of attributes possessed by a laser beam.

CAPABILITIES OF A LASER BEAM

A properly controlled laser-beam radiation has many advantages over the conventional methods used in industry, and in the medical and dental fields. Most of the following laser capabilities are utilized with the beam focused optically.

1. A laser beam can weld microelectronic devices, such as transistor-package caps, transistor leads, diode leads, microresistor leads, capacitor leads, integrated-circuit leads, and similar elements, to interconnections of printed-circuit boards without causing any cracking at the weld interface, as is now experienced with resistance welding or ultrasonic bonding.
2. Laser bonding can replace thermocompression bonding of microcircuit gold or aluminum leads to semiconductor-wafer chips, and gold-plated sites. Laser bonding eliminates the effect of heat zones and prevents intermetallic formation at the bond interface.
3. A laser beam is capable of welding, with proper instrumentation, certain structures which are remote from the welding machine.
4. It can weld aircraft-fuselage skin in the field. It can also weld missile housings and automotive parts conveniently and effectively without forming significant heat-affected zones, thereby eliminating the need for heat normalizing subsequent to welding, as is now necessary with gas-torch welding.
5. It can remove metals by vaporization. Gyros and the balance wheels of watches and clocks can be balanced in this manner.
6. A laser beam can weld delicate parts embedded in glass or plastic without harming the contiguous areas.
7. It can weld parts enclosed inside a glass envelope, such as broken electrodes in electron tubes.
8. It can trim thin- and thick-film resistor elements in a microcircuit.
9. It can weld jewelry parts and mountings made of gold, brass, silver, ceramic, or similar materials.
10. It can weld Mylar-embedded electronic interconnections to printed-circuit boards without necessitating the removal of the Mylar insulation.
11. Unlike conventional welders, laser welders can weld and produce thermocouple points without creating undesirable oxidation by-products.

12. A laser beam can repair cracks, discontinuities, and voids in castings and forgings, as well as in weldments.
13. It can weld various thicknesses of similar or dissimilar materials, such as Kovar, nickel, stainless steel, copper, silver, gold, gold-plated sheets and leads, silver, Inconel, titanium, aluminum, magnesium, brass, etc., without using a flux.
14. It can perform butt-welding of sheets and rods.
15. It can perform seam welding in a continuous-weld structure.
16. It can weld certain types of plastic materials.
17. When a laser beam is used with a proper waveguide, it can perform bloodless surgery, remove tumors from the brain and body cavities, and perform bloodless operations on the kidney, liver, lungs, stomach, and pancreas. It can remove tattoos from human extremities, and it can drill holes, cauterize tissue, and strengthen enamel in dental work.
18. It can transmit messages and technical data from one location to another.
19. It can be used to measure distances, align structures, survey land, detect flaws in materials and parts, scribe ceramic and glass (under controlled conditions), and sterilize milk.
20. A laser beam can be used to verify credit cards and fingerprints and to detect counterfeit money, paintings, etc.
21. It can be used in quality control to nondestructively test and gauge parts and components.
22. It can be used for cutting garments and sewing certain plastic materials.
23. It can drill tunnels and help in underground pipe laying.
24. It can brand cattle and salmon rapidly and almost painlessly.
25. It can be used as a short-range radar transmission and receiving vehicle.
26. It can be used in multiple wavelengths in color television to form the principal color beams.
27. It can be used to direct the blind, in the form of a cane adapted to sense distance and objects.
28. It can be used in spectroscopy, interferometry, and chemical analysis.
29. It can be used in a night-vision camera to take pictures in the dark because it can illuminate the ground with infrared in darkness.

30. It can be used as a fire-detector beam in an alarm system.
31. It can be used in a burglar alarm.
32. It can be used as a safety alarm in swimming pools, to detect the accidental fall of an adult or child into the pool.
33. It can be used as a typewriter eraser, stenographic eraser, etc.
34. It can be used in military tactics for destroying targets or for harmlessly and economically training soldiers in the field.
35. It can be used for security surveillance in hospital grounds, military installations, and rehabilitation institutions.
36. It can be used for annealing or normalizing microelectronic materials.
37. It can be used in holography for nondestructive analysis of strains and stresses in metals and alloys. It also can be used for aesthetic purposes in museums or art galleries.
38. It can be used to indicate changes in the earth's North Pole.
39. It can be used as a gyroscope with no moving parts.
40. It can be used for sending wire photos via space or via waveguides.
41. It can be used to split rolls of paper, metal, and plastic.
42. It can be used in projecting three-dimensional images on a screen.
43. It can be used as a sound decoder in motion pictures.
44. It can be used to process computer data and to code and decode messages.
45. It can be used to drill holes in baby nursing-bottle nipples.
46. It can be used in automated machining and fabrication.
47. It can be used in seismometers.
48. It can be used in optical recording systems.
49. It can be used in particulate sampling.
50. It can be used in positioning systems for automated machines and fabrications.
51. It can be used as an optical aid for performing a variety of experiments in physical laboratories.
52. In a communications broadcast, laser beams can traverse the critical media of hot ionized gasses or plasma surrounding a spacecraft, unlike radio waves which black out in this situation.

There are many other applications of laser beams, some of which are still under experimentation and others not yet discovered. All optical functions performed by visible light and infrared, and certain functions of ultraviolet radiations, can be performed by laser beams, in some cases with improved efficiency and at lower cost. In the sections accompanying this chapter, many current and future applications of laser beams will be discussed and illustrated with photographs and schematic diagrams.

The discussions will begin with laser welding systems since they have become so well known in industry, medicine, and dentistry; however, although well known, they have not been universally adopted because the systems are inflexible and because the system designs fail to implement laser concepts, which are theoretically well established.

POWER INPUT AND LASER ENERGY

Power-Supply Energy

It has been shown earlier that in order to produce a laser radiation, the lasing element must be optically pumped by means of a flashlamp. The flashlamp receives its illumination energy from a power supply. The higher the flashlamp intensity required, the greater the energizing power that must be furnished by the power supply. This energy may be either a continuous-wave type or a pulsating type, depending on the type and the threshold energy of the lasing element. Since the efficiency of most solid-state lasing rods is 1% or less, it is obvious that large amounts of power are required to sustain a nominal laser output from the generating system.

For a continuous-wave laser output, the power supply is usually a resonance type; for a pulsed laser output the power supply contains high-capacity condensers at high voltages. Part of the energy applied to a flashlamp is used for producing light, and the remainder is dissipated in the form of heat. During operation, the laser element becomes heated by the radiation from the flashlamp, whereupon the laser rod loses its efficiency of laser emission. Therefore, both the flashlamp and the laser rod must be cooled during their operation. This is accomplished by passing a stream of cool or refrigerated, purified, and deionized water through the jacket or the housing enclosing the flashlamp and the lasing rod; the cooling is regulated so that a constant temperature is sustained at all times by the lasing rod and so that its output can be kept constant.

There is no set formula for definitely stating how much flashlamp power is required to produce a laser radiation of desired energy value, since to determine this precisely, the type of lasing rod, its size, its optical threshold characteristics, and the flashlamp wavelengths must be considered; in addition, the pulsing time and the type of radiation (Q-switched or non-Q-switched), and other physical factors enter into the situation. However, an approximation can be made by generalizing the relationship of power-supply input to laser output from a given solid-state laser system. For a general-use pulsing power supply, comprising a bank of capacitors and stabilizing resistors energized by a high dc voltage, the following relationship may be given to calculate the laser output from a laser system; this relationship is only for the benefit of the uninitiated in the laser field.

Let us assume that the power supply has six 200-microfarad pulse-forming capacitor sections sustained at 2000 volts or 2 kV dc. The total electrical energy, P_t, supplied by the power circuit will be:

$$P_t = \frac{CV^2}{2} \times n \qquad \text{(Eq. 3-1)}$$

where,
P_t is in joules,
C is in microfarads,
V is the charging voltage in kilovolts,
n is the number of pulse-forming sections.

The maximum electrical energy of the system is:

$$P_t = \frac{200 \times 2^2 \times 6}{2}$$

$$= 2400 \text{ joules}$$

Now, what maximum laser output can be expected from 2400 joules of applied energy to the flashlamp? Again a great many factors enter into the calculation of an accurate answer to this, but a rough approximation can be made, for example, for a ruby rod of 15 millimeters in diameter and 10 centimeters long. It is reasonably safe to state that it takes 1 joule of flashlamp input energy to produce from 0.003 to 0.005 joule of laser energy above the emission threshold energy varying roughly from 300 to 340 joules. Thus, laser energy J in joules obtained from the stated laser unit will be:

$$J = (2400 - 320) \times 0.004 \text{ (average)}$$

$$= 8.32 \text{ joules}$$

The capacity of the equipment, therefore, is said to be 8 joules. It must be noted that such a calculation is only for making a quick estimate of the laser output of the equipment, when the input energy is given.

Laser Generation

Fig. 3-1 illustrates a simple setup for producing a laser beam from ruby rod R, which is irradiated with xenon flashlamp F, which is energized by power-supply energy E. End M_1 of the ruby rod is heavily coated with a reflecting material, such as silver or gold, and end M_2 is lightly coated with a reflecting material consisting of a multilayer dielectric substance which acts as a partial mirror and partially transmits the generated laser beam from the rod.

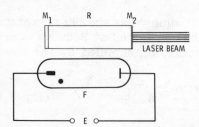

Fig. 3-1. A simplified setup for laser generation.

When flashlamp F is energized, an intense greenish light illuminates (pumps) the ruby rod, which is sensitive to the green wavelength of xenon light. Some of the chromium atoms, which are normally at their low-energy state in the rod, become excited by the photonic energies in the xenon radiation. The excited atoms are in an unstable state, and as the xenon-light pulse (having a duration of a few milliseconds) stops illuminating the rod, the excited atoms spontaneously fall back to their original normal states. In this transition from a higher energy level to a lower energy level, the excited atoms radiate a red light (characteristic of ruby). During the radiation of the red-light photons, they oscillate by reflecting from one mirror to the other. During this oscillation, the light particles, or photons, collide with other excited atoms and cause them to produce additional photons with energies equal to the energies of the colliding photons and with vibrations in phase. The photonic collisions increase the amount of photons in the resonant optical cavity. When the energy of the oscillating photons exceeds the threshold of the resonant system, a beam of amplified ruby light emission projects out of partially mirrored end M_2. This emission is the familiar laser beam.

The energy of each photon is given by hν,

$$\text{Photonic Energy} = h\nu = \frac{hc}{\lambda} \qquad \text{(Eq. 3-2)}$$

where,

h is Planck's constant equal to 6.625×10^{-27} erg-second,
ν is the frequency of the photon traveling with the speed of light c,
λ is the wavelength of the photon.

Equation 3-2 shows that the shorter the wavelength of a photon, the greater its energy. Since energy hν depends on the value of frequency ν, h being constant, then the greater the frequency of a photon, the higher its energy. Thus, in the laser spectrum, the energy of the photons increase from infrared to ultraviolet. Because of the energy and frequency difference of the wavelengths in the laser spectral range, different materials are compatible with different types of wavelengths. For instance, a ruby laser beam is compatible with glass and some types of plastic fiber optics, while a carbon dioxide laser beam is not compatible with plastic or certain glass fiber optics. Furthermore, while ruby wavelengths are weakly absorbed by the human blood, argon- or carbon dioxide-laser wavelengths are highly absorbed by the blood and are particularly recommended for photocoagulation in medical surgery. Therefore, argon-laser wavelengths can be transmitted through fiber optics to the work area in surgery. On the other hand, a carbon dioxide laser beam is recommended in metalworking because of its high power; however, its principal disadvantage is its 106,000-angstrom wavelength, which is highly reflective on metal surfaces. The optical elements usually used for focusing a carbon dioxide laser beam are absorptive, and lenses made of germanium, silicon, or gallium arsenide must be used.

Thermal Considerations

As stated in the preceding section, most of the energy expended in producing laser radiation is in the form of heat. Again taking the ruby as an example, the heat from the energy applied to a xenon flashlamp is almost 50% expended in the walls of the xenon discharge tube; another 25% is expended in the resonant cavity, and about 25% is expended in the housing enclosing the ruby and the flashlamp. This means that a large amount of heat has to be removed from the bulk of the laser-generating section. When this amount is multiplied by the number of pulses per minute and if no provision is made to remove the heat, it is obvious that the temperature will rise enormously. For example, if an energy input of 1600 joules per pulse from the capacitor network is applied to the flash-lamp at a repetition rate of 10 pulses per minute, the total energy input will be 16,000 joules, which is roughly 4000 calories. This heat must be dissipated to the outside of the system by conduction, convection, and radiation, if no other means exists.

Let us assume that the above system weighs 1000 grams and has an average specific heat of 0.15 cal/gm. The heat capacity of the system will be 150 calories, and the temperature rise of the system will be $4000/150 \cong 27°C$. If the system at the start was at an ambient temperature of 25°C, the final temperature of the system will be approximately 52°C, which will considerably decrease the emission efficiency of the ruby laser. After a few minutes of running the equipment in this manner, the ruby will cease emitting and may even crack.

It is obvious that the system must be cooled. This is usually accomplished by passing through it a liquid cooler, such as pure deionized water, at the rate of $1\frac{1}{2}$ to 2 gallons per minute. If electrical insulation of the laser-generating system is a problem, liquid silicone or a fluorochemical can be used to maintain the system at ambient room temperature or lower. Cold water from the water line may be run continuously, or a closed-circuit refrigerated water system may be used, the latter being preferred. Thus, it is evident that during the planning stages of a laser system, careful calculations must be made to provide a suitable cooling system.

Laser-Energy Amplifiers

Ordinarily, laser-rod materials provide the highest output of laser energy for solid-state lasers. The amount of laser energy produced is dependent on the effectiveness with which the laser rod is optically pumped. The optical-pumping effectiveness is directly proportional to the surface area of the laser rod that efficiently absorbs the optical-pump energy. Thus, the energy output is principally determined by the size, geometry, and type of the rod material. A physical factor to be overcome with such a rod material is the pump-radiation reflection losses at the laser rod and air interface, which become particularly significant with high-energy laser generators. The coherence or directionality of the emitted laser radiation is mainly dependent on the geometry of the rod and the resonant cavity of the laser optical system.

With presently used circular laser rods, increased laser emission output is obtained by increasing the length and the diameter of the rod and, hence, its cross-sectional area, as well as increasing the optical pumping energy. While the concept at first appears very attractive, inherent limitations are imposed on the amount of increase that is possible in these factors. These limitations are:

1. The optical-pump energy needed to produce metastable quantum states and make the rod operate as a tubular body is effective only to a limited depth into the laser rod.
2. The core of the rod absorbs the heat from the optical pumping energy, which tends to counteract the formation of excited metastable states.
3. The laser excitation at the core of the rod is reduced to nothing and the thermal radiation, emitted radially from the center of the rod, further favors the reduction of emission.
4. Upon exceeding a certain rod length and the resultant emission gain, a condition of spontaneous avalanche occurs which adversely affects the directivity in the radiation.
5. The formation of a nonuniform temperature condition within the rod produces distortion in the optical path, and this effect further increases with heterogeneity in the rod material.
6. The attempt to obtain a high laser output in this manner (by increasing volume and optical-pump energy) can ultimately lead to the destruction of the laser rod.

Accordingly, these problems must be overcome before an amplification in the laser output can be realized.

Several methods have been utilized to preclude the adverse effects of obtaining a high gain in laser emission level. One simple method has been to drill an axial bore located centrally to the rod. This method alleviates the production and radiation of heat emitted radially from the core of the rod, thus reducing the threshold of the metastable states and increasing the laser emission level. Another method has taken advantage of the geometry of the rod by constructing it in a quadrangle or in a square in cross-sectional dimension; this condition increases the surface area exposed to the optical-pump illumination and reduces the thermal effect of the core upon the atomic excitation by more-efficient radiation of heat from the rod. The difficulty in the latter method has been in obtaining optically flat surfaces and homogeneous rod material, which require special techniques that are slow and costly. Therefore, the ideal laser element for obtaining amplified laser radiation is one that will: not require homogeneous laser material, eliminate thermal effects on the core of the laser element, offer the greatest possible surface exposure to the optical radiation, eliminate lens effect in the laser element, and produce a uniform temperature distribution and thus homogeneous metastable states throughout the rod. Such conditions have been obtained by using thin plates of laser material of quadrangular or oval configuration and arranging the plates in an axial array perpendicular to the axis of the array or at some suitable angle for particularly eliminating surface reflection losses from the laser plates. Laser amplification of a high order of magnitude, depending on the technique used, has been achieved by using such a method. At least two companies (General Electric Co. and American Optical Corp.) have introduced this system arrangement in the laser market, and later variations and modifications have been successfully put into use. Two examples of the general design are illustrated in Figs. 3-2 and 3-3.

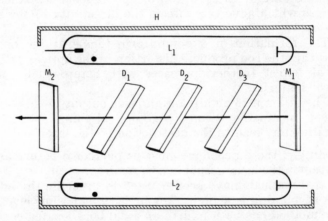

Fig. 3-2. Brewster-angle arrangement of parallel-surface discs.

In Fig. 3-2, rectangular housing H contains two flashlamps, L_1 and L_2, for illuminating laser discs D_1, D_2, and D_3, which are square and have parallel surfaces angularly positioned in the housing to eliminate plate-air interface reflection losses. The plate angle with respect to the axis of the housing is between 57° and 60°; this plate angle is also known as the Brewster angle. For practical purposes, the tangent of this angle is equal to the refractive index of the laser disc. At each end of the housing are located the familiar mirrors. Mirror M_1 is heavily coated, and mirror M_2 is partially coated to allow the resultant laser beam to traverse to the outside of the resonant

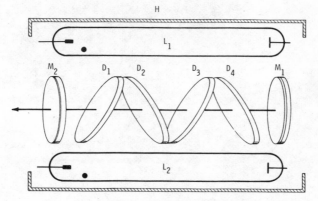

Fig. 3-3. Zigzag arrangement of laser discs.

system. The laser disc is made of silicon glass with 3% neodymium. For a pulsing mode, xenon flashlamps are used; for a continuous mode, electric arc lamps are used. The radiation from this laser system is collimated and highly coherent with a wavelength of 10,600 angstroms in the infrared spectrum. Such a system may be considered a module, and several such modules can be optically coupled in series to produce a high-power laser generator. The system is water-cooled; a stream of deionized distilled water circulates through it at a rate of 1½ to 2 gallons per minute per module. The operation of such a system is similar to a ruby or a neodymium-YAG laser generator.

In Fig. 3-3, discs D_1 through D_4 are arranged in a zigzag manner at 45° angles with respect to the axis of the housing, and the operation of the discal system is similar to that shown in Fig. 3-2. Although there is some controversy regarding the efficiencies and laser outputs between these two modules, the difference in output would be generally due to a difference in design configuration. Although this method does not enjoy the elimination of interface reflection losses, it has the advantage of utilizing secondary emissions cumulatively in the resonant cavity. By extending the length of flashlamps L_1 and L_2 and by replacing mirror M_1 with a ruby or neodymium-YAG laser, the author has obtained increased cumulative laser emission with only a slight loss in coherence.

CHAPTER 4

Industrial Laser Welding Systems

In order to use a laser beam in welding operations, one must first be acquainted with certain essential requirements related to the beam and the equipment utilizing the beam. Any significant deviation from these requirements will lead to total failure in accomplishing the purpose and in utilizing the many advantages of laser welding over other types of welding methods now in use. The following are the requirements:

1. The laser beam must be of sufficient energy to transmit heat to the material to be welded.
2. The time of welding (i.e., the pulse width) of the laser beam must be relatively long—a few milliseconds—to conduct the heat through the material.
3. The wavelength of the laser beam must be selected for optimum absorption by the particular material. For instance, some materials may require a beam from a neodymium-YAG laser, while others may require a ruby laser beam; and still others, such as microelectronic hybrid-circuit devices, may not work with a carbon dioxide laser.
4. A very close contact must be maintained between the contiguous weld surfaces. If necessary, some pressure can be exerted on the material, but not so much as to distort or mar it with the pressurizing instrument.
5. The pulse shape of the beam must be controlled precisely.
6. The focus of the beam must be adjusted for the wavelength and intensity of the laser beam and also must be adjusted to the thickness of the material being welded.

7. Human error in focusing the beam must be eliminated by electronic or mechanical means, which are automatic and consistent with each pulse of the laser beam and with the weld formed by the laser.

8. Ideally, all safety goggles must be eliminated so that the operator can work freely without being restricted by improper visualization of the workpiece being welded.

9. The equipment should be provided with a means of automatically regulating the line power to the laser-stimulating system so that each laser pulse will contain precisely the amount of energy as the one following it or preceding it. Any deviation from this rule will result in disappointment because slightly more laser energy than that required may produce a hole instead of a weld, and slightly less energy may produce nothing or a surface blemish. This means that control over laser energy is very essential.

LASER WELDING SYSTEMS

A typical laser welding machine should consist of a laser-beam generator, a power supply to energize the generator, a laser-triggering section, an optical system to shape and focus the laser beam on the workpiece, an electrical control panel with control instruments, a workbench on which to perform the laser welding, and a cooling system to sustain the laser-generator temperature at a level favorable to efficient laser

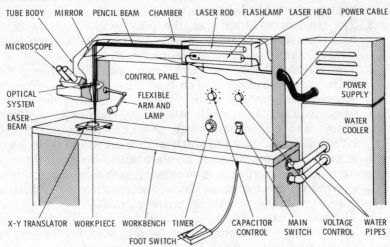

Fig. 4-1. A laser welding system.

emission. Other auxiliary equipment may also be added and will be considered with the particular type of laser system discussed in this chapter.

The diagram of a laser welding system in Fig. 4-1 illustrates an enclosure containing a power-supply section and a water-cooling system. The water-cooling system is connected through water pipes to the laser head which is constructed integrally with an electric control-panel section supported on the workbench. The laser head contains a laser rod which is optically pumped (illuminated) by a flashlamp that receives its energizing power through a cable from the power-supply section. The power supply is controlled by a capacitor control and a voltage control.

A main switch turns on the power to the power-supply section and to the cooler section. A footswitch triggers the flashlamp which illuminates the laser rod and causes emission of laser radiation. This radiation is projected from the laser rod into the chamber as a pencil beam, and after reflecting from the mirror or reflector at 90°, this beam passes through the optical system which focuses it on a workpiece placed on an X-Y translator. A binocular microscope is attached to the laser head, and the laser beam passes through the tube body and the optical system and converges on the workpiece. A flexible arm with a lamp illuminates the workpiece area during operation of the unit. A timer on the control panel selects the laser welding time in milliseconds, depending on the type of material being welded.

Fig. 4-2 illustrates the schematic of the entire laser system, which corresponds to the parts in Fig. 4-1. A rectifying system converts the alternating current into direct current to charge the pulse-forming capacitor network. A water pump circulates deionized distilled water through the laser head chamber to cool the laser rod and the flashlamp.

It will be noted from Figs. 4-1 and 4-2 that there is a considerable distance between the lens and the workpiece, and the welding is accomplished without contact of the laser head with the workpiece. Stabilizing the workpiece is performed by using either holding jigs or a pair of tweezers manipulated by the operator. Since both the primary (direct) laser bean and the secondary (reflected) laser beam are visible to the eye, laser safety goggles must be worn by the operator during the operation of the laser system. Another characteristic of the equipment, similar to all other laser welding systems, is that the laser beam traverses the microscope-tube body to the workpiece. A shutter is provided in the microscope-tube body so that after focusing, the shutter is closed to prevent the operator from looking directly at the laser beam reflecting from the workpiece.

The Holobeam laser welder-driller shown in Fig. 4-3 is designed for welding and drilling small precision parts at production speeds up to 100 per minute and with pulse duration from 1 to 6 milliseconds. It has a colinear, binocular viewing system with a fail-safe eye shutter. Sheet stock as thick as

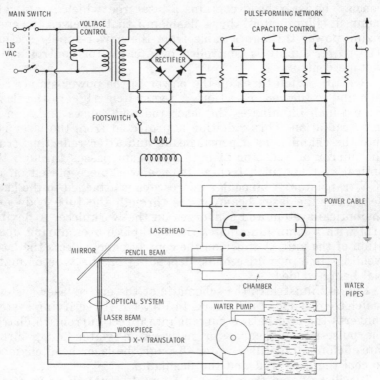

Fig. 4-2. Schematic of a laser welder.

0.05 inch and wires with diameters up to 0.07 inch can be welded with a focus-spot size varying from 0.001 to 0.06 inch. The system can drill holes in materials up to 0.3-inch thickness, and the hole sizes can range from 0.0005 to 0.06 inch; a hole depth-to-width ratio of 25 can be obtained with the equipment. The unit operates from a 220-V, 60-A, 50- to 60-Hz, single-phase power source. It is water-cooled by means of a water-to-tap water heat exchanger requiring 1 gpm of tap water at 20 psi. Refrigerated-type cooling is also available.

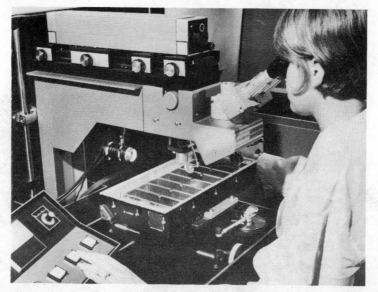

Fig. 4-3. A commercial laser welding system.

Fig. 4-4 shows a laser welding system manufactured by GTE Sylvania, Inc. The Model 1610 system is rated to operate at an average power of 150 watts, using a neodymium-YAG laser rod with pulse energies of 3 to 20 joules at pulse lengths of 1 to 6 milliseconds. It has a pulse rate of 100 Hz for the lowest energy and 15 Hz for the highest energy. The system can be operated either in single- or repetitive-pulse modes, with manual or automatic remote control for on-line production. Coaxial alignment is accomplished with a binocular microscope having alignment crosshairs for viewing the workpiece and for aligning and focusing the laser beam relative to the workpiece. Its integrated power meter gives a continuous power reading from 0 to 200 watts. Its manufacturer claims that it welds microcircuits and microcircuit leads, with a spot diameter varying from 0.01 to 0.04 inch. The equipment operates from a 220-volt, 50-ampere, 3-phase, 60-Hz power source and has a cooling system from the same power source using 2 amperes. The cooling system is a closed-loop type using 4.5 gallons per minute of clean filtered water at 20 psi.

WELD FORMATION WITH A LASER BEAM

With a given thickness of material to be welded, several things occur: the specific parameters of laser-emission energy

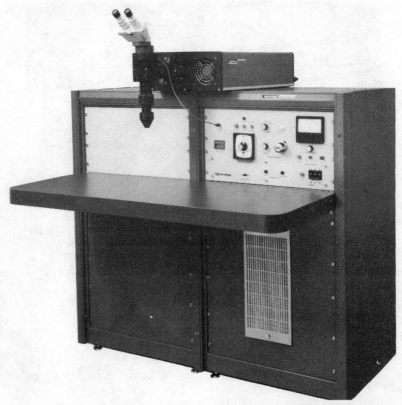

Fig. 4-4. GTE Sylvania laser welding system Model 1610.

are set by the panel controls shown in Fig. 4-1; the lens focus
is adjusted with the optical system; and the laser generator
is triggered with the footswitch to project a laser pulse on
the workpiece. The focusing of the laser beam on the workpiece is performed indirectly; that is, a light source, not shown
in Fig. 4-1, is directed through the laser optical system, preliminary to triggering the laser, and is focused on the workpiece. During laser triggering, this light beam is cut off from
view; simulaneously an optical path for laser transmission is
opened so that when the laser is triggered, the laser beam is
in focus on the workpiece. Although this operation may at
times become cumbersome, it is obviously necessary to protect
the operator's eyes from exposure to the laser radiation. In
addition to the inconvenience of this type of arrangement
which is typical of such laser welding equipment, it is highly

improbable that the incident-beam focus will have a precise identical diameter each time an operator sets the focus with the visible light. Furthermore, it is doubtful whether different operators will obtain the same size focus when they are focusing the beam on the workpiece. In other words, precise and identical focus size is essential for obtaining a uniform weld quality.

Experience with different laser-welding operators has shown that with a constant lens focal length and constant electrical parameters for laser emission, the welding results obtained are variable from one operator to another. The same laser energy that may form an acceptable weld with one operator could form a hole with another operator's focus, or even no effect may be noted on the work of still another operator; this is because each operator focuses differently. For instance, let us assume that one operator has properly focused the laser beam on a given workpiece. It is found that the same laser energy that produced a large hole in a thin sheet has formed a small weld in a thicker sheet of the same material. By maintaining a constant sheet thickness and by gradually increasing the electrical parameters (and hence the laser output), the heat-affected area will vary successively from a slight dent, a small weld, and a large weld, to finally a hole. A further increase of the laser output will produce an increasingly larger hole.

The variation of the character and of the size of the heat-affected area is expected from physical principles. However, the particular point of interest here is that the laser welding method is flexible in obtaining a given-size weld or hole; either the thickness of the material, the lens-to-workpiece distance, or the electrical setting can be varied. This means that where the electrical setting is not sufficiently flexible to produce the desired result, the thickness of the workpiece can be varied to compensate for the desired electrical setting. Conversely, where the thickness of the workpiece cannot be changed, a variation in electrical parameters may be made to obtain the desired result, provided that all other factors are kept constant and that the capability of the equipment is within this requirement.

With a given focal-length lens at a constant-emission state, experience has shown that the distance between the lens and the workpiece directly influences the size of the weld, the depth of the weld nugget, and the metallurgical quality of the weld structure, as illustrated in Fig. 4-5. This implies that an improperly distanced weld zone may result in the formation of a hole (Fig. 4-5A), a concave weld with a puncture in its cen-

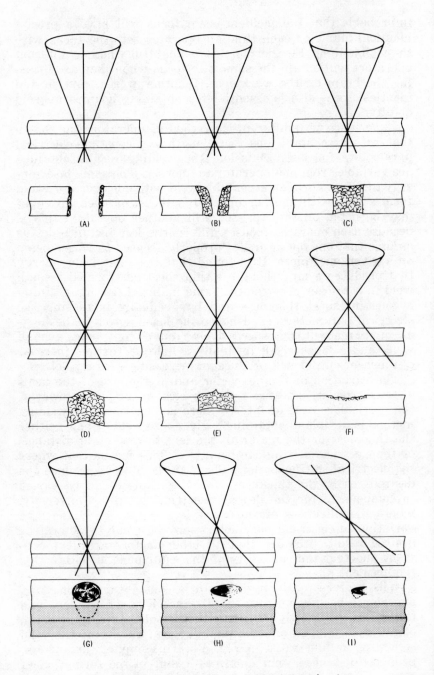

Fig. 4-5. Various weld shapes or holes due to focus location.

ter (Fig. 4-5B), a concave weld (Fig. 4-5C), a convex weld (Fig. 4-5D), a convex weld with an apex in its center (Fig. 4-5E), or an oxidation (burning) effect in the heat-affected area (Fig. 4-5F). The lens-to-focus angular attitude with respect to the normal indicates dependence of the weld configuration on this condition; for instance, a transition from a normally expected circular area (Fig. 4-5G) to one of an ellipse (Fig. 4-5H), more elliptical configuration (Fig. 4-5I) occurs. Consequently, these conditions point to the critical nature of the relationship between the optical positioning and the resultant thermal transition of the heat-affected area. These conditions are prevalent at the present time with many of the commercial laser-welding operations, which is why some equipment manufacturers have failed to make headway in the market. Therefore, the need for a self-focusing, self-distancing, and self-setting laser welding system with high flexibility of manipulation of the laser beam is obvious.

Self-Focusing Laser Welding System

A laser welding system was developed by Laserkinetics Corporation to eliminate human errors and to incorporate as much flexibility as possible into a laser welder. The laser system comprises a single-unit console containing a laser generator, a power-supply unit with a pulse-forming network, a closed-circuit water-cooling system, a laser head embodying the laser optical mechanism, controls for laser intensity and pulse-width adjustment, and electrical meters to indicate the various parametric settings and the temperature condition of the laser head. A foot treadle is used to move the laser head to and from the workpiece and simultaneously to trigger the laser radiation when the laser head contacts the workpiece; this latter feature protects the operator against laser reflections and eliminates the shutter mechanism provided on conventional laser systems. An auxiliary laser waveguide of special construction is also provided for weldments, cutting, and drilling to be performed remote from the console.

This laser system is more than just a laser welding machine. It is an efficient and compact laser welder, driller, cutter, scriber, and trimmer. The system can be used for welding sophisticated circuit parts, for bonding and cutting plastics, and for cutting other synthetic materials, such as garment materials, with slight component modification. Some of the metals on which this system can be used are: gold, silver, stainless steel, nickel, titanium, aluminum, copper, tungsten, zinc, tantalum, beryllium, and alloys of these metals. All types of metallic and semiconductor materials, aircraft and space materials, and parts used in the microelectronic and semiconductor industries can be welded, drilled, and cut by this system. The thickness of the materials on which this laser system can be used is dependent on the density, thermal conductivity, reflectance, and light diffusivity of the materials. Generally, thicknesses between 0.001 to about 0.4 inch can be worked with this system, using 1 to 40 joules of laser energy. Higher-energy systems are also available using high-power input supplies to work thicker materials.

The following are some of the principal advantages of the system:

1. The laser focus on the workpiece is automatically adjusted, is precise, and cannot vary from one operator to another once the parameters are set.
2. Weldments, cuttings, and holes are sharp, clean, and rapid.
3. Because the laser head contacts the workpiece for welding, no stray laser radiations are visible to the operator —a safety factor.
4. There is no need to hold down the workpiece with jigs or tweezers during welding and drilling, since the laser head performs this.
5. No microscope is necessary for focusing the laser beam, thus eliminating another human error that may occur when focusing is done visually.
6. The laser beam can be directed by means of a proprietary waveguide onto a workpiece located as far away from the console as five feet.
7. The laser beam can be transmitted to areas and corners inaccessible by conventional welding machines.
8. Operator training is reduced to a minimum, and human error is practically nothing.
9. A binocular microscope located on the laser head is for locating and magnifying the workpiece and not for focusing the laser beam. The microscope magnification varies from 10x to 100x.
10. The beam can be focused above the workpiece, within the workpiece, or on the surface of the workpiece.
16. The laser head can rotate 360° in the vertical plane; thus, the beam can be directed at any angle from the console.
12. The system is a single-unit apparatus and is portable on special wheels provided under the console.

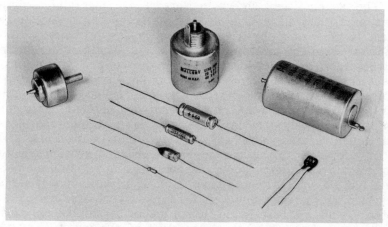

(A) Capacitors.

(B) Semiconductors.

(C) Integrated circuits.

Fig. 4-6. Some electronic parts and assemblies that can be welded with a laser beam.

Some of the parts that can be worked with this system are shown in Fig. 4-6, and the cross sections of welded materials are shown in Figs. 4-10 and 4-16. Table 4-1 gives an example of how the parameter settings for a new material can be determined for welding, cutting, or drilling holes.

The various items shown in Fig. 4-6 are generally used in the microelectronics field. The welding of the capacitor is usually performed by seam welding which provides a continuous series of overlapping spot welds. The resultant weld structure is virtually identical with electric arc welding, except that with the proper weld schedule there should be no microcrack in the welded area. The semiconductors and integrated circuits are welded by the spot-weld method. Only one or two spot welds per lead are sufficient to attach the leads of the integrated circuits, switch terminals, capacitors, and semiconductors to the printed-circuit board. Experience with printed-circuit component attachments using resistance welding has shown that more than 50% of the component leads develop microcracks. Some of these microcracks are harmless; others, such as those found in equipment on shipboard, gradually grow because of the interaction of the metal (Kovar) with the moisture in the sea air. After a while, the lead material develops corrosion, which results in the opening of the circuit and in the consequent malfunctioning of the circuit-board

Fig. 4-7. An IC gold-plated Kovar lead, resistance-welded on a circuit-board interconnect (magnified 40✕).

assembly. If the leads are laser welded, the condition occurs in less than 1% of the welded leads. This can be attributed to a variety of factors, the principal one being poorly deposited or porous lead plating. A circuit-board failure due to lead corrosion resulting from microcracks is shown in Fig. 4-7. The gold-plated Kovar lead shown in the center is pushed aside to show the badly degraded and corroded weld interface. This is one of the many examples of similar failures occurring in computer equipment installed on a ship. For reasons of this type, this particular contract with the customer was changed so that all component leads were solder joined to the printed-circuit boards, with a solder material having a melting point of 450°F. The reason that solder-joining of component leads is not favored in some cases is because the equipment operates at air-cooled high temperatures at which low melting-point solders melt, causing the microcircuits to open and the equipment to fail.

In contrast with resistance welding, an example of laser welding is shown in Fig. 4-8, in which integrated-circuit (IC) leads are laser welded to a printed-circuit board. Note that

Fig. 4-8. Laser-welded gold-plated Kovar leads on a circuit board (magnified 15 X).

two welds are made on each gold-plated lead, which is 30 mils wide. The diameter of each weld is about 15 mils, and by pulsing two welds on each lead, the weld interface area increases with an increase in holding strength.

The welding schedule for this work was 1.4-joule laser energy and 3-millisecond pulse time, using a 25-mm focal-length planoconvex lens. Considering that the equipment used was only a prototype laser system, note the uniformity of the weld size and weld location on the leads. A pull test on a single weld of this size will yield from 3500 to 4000 grams, which is actually greater than a resistance weld of equal size.

Fig. 4-9 is the top view of a typical laser weld on nickel. The coaxial circular lines represent the mechanism responsible for instantaneous melting and cooling of the metal during welding. The pattern indicates how the thermal pulse propagates radially from the center outwards during melting, and its path solidifies as the cooling proceeds from the periphery to the center. The black outer circular area is the residue of the charred surface contaminants.

Fig. 4-10 is the cross-sectional view of the laser weld shown in Fig. 4-9. The view shows the microstructural pattern after

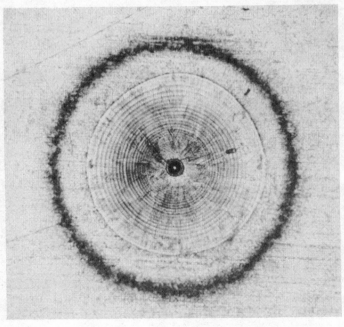

Fig. 4-9. Top view of a laser weld on nickel sheet (magnified 375✕).

Fig. 4-10. Cross-sectional area of the weld shown in Fig. 4-9
(magnified 375×).

the metal has melted and suddenly solidified. Each sheet is
2-mil thick nickel, welded with a 40-mm focal-length lens. The
cross section is polished and etched with nitol. Note the ar-

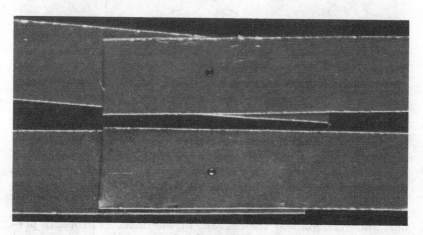

Fig. 4-11. Pull-test specimens for determining
weld strength.

rowhead shape of the weld nugget, which follows the penetrating heat pattern. Good penetration is indicated, the dark spots representing traces of porosity in the material. Fig. 4-11 shows photographs of the pull specimens used to test weld strengths. Fig. 4-12 shows the Laserkinetics Laser System Model ME-101.

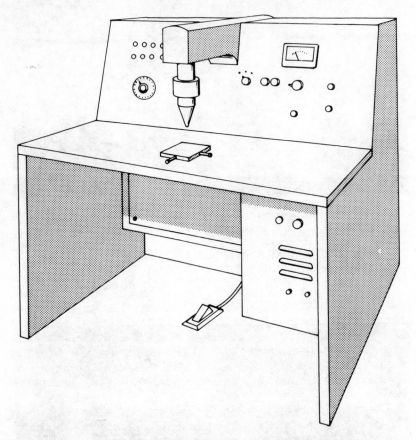

Fig. 4-12. Laserkinetics Laser System ME101 for welding, drilling, scribing, and trimming resistors.

LASER DRILLING AND CUTTING

A laser beam can drill through metal, plastic, ceramic, rubber, and even glass if the surface of the latter is properly prepared. For drilling operations, the focus of the beam from a long focal-length lens is usually used. To reduce the tendency of the beam to form a conical hole, the laser beam can be jet-assisted by using either an inert or an active gas. The inert gas, such as helium or argon, is used to obtain sharply cut edges when drilling or cutting plastic and paper materials. An active gas, such as oxygen, is used to reduce the kerf (width of the cut) when drilling and cutting metals and alloys. A laser drilling or cutting scheme is shown in Fig. 4-13.

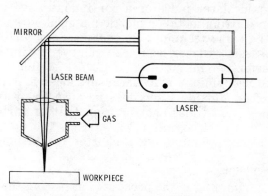

Fig. 4-13. Illustration of a laser cutting system.

In drilling with a laser beam, either ruby, neodymium-YAG, or carbon dioxide lasers can be used, and the delivery of the laser beam to the work material can be either pulsed or continuous. Short high-intensity pulses from a ruby or a neodymium-YAG laser will vaporize the material to make the hole, the size of which may be varied from 0.01 mm to 1.0 mm in diameter, depending on the power level of the laser equipment and the thickness of the material. Carbon dioxide gives the highest depth-to-diameter ratio when an active jet assist is used. The jet assist increases the heat at the focus by oxidizing the material, and the hole edges are smooth and sharp and have a narrow kerf.

The mechanism of hole drilling may be explained as follows: the incident laser beam on the surface elevates the temperature of the material at a rate approaching 10^{10} degrees per second, vaporizing the surface material to a depth of a few microns. The metal below the surface melts, and together with the vaporizing metal, an enormously high pressure of several-hundred atmospheres is formed in the hole. The pressure results in the expulsion of the metal at high velocity from the hole in the form of a plume. This process, which takes less than a second, continues until all the metal is removed from the hole area. The gas jet further aids in the removal of the vaporized metallic particles, thus cleaning the hole. With plastics, the material is removed by burning, and clear-cut edges are formed by the expulsion of the burned material with an inert-gas jet assist.

As the material is drilled or cut, the beam focus is gradually moved inward to the material, and a depth-to-hole diameter ratio of up to 250 to 1 can be obtained with a Q-switched carbon dioxide laser pulse or a continuous-wave neodymium-YAG laser. Cutting metal or plastic material with a laser beam requires the same technique as that used for drilling, except that a gas-assisted laser beam can achieve cutting-speed rates up to 1 meter per minute in $\frac{1}{2}$-cm-thick stainless steel or titanium. A neodymium-YAG laser produces a narrower kerf than a carbon dioxide laser does because the wavelength of the former is ten times shorter than that of carbon dioxide. However, in the neodymium-YAG laser, the optics must be brought closer by employing a shorter focal-length lens.

Resistor Trimming

Resistor trimming is the process of adjusting the resistances of thin- or thick-film resistors to permissible tolerances. During the manufacture of the resistors, it is difficult to control the film resistance values. The manufacturer fabricates the resistors with lower resistance than intended and then trims (to increase resistance) them to the required resistance, thus allowing close resistance tolerances to be achieved. There are three types of resistor trimmers in general. The first type, the abrasive trimmer, uses an abrasive-powder jet to abrade the metal and is closely watched to eliminate contaminants from the microcircuit. The second type, the capacitive trimmer, projects an electrical pulse on the metal to melt and remove it; but because of the difficulty of obtaining repeatable trimming performance, the industry has not fully adopted it. The third type is the laser trimmer which offers the following advantages: (1) precise control over the resistance value that can be achieved; (2) a very small spot size (10- to 30-micron kerf) which allows a narrow line to be made through the resistor (Fig. 4-14); (3) only negligible heating so that the characteristics of the contiguous structures in the microcircuit are not amenable to changes; and (4) little or no residue after trimming. The cleanliness of this process outweighs all other trimming methods. In addition to trimming resistors, a laser trimmer (Fig. 4-15) can also fabricate cylindrical resistors by cutting spiral elements from the nickel-chrome coating of the cylinder.

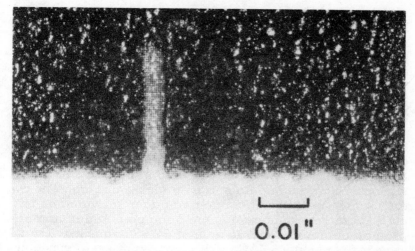

Fig. 4-14. Typical laser-trimmed resistor cut.

The Laser trimmer shown in Fig. 4-15 is manufactured by Quantrad Corporation. The system is a pulsed xenon laser, which is ideal for thin-film hybrid microcircuit adjustment, ferrite micromachining, ROM encoding, and for the removal of photographic emulsion without damaging the film. The

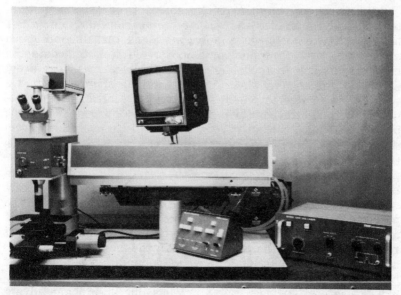

Courtesy Quantrad Corp.

Fig. 4-15. Laser resistor trimmer.

radiation from the laserhead is green (5000 angstroms) and is suitable for photographic error correction and trimming of nickel-chrome (NiCr) resistor films on silicon substrates which require narrow kerf, to about 3 to 10 microns. The equipment can also trim thick-film hybrid circuits using a Q-switched YAG laser and scribe IC silicon wafers with a kerf of 10 to 30 microns. The YAG laser is optically pumped by krypton flashlamps.

While ruby, neodymium-YAG, argon, and carbon dioxide lasers can be used for trimming resistors, only two types— Q-switched neodymium-YAG and Q-switched carbon dioxide lasers—have been chosen for their practicality and fast repetition rates of trimming. Ruby is used for manual and slow operations where the need is selective rather than routine production. Both neodymium-YAG and carbon dioxide lasers are pumped and repetitively Q-switched during trimming. The Q-switched neodymium-YAG produces pulses of nanosecond duration and eliminates substrate heating. The carbon dioxide laser produces a relatively larger spot, or kerf line, because of its longer wavelength. It requires an expensive optical system using germanium or silicon lenses; however, its operating cost is low. Both lasers are adaptable to automatic trimming of resistors on a continuous basis, limited only by the X-Y table speed and the bridge response time.

A laser-trimmer unit typically consists of: a laser generator; a neodymium-YAG (Nd:YAG) or carbon dioxide (CO_2) lasing material; a power supply; standard focusing optics; a workbench with a manual or a motorized X-Y translator; a microcircuit substrate holder; a binocular microscope; a set of probes for sensing the resistance during trimming; and a wheatstone bridge to which the probes are attached and, together with the resistor being trimmed, are made a leg of the bridge. The laser output is focused at a given spot size—from several mils down to microns—on the resistor film to be trimmed, and the metal is removed as the X- or Y-translator is moved in a straight line along the resistor. The probes continuously monitor the resistance, and as soon as the preset resistance value is achieved, the bridge is balanced and the movement of the translator and the laser emission stop immediately. The translator table is returned to another resistor for adjusting it to the preset value in the same manner. This action may be manual or automatic, depending on the rate of production required by the manufacturer.

The use of CO_2 laser trimming has one significant advantage: the reflections of 106,000-angstrom radiation are harmless to the human retina. However, for absolute safety, proper eye glasses (ones that are opaque to the carbon dioxide wavelengths) should be worn while using the laser equipment. With Nd:YAG laser radiation, safety glasses must be worn at all times unless the equipment has a built-in safety device, such as a television viewer, which can be viewed directly without safety glasses. Both laser beams pulse with high peak power, but the Nd:YAG beam has the added advantage of focusing to a spot 10 times smaller than that of the CO_2 laser. Also, its radiation is more readily absorbed by the resistor material, which may be nickel-chrome, palladium, or a mixture of silver-gold and other metallic powders formed into a cementing ink which makes up the resistor material.

Semiconductor Scribing

Laser scribing is usually performed on semiconductor wafers made of silicon dioxide, ceramic, sapphire, and similar crystalline substances. Ceramic or sapphire wafers of 1.25 to 3 inches in diameter are processed on one of their surfaces by coating them with a layer or layers of n-type and p-type active silicon material from which miniature electronic circuits are made. This is accomplished by vapor-depositing metallic (aluminum or gold) leads which are externally bonded to Kovar leads for soldering on printed-circuit boards. From 250 to 400, or more, individual circuits are processed on each wafer, each circuit having the configuration of a square or an oblong. The processed wafer is mounted on a scriber, and thin scribe lines are made in the wafer. The square or oblong sections are broken with tweezers or a knife blade from the back side of the wafer to obtain the individual microcircuits, which may be transistors, diodes, or integrated circuits of these components.

Ordinarily the scribing is performed with a diamond scriber. However, the diamond scriber sprays fine particles of the silicon substrate on each side of the kerf. These particles sometimes are difficult to clean off by conventional cleaning processes. And when they become included in the fabricated-circuit package, they may contaminate the circuit components by reacting with the package atmosphere to form conducting particles. These particles may cling between any two circuit conductors and cause destruction of that section by short-circuiting.

The wafer can be scribed with a high-intensity fine-focus laser beam to obtain thin scribe paths. The beam may be used to make a straight line or a series of fine holes—about 10 holes to a millimeter—to a depth of ¾ or more of the ceramic wafer thickness. In either case, no contamination or crystalline particles are thrown onto the circuit surface; cleaning of the square circuit chips may or may not be necessary. The laser-scribed wafer is broken into the square chips in the same manner as when the wafer is scribed with a diamond point. A laser scriber is similar to a laser cutter except that the scriber does not have to be provided with a gaseous jet.

THEORETICAL CONSIDERATIONS

In welding two pieces of metal together, the temperature of the metal must be raised to the melting point. The energy used to melt the metal must come from the laser beam. However, not all the incident laser-beam energy on the metal is used in melting the material. Some of the energy is dissipated by reflection from the surface of the metal; some is conducted to contiguous areas; and the remainder is used in raising the temperature of the metal. As stated earlier, the laser rod receives its energy from the flashlamp which energizes it to radiate. But, in practice, only about 1% of the energy received by the laser rod (for example, a ruby rod) is converted into laser radiation. Other physical parameters also enter into this relation, but they will be neglected for the time being in order to simplify the discussion.

As an example, suppose 1 joule of laser-beam energy is incident on a 2-mil thick Kovar sheet and is focused on an area 2 mils in diameter. The following thermal conditions will exist:

The heat content of the incident 1-joule laser beam will be:

$$H = \frac{1}{4.186} \text{ calorie}$$

$$= 0.24 \text{ calorie} \qquad \text{(Eq. 4-1)}$$

Assuming that the radiant energy, upon incidence on the Kovar, has incurred no loss by reflection or by secondary radiation, the energy absorbed by the Kovar may be calculated as follows:

$$\text{The volume (V) of Kovar heated} = \pi \left(\frac{d}{2}\right)^2 \times t$$

or,

$$= \pi r^2 t \qquad \text{(Eq. 4-2)}$$

where,
    d is the diameter of the weld in mils,
    r is the radius of the weld in mils,
    t is the thickness in mils of the Kovar.

Substituting values for these quantities, we have:

$$V = 3.1416 \ (0.001)^2 \times (0.002) \ \text{in}^3$$

Expressing this relation metrically, we obtain:

$$V = 3.1416 \ (1 \times 10^{-6}) \times (2 \times 10^{-3}) \times 16.387 \ \text{cm}^3$$
$$= 102.96 \times 10^{-9} \ \text{cm}^3$$
$$= 1.03 \times 10^{-7} \ \text{cm}^3$$

The weight (W) of the Kovar (density = 8.35 gm/cm^3) will be:

$$W = 1.03 \times 10^{-7} \times 8.35$$
$$= 8.6 \times 10^{-7} \ \text{gram}$$

The heat (H), in calories, required to raise the temperature of 8.6×10^{-7} gram of Kovar 1°C will be:

$$H = 8.6 \times 10^{-7} \times \text{specific heat of Kovar}$$
$$= 8.6 \times 10^{-7} \times 0.105 \ \text{calorie/°C}$$
$$= 0.903 \times 10^{-7} \ \text{calorie/°C}$$

The melting point of Kovar is 1450°C, and its heat of fusion is 64 calories per gram. Therefore, to raise the temperature of 8.6×10^{-7} gram of Kovar to its melting point, the heat required will be:

$$H = 0.903 \times 10^{-7} \times 1450 + (8.6 \times 10^{-7}) \times 64$$
$$= 1309.35 \times 10^{-7} + 550.4 \times 10^{-7}$$
$$= 1859.75 \times 10^{-7}$$
$$= 1.86 \times 10^{-4} \ \text{calorie}$$

In order to heat the two layers of Kovar that are to be welded together, the heat required will be doubled as follows:

$$H = 1.86 \times 10^{-4} \times 2$$
$$= 3.72 \times 10^{-4} \ \text{calorie}$$

or,

$$J = 0.156 \times 10^{-2} \ \text{joule}$$

On the basis of the above assumptions (which do not take into consideration the heat dissipation by conduction, reflection, diffusivity, etc.), it is evident that 1-joule laser energy of 0.24 calorie equivalent is much greater than the required welding thermal energy and that instead of producing a weld, it will produce a hole through the two layers of Kovar. However, the laser energy must be attenuated as shown by our calculations. The usual method of attenuating the laser energy is to reduce the flashlamp input energy from the power supply in accordance with Equation 3-1.

Laser-beam energy emanating from the laser rod or from the optical head can be attenuated by several means. One of the most common methods is to regulate the voltage or the capacitance, or both. This can be calculated from Equation 3-1. Another method is to regulate the size of the focal spot incident on the workpiece; however, this imposes restrictions on the wavelength of the laser beam and on the thickness of the material being welded. An equation to calculate the focal spot size (area) is given by:

$$A = 1.169 \left(\frac{f}{a}\right)^2 \times \lambda \qquad \text{(Eq. 4-3)}$$

where,

A is the focal spot size,
d is the diameter of the focal area,
f is the focal length of the lens,
a is the diameter of the laser rod,
λ is the radiant-beam wavelength.

When the expected area or the diameter of the microweld is known, the following relation may be equated to determine the focus-to-workpiece distance, S_f:

$$S_f = \frac{da}{2} \sqrt{\frac{\pi}{1.7\lambda}} \qquad \text{(Eq. 4-4)}$$

If the materials being welded are gold, silver, copper, and aluminum, or if the materials are platings of the first three metals, the diffusivity characteristics and the high conductivity of these metals play important roles in joining them together or to other metals. This relationship is given by the following expression:

$$\alpha = \frac{\varphi}{\rho H_s} \qquad \text{(Eq. 4-5)}$$

where,

α is the thermal diffusivity of the metal in cm² sec,
φ is the thermal conductivity, cal/cm/sec/°C,
ρ is the density of the metal in gm/cm³,
H_s is the specific heat, cal/gm/°C.

Steel, stainless steel, nickel, Kovar, Inconel, zinc, beryllium, chromium, and tantalum, all of which have low diffusivities and thermal conductivities, are more readily welded than aluminum, magnesium, and the noble metals, all of which are more difficult to weld unless their surfaces are treated with a readily removable substance. A laser beam ordinarily has no effect on glass because the latter is transparent to the beam; but glass can be drilled after its surface is treated with a low thermal-conductivity material. Nontransparent plastic materials are also easy to weld, even when a large-diameter focal spot is used on the workpiece.

Determination of Welding Schedules

With materials that do not have welding schedules specified by the laser-equipment manufacturer, one can use the pertinent equations given in the preceding sections to calculate the kilovoltage, capacitance, and time parameters, since the thickness of the material can be measured directly. The optical system remains constant after its selection by the operator, using a short focal-length lens for thin materials and a long-focal length lens for thick materials. Also, a fast, approximate estimate of the welding schedule can be determined by trial, by using nominal voltage, capacitance, and pulse-width values. If these trials are not successful, then other exploratory schedules may be tried in accordance with the form given in Table 4-1.

The Remarks column in Table 4-1 indicates the result of the trial schedule. The schedule that shows the optimum result for the material under trial would be the values shown by the X's located horizontally across from the favored result. The focal length of the lens can be stated in the title of the experiment, since it will remain constant. It is suggested that for each lens focal lengh, a new table be constructed for the welding schedule explored.

For low thermal-conductivity materials, the laser energy level that is selected should be in the lower range of the equipment and the pulse width should be long. Conversely, for high thermal-conductivity materials, the laser energy level should be high and the pulse width should be short. The pulse time for nominal-energy equipment is usually between two milliseconds to eight milliseconds. Therefore, when a short pulse time is selected, it will be closer to two milliseconds, and when a long pulse time is selected, it will be closer to eight milliseconds for that particular equipment. The energy ratings and the pulse-time range are given in the manufacturer's data sheets that are furnished with the equipment when it is purchased.

Table 4-1. Laser Feasibility Test Firings for Kovar (Lens Focal Length is 20 mm)

Thickness in Mils					Voltage in kV				Capacitance in μF				Weld Size in Mils*	Energy Input in Joules**	Laser Output in Joules†	Remarks — Weld	Remarks — Hole
1	2	3	4	5	1.1	1.2	1.5	1.8	200	400	500	600					
X					X				X								
X					X					X							
X					X						X						
	X					X			X								
	X					X				X							
	X					X					X						
		X					X		X								
		X					X			X							
		X					X				X						
			X					X	X								
			X					X		X							
			X					X			X						
				X			X			X		X					
				X			X			X		X					
				X			X			X							
X						X				X							
X							X			X							
X								X	X								

Notes:
(*)   Measure weld size with microscope and place across appropriate X.
(**) Calculate input energy in joules and place across appropriate X.
(†)   Calculate output laser energy using Equation (3-1) and place across appropriate X. Any variation of this table may be tried for other electrical inputs and laser outputs.

Choice of Laser Equipment

Prior to the purchase of laser equipment, the purchaser must become familiar with the types of materials he intends to weld with the equipment so that the proper choice of the laser generator may be provided in the equipment. Certain lasing elements, while being successfully employed for welding certain materials, may not produce acceptable results with other materials. For instance, Equation 4-3 shows that the laser-beam spot size is determined not only by the focal length of the lens but also by the wavelength of the laser beam used. Wavelength also affects the absorption characteristics of the material; some materials absorb longer wavelengths more easily than shorter wavelengths. The equation indicates that the focal spot size for most diffraction-limited laser elements is directly proportional to the focus-to-workpiece distance and the wavelength of the laser radiation, and that it is inversely proportional to the laser aperture (diameter of the rod). That is, when two laser beams are compared, such as neodymium-YAG having a wavelength of 10,600 angstroms and carbon dioxide radiating with a wavelength of 106,000 angstroms, a lens should be chosen for the neodymium-YAG with a focal length 10 times that chosen for the carbon dioxide.

While a short focal-length lens is suitable for thin metals, such as thin-film microcircuits, for thicker metals a longer focal-length lens is required. This is because of the deeper penetration obtained with a laser beam focused with a long focal-length lens. Also, the possible contamination of the optical system from weld effluents will be minimized or eliminated by use of the latter type of lens. Accordingly, a carbon dioxide laser unit with a long focal-length lens will be preferable for welding (and cutting) thick metals, and neodymium-YAG or ruby will be preferable for welding thin microelectronic devices, sheets, and microcircuit films.

Thus, it is seen that a great number of parametric factors enter into obtaining properly bonded weld structures. In addition to the dependence of the metal characteristics expressed in Equations 4-4 and 4-5, the beam divergence and hence the beam irradiance must also be considered as follows:

$$\text{Irradiance at laser aperture} = \frac{\text{Total laser output}}{\text{Area of aperture}}$$

or,

$$P_a = \frac{P}{\pi (D/2)^2} \qquad \text{(Eq. 4-6)}$$

where,

P_a is the irradiance in watts at the laser aperture,
P is the laser output in watts from the laser element,
D is the diameter, given in centimeters, of the laser beam at
the aperture.

The divergence of the laser beam after emerging from the laser aperture is also an important factor and varies with different lasing (laser-producing) materials. This factor is usually specified in the manufacturer's data sheet for the laser equipment, and it may be given in equation form as:

$$D_s = S\theta + D_a \qquad \text{(Eq. 4-7)}$$

where,

D_s is the diameter of the diverged beam at distance S measured in centimeters from the laser aperture,
D_a is the diameter of the laser aperture given in centimeters,
θ is the beam divergence given in radians.

The irradiance at a distance S is given as:

$$P_s = \frac{P}{\pi (D_s/2)^2} = \frac{4P}{\pi (D_s)^2} \qquad \text{(Eq. 4-8)}$$

where,

P_s is the irradiance in watts per square centimeters.

For example, what will be the diameter of divergence of a laser beam at a distance of 50 feet from the laser aperture if the angle of divergence is 1 milliradian and the aperture diameter is 0.2 centimeter? What will be the laser irradiance at 50 feet if the laser power output is 5 milliwatts?

The diameter of the laser divergence will be:

$$
\begin{aligned}
D_s &= S\theta + D_a \\
&= (50 \times 30.48 \text{ cm}) \times 0.001 \text{ radian} + 0.2 \text{ cm} \\
&= 1524 \times 0.001 + 0.2 \\
&= 1.724 \text{ cm}
\end{aligned}
$$

The irradiance at 50 feet will be:

$$
\begin{aligned}
P_s &= \frac{P}{(D_s/2)^2} = \frac{4P}{(D_s)^2} \\
&= \frac{4 \times 0.005}{3.14 \times (1.724)^2} \\
&= \frac{0.020}{9.32} = 0.0021 \\
&= 2.1 \times 10^{-3} \text{ watt/cm}^2
\end{aligned}
$$

The last quantity also indicates whether the laser energy at 50 feet from the source will be safe for direct viewing. Since the safety factor for laser viewing is given as 5×10^{-5} watt/cm² by the American Conference on Government Industrial Hygienists, it would definitely be unsafe to look directly into the beam because it might permanently damage the retina of the eye.

To recapitulate the laser welding process and the lasing elements most favorable for the particular work, the following quick and approximate rules may be given, from which deviations are possible after having a working understanding of all types of laser elements, equipment, and ancillaries.

A ruby laser is capable of delivering high-average laser power, with pulse energies on the order of 5 to 50 joules at rates of 1 pulse per second or less to prevent the laser rod from becoming too hot and losing emission efficiency with an increase in beam divergence. A warm-up pulsing time is necessary for continuous pulsing in production with adequate cooling of the ruby rod. On 10- to 20-mil-thick Kovar leads, moderate energies (between 2 to 10 joules) allow continuous-pulsing operation to be performed, and seam welds on sheet material can be made by overlapping the spot welds, as shown in Fig. 4-16. An average pulse energy of 6 joules at 4 to 5 milliseconds, pulsing at 60 pulses per minute, can be used with continuously water-cooled equipment.

Another type of laser rod, neodymium-YAG, is also applicable to continuous welding of metals and certain types of plastics, although an argon-gas laser would be preferable for plastic welding. Neodymium-YAG is particularly suitable for

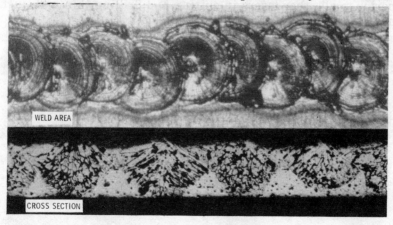

Fig. 4-16. Laser seam-welded Kovar.

seam welding because laser-energy powers of hundreds of watts can be obtained from the laser rod. Because of the high efficiency and the availability of a small focal spot from neodymium-YAG, it can be used for miniature circuits and for scribing semiconductors.

Neodymium-glass is another candidate for laser-welding operations. It has laser output energies in excess of those from a ruby rod. Because of the low thermal conductivity of the neodymium-glass material, the pulse repetition is restricted to about 10 to 15 per minute. After a warm-up pulsing time, the laser rod can be continuously pulsed at higher repetition rates.

The carbon dioxide laser operates with the highest efficiency and at high laser power output in a single mode. This gas may be operated continuously at high-energy pulses and at long wavelengths which are easily absorbed by low-conductivity metals and various nonmetals. By pulsing the laser energy at rates of 100 pulses per second or less, deep penetration in seam welds of heavy materials, such as stainless steel, nickel, Kovar, titanium, and rubber materials, can be performed because reflectivity losses become negligible at the infrared wavelengths of 106,000 angstroms. However, the laser beam from carbon dioxide is highly absorbed by most optical systems. For this reason, the lenses must be made of costly silicon, germanium, or gallium arsenide for nondestructive beam transmission; or, reflective optical systems must be used to focus the beam on the workpiece. This laser beam should not be used for welding miniature microelectronic circuits or devices; however, it is suitable for scribing semiconductor wafers and trimming thin- and thick-film resistors. The carbon dioxide laser is found superior to all other lasers in cutting and drilling thin and thick metals, and sheets of nonmetal materials.

CHAPTER 5

Laser Instrumentation in Medical Surgery

During the past several years, scientists have been intensely interested in the biological effects of laser beams on the human body, and considerable study and investigation have been conducted in determining the behaviors of laser radiations from different laser-producing elements. Since the development in 1959 of the first helium-neon maser using microwaves for excitation, many materials have been tried as laser sources. Those found as effective lasing materials are: ruby, neodymium glass, neodymium-YAG, carbon dioxide, nitrogen, argon, xenon, krypton, germanate glass, lanthanate glass, sulfur glasses, and a gamut of other laser sources, which have been investigated for application in the biological sciences. One of these applications that is of particular interest is bloodless surgery in medicine.

To date, the study and investigation of laser beams for medical use have been confined to various research centers and hospitals throughout the United States and abroad. Investigations have also been directed to the characteristics of various types of laser beams and to varied techniques of manipulation, in an attempt to create specialized applications for each particular type of laser radiation. The findings have disclosed that laser radiations of different wavelengths have significantly different effects on different body tissues, as well as on elemental substances inherent in body tissues.

The findings have further disclosed that laser types used on tissue structure must be selectively chosen. That is, a laser beam from a ruby rod is readily absorbed by retinal tissue and, therefore, it is effective in attaching a detached retina (photocoagulation). At this writing, more than 60,000 patients have been treated with laser beams for retinal attachment; this condition is common in diabetics. Because the ruby laser beam is visible, it is focused through the pupil of the eye. However, the beam is absorbed only weakly by blood cells. The visible beam from argon is highly absorbed by the visceral tissue and is very effective for photocoagulation. Since the argon laser beam is compatible with fiber-optic material, it can be used continuously or in long pulses as a surgical scalpel. The neodymium-YAG laser is also a powerful surgical tool when conducted through a properly selected waveguide or a fiber-optic bundle. While carbon dioxide is the most powerful lasing material for use in medical work for cutting and cauterizing small blood vessels in the liver, the kidney, and the stomach, its principal drawback is its long infrared wavelengths which are highly absorbed by the focusing optics of the laser unit and are not compatible with ordinary fiber-optic waveguides. Therefore, expensive lens material or less costly but bulkier reflective optics must be used with it. Efficient waveguides for high-power laser beams for medical use will be taken up separately in a later section.

Medical surgery has already employed various types of laser beams in the fields of dermatology, oncology, hematology, ophthalmology, and recently in surgery on brain tissues, on neural nodes or trunks, on the liver, on the kidney glomeruli and related renal areas, and on gastric ulcers. Polyps and nodules in the esophageal tract, cancerous growths in a body cavity, carcinoma of the vocal cords and the breast have also been treated with laser beams. Superficial and visceral cancer, coagulation of blood in surgical incisions, photocoagulation in ophthalmic affections, and in benign tumors in various body locations are among those that can be surgically treated by laser beams.

BLOODLESS SURGERY ON VOCAL CORDS

At Boston University, a team of surgical specialists have reported that they have effectively used a carbon dioxide laser beam in the removal of horny growths, polyps, and nodules from human vocal cords.[7] The surgery has been highly precise and bloodless; healing has been prompt and has been accomplished without damage to the vocal cords or to voice

---

[7] See references on pages 83 and 84.

quality. The specialists have also removed a huge tumor from the vocal cords of a 14-year-old boy who had undergone 24 previous unsuccessful, routine operations. It is further reported that the boy has acquired a normal voice for the first time in his life, subsequent to the laser treatment.

APPLICATIONS OF VARIOUS TYPES OF LASER BEAMS

At the University of Cincinnati, the use of the carbon dioxide laser beam has become a routine procedure in the removal of cancerous tissues, growths, and nodules.[1] For dark, black-colored malignant growths, it was found that a laser beam from ruby, neodymium-YAG, argon, or carbon dioxide was equally effective, with the exception of healing time. Malignant melanomas (tumors) of the skin were treated with a pulsed ruby laser and also with a continuous-wave carbon dioxide laser beam. The areas treated with the carbon dioxide lasers healed more slowly than when a pulsed ruby laser at 1500 J/cm^2, or a neodymium-glass laser at 380 J/cm^2, or an argon laser at 5 W was used. The patients had previously been treated with conventional methods, and no significant healing of the lesions was apparent. Therefore, they voluntarily submitted to the laser-radiation treatment, which was effective, painless, and resulted in the healing of the tissues. During treatment, when pain was sensed by the patient, local anesthesia by means of a nerve block was administered.

Comparative experiments were also conducted using conventional scalpel, electrosurgery, electroexcision biopsy, excessive exposure to sun, and x-ray therapy. It was concluded that the laser-beam treatment was superior since it was practically bloodless, rapid, and effective. Thermal-coagulation necrosis using a carbon dioxide laser beam was administered in the spreading melanoma and found to be of no particular advantage over the other laser beams. However, the carbon dioxide laser beam was very effective and superior to its rival, electrosurgery, for profusely bleeding areas. These experiments have also shown that the use of laser radiation for cancer surgery in profusely bleeding organs, such as the liver, the lungs, the heart, and the stomach, is most necessary; accordingly, the work is said to be continuing in this direction.

A team of scientists from Stanford Research Institute and Coherent Radiation, Inc. has developed an argon photocoagulator for the treatment of retinopathy, a pathological deterioration of the retina due to advanced diabetes. In the treatment, Coherent Radiation's Model 800 argon laser is used.

The system has a laser output that can be varied continuously from 0 to 1 watt at the region of the cornea. The beam is transmitted through an articulate arm having reflective optics into a microscope directed to the patient's eye. With this microscope, the physician adjusts the focus size of the laser beam on the retina through a contact lens over the cornea. The focus size can be varied from 1 millimeter down to 50 microns in diameter. The laser treatment requires no anesthesia since the treatment is painless.

One such laser system has been installed at the University of Illinois Medical Center for treating patients with retinal trouble. The argon-laser photocoagulation treatment is under the direction of Dr. Morton F. Goldberg, the head of the Department of Ophthalmology, University of Illinois College of Medicine. It is reported that hundreds of diabetic patients are being treated annually at the Medical Center. More than 90% of the approximately six million diabetic persons in the United States are said to require photocoagulation treatment ultimately. While early treatment of retinal disease is important, a physician using the laser photocoagulator must learn to know the exact dosage to be administered to any one particular patient, according to Dr. Goldberg.

LASER APPLICATION IN BRAIN SURGERY

At the University of Pittsburgh, another medical team of researchers has successfully used a laser beam for removal of a malignant growth in brain tissue.[2] In this operation, the laser beam has been used to destroy the cancerous tissue, and then the mass has been removed by conventional methods. Many patients with Parkinson's disease (shaking palsy), which affects the nerve ganglia at the base of the brain, are reported to be aided by treatment with a laser beam. The laser-beam treatment precludes the necessity of extensive surgery or probing the brain with an electrode.

REMOVAL OF TATTOOS, WARTS, AND SKIN BLEMISHES

Cosmetically speaking, the laser beam has also been routinely employed in the removal of tattoos and skin blemishes from human skin. At the University of Cincinnati, this procedure has become routine.[1] The mechanism of laser interaction with a tattooed area consists of injecting a beam of ruby laser (for its better absorption quality) into the tattooed area or spot. The beam penetrates the translucent skin with little or no harm and vaporizes the dark dye pigment by absorption into the pigment. It is reported that at the Laser Laboratory of the university, the carbon dioxide laser has become a standard device for removing skin blemishes, warts, etc., from the legs, the chest, the arms, or any other cutaneous part of the body. And in some cases, the laser beam has been found to be a substitute for high-voltage x-rays, radium, or radioactive cobalt in the treatment of deep-seated cancer.

LASER MICROSURGERY BY SWEDISH RESEARCHERS

The researchers at Uppsala University in Sweden have been trying to perfect a laser microsurgical device that will correct faults in nerves and intricate body organs. Experiments with live animals have disclosed that such microsurgical techniques are feasible even on the labyrinth of the ear, which could be easily damaged, resulting in deafness. One main problem has been that the laser beam they have been using for the job has been producing a mechanical shock through induced acoustic cell oscillation. The degree of shock has been enough to cause the cells to explode and damage the contiguous structures. Apparently, the United States researchers have not experienced this phenomenon in their laser research on live biological specimens, such as the human nervous center, the brain.

OTHER INSTITUTIONS USING THERAPEUTIC LASER BEAMS

In California, several institutions—the University of Southern California, California University at Los Angeles, Pasadena Medical Foundation, Stanford Institute, and others—are conducting laser treatment on cancerous growths, skin blemishes, brain anomalies, nerve necrosis, gingivitis, and similar conditions.[3] Work with the laser is widespread over the continent, and some of the work as yet is incomplete at this writing. The University of California at Los Angeles has been conducting investigations on restorative dentistry for several years on human teeth in vivo and in vitro, with high success.[4] Similar work is being carried on at other institutions. The laser has become a biological tool in both medical and dental applications.

DIFFICULTIES WITH PRESENT LASER EQUIPMENT

One common problem that all researchers have encountered in the administration of laser beams in the medical and dental fields is the lack of versatility of the laser equipment used. This shortcoming has deterred many investigators from achieving the maximum use and effectiveness of the laser beam. These investigators have been searching among laser manufacturers for a laser instrumentation scalpel that will have the flexibility of an electrosurgical scalpel but have greater effectiveness and utility. The present use of tubular conduits with reflectors, prisms, mirrors, or similar contrivances for delivering the laser from its source to the work area has been cumbersome and time consuming. The enormous size of the instrumentation apparatus, the irregularity of configuration, and the inflexibility of its reach in corners or curved areas have limited its use as standard equipment in medical work.

Foreseeing these problems, the author's organization has taken steps to develop and patent laser aids and auxiliary devices that should contribute to the versatility and effectiveness of the laser beam as a tool for medical and dental applications. The accompanying illustrations only restrictedly display the principle of Laserkinetics' laser equipment and pertinent manipulative instruments. Fig. 5-1 shows a Laserkinetics Medical Laser Model ML-102.

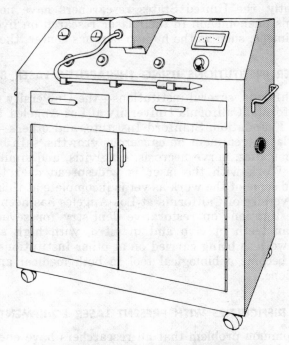

Fig. 5-1. Laserkinetics' medical laser Model ML-102.

CONVENTIONAL LASER WAVEGUIDES IN MEDICAL SURGERY

The Hartford Laser Laboratory of the University of Cincinnati Medical Center has developed a sterilizable laser-beam probe using a neodymium-YAG laser which furnishes 200 watts in the 10,600-angstrom infrared range.[1] The beam is used for surgery on profusely bleeding organs, such as the liver, the heart, the lungs, and the stomach. Because of its high absorption coefficient for colored tissues, tattoos, and black tumors, the beam selectively destroys the affected tissue cells without severe damage to the surrounding healthy tissues.

The laser probe is a fiber-optic conduit with a transmission capability of 80% and a beam divergence of 10 milliradians. Its researchers claim that the laser probe can deliver, to the work area, energy that is several orders of magnitude greater than ordinary fiber-optic materials; the focused power density is about 700 watts/mm² at the 0.4-mm focus of a 50-mm focal-length lens. For aiming the infrared laser to the work area, a helium-neon laser beam is used through the focusing probe to locate the point of the neodymium-YAG laser beam. The investigators further claim that the neodymium-YAG laser is superior to the carbon dioxide laser in transmitting the beam through the fiber-optic bundle. Also, by Q-switching the neodymium-YAG and operating the laser beam at its longer wavelength (13,000 angstroms), its cutting capability is improved. However, they believe that "an ideal laser surgical instrument is not yet available." They also admit that perhaps the development of the ideal laser surgical instrument will not come from reluctant laser manufacturers because of the presently restricted market feasibility of the probe. However, they are highly anticipative that the laser probe will some day be an indispensable tool in medical and dental surgery. An illustration of the fiber-optic probe using a He-Ne aimer is shown in Fig. 5-2.

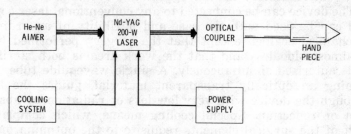

Fig. 5-2. Laser probe with He-Ne aimer.

Another fiber-optic scalpel has been developed by scientists at Munich, West Germany. They say it is capable of transmitting 20 times more light energy before it breaks down than existing fiber-optic materials can. This fiber-optic scalpel was demonstrated at the European Electro-Optics Markets & Technology Conference and Exhibition held in September 1972. The developers contend that the fiber-optic bundle can transmit powers up to 100 kW at 5000 pps. The device is connected to a 200-W neodymium-YAG laser to deliver high peak powers. In its preliminary application, it has been used in human dermatology. The device is also being considered for the coagulation of bleeding in the field of endoscopy.

LASERKINETICS LASER WAVEGUIDE FOR SURGERY

A unique laser waveguide, developed by Laserkinetics Corporation for use with medical surgery and dental restorative work, is shown in Fig. 5-3. The versatile laser waveguide is

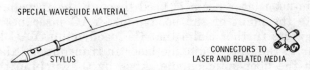

Fig. 5-3. Laserkinetics' surgical laser stylus.

provided with a novel laser-transmitting conduit, which conducts both a laser beam and a fluid for anesthetizing the area to be treated by the laser beam. Radiations emitted from ruby, neodymium-YAG, carbon dioxide, argon, or nitrogen lasers can be transmitted through the waveguide because of the compatibility of the waveguide with the wavelengths of these laser beams. With selective use of waveguide materials, no degradation of the waveguide or solarization effects exist to wear out or destroy the waveguide.

The device can be connected to any conventional laser source and can be used with the ease and flexibility of an ordinary mechanical scalpel, except that the surgery performed by it is almost bloodless and that the work area is both sterilized and cauterized simultaneously. A single waveguide tube, containing an optically transparent material, guides the laser through the device with very low loss of radiation by absorption or reflection. Special cooling means, which comprise a part of the surgical elements requisite to the optimum operation of the surgical stylus, are provided so that high-intensity energy levels up to several-hundred watts or 80-joule pulses without Q-switching are possible. Fingertip push buttons regulate the focal point of the laser beam incident on the work area and the flow of the fluid jet through the instrument into the patient's affected region in the visceral, the nervous, and the blood-containing organs of the body. The focus of the laser plasma on the work area can attain a temperature up to 14,000°C.

REFERENCES AND COMMENTS

This chapter is not intended to instruct the reader how to administer laser treatment to the human body but rather to present a treatise for an appreciation of the application of the laser in the treatment of various sufferings of the human body. The principal objectives of the text are to point out: (1) The necessity of the design and development of a laser system of maximum utility for the medical surgeon. (2) The incorporation of ease and flexibility of use into the laser equipment for the delivery of the laser beam from its source to the work area. (3) The provision of laser safety into the equipment to eliminate protective apparel now worn by the surgeon. (4) The importance of the scientist and the physician working together as a team to formulate proper laser treatment methods and dosages.

The author further calls the attention of the reader to the progress made with lasers in the medical field and gives examples of the investigative and routine work now being conducted by the following foremost medical and laser research workers, whose contributions to the field of surgery have formed the basis for the medical aspects of this text.

1. Dr. Leon Goldman, M.D., director of Laser Laboratory and Medical Center, University of Cincinnati, professor and chairman of the Department of Dermatology, who has written numerous books and papers on the biomedical aspects of lasers; and his colleagues, Dr. Zdenek Naprstek, director of Investigative Cardiovascular and Liver Surgery, and the directing physicist, R. J. Rockwell, Jr., the president of the Laser Institute of America.
2. Dr. Hubert L. Rosomoff, professor of Neurological Surgery, University of Pittsburgh, who conducts medical laser work at the Presbyterian University Hospital.
3. Dr. Ronald R. Rounds, Pasadena Foundation for Medical Research, California.

4. Laser researchers at the University of California at Los Angeles.
5. Dr. Malcolm L. Stitch, laser physicist, University of Southern California, Los Angeles.
6. Dr. William L. Benedict, M.D., laser photocoagulation specialist, New York Eye and Ear Infirmary, New York.
7. The medical team at Boston University, Massachusetts.

CHAPTER 6

Laser Instrumentation in Dentistry

INTRODUCTION

Since 1960, considerable investigation has been conducted on dental specimens both in vivo and in vitro, using a laser beam both from a Q-switched ruby rod (6943 angstroms) and from a Q-switched carbon dioxide laser (106,000 angstroms). The investigators include laser scientists and dental specialists working in research institutions and dental laboratories both in the United States and abroad.[2] The investigative work covers the restorative anatomy of dental structures and dental diseases, using pulsed laser beams. This endeavor has led to laser-induced inhibition of caries (tooth decay) and is centered on the effect of the laser beam on dental soft tissues, the degree of laser safety necessary, and the potential applications of laser radiations in dentistry.

To date, the principal drawback in routine use of a laser beam in dentistry has been that of building suitable laser systems which would afford the greatest versatility of instrumentation, compactness, efficiency, and effectiveness as a dental tool. This chapter describes the investigative work done, the present difficulties encountered, and how these difficulties may be overcome by the use of a laser system which is a versatile and very effective dental tool for routine applications in clinical and in prosthetic practices.

The discussion in this chapter further indicates why a laser beam should be used in both the restorative and the therapeutic work in dentistry and the resultant benefits derived from such

---

[2] See references on page 95.

applications.[1] It is believed that the standard application of a laser beam in the dentist's office to date has been retarded because of the lack of adequate equipment and an instrumentation facility. To this end, much work has been done by the author's firm to advance the state of the art of laser implementation.

DENTAL STRUCTURE

The alveolar processes of the maxilla and the mandible contain sockets covered by a dense, insensitive, fibrous, mucous membrane (the gums). The sockets, or alveoli, are lined by the periosteum which, together with the gums, serves to attach the teeth to their sockets and provide a source of nourishment for the teeth. Each tooth has three main sections: the root, consisting of one or more fangs; the crown, which is beyond the level of the gums; and the neck section, which occupies the region between the root and the crown, as illustrated in Fig. 6-1.

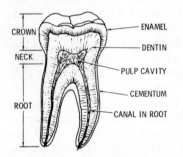

Fig. 6-1. Longitudinal section of a human tooth.

As shown in the illustration, each tooth consists of a central structure—the dentin—which encloses an internal pulp cavity and is capped by a dense layer of enamel. A layer of cementum interfaces the dentin and the enamel. These three substances are harder than bone, enamel being the hardest. The pulp cavity is continuous with a canal containing blood vessels and some nerves. The enamel is composed of 98% inorganic substance and 2% organic matter. The dentin contains approximately 30% organic matter.

The most common dental disease is caries. The carious process may start at an exposed area of the cementum, or at a weak point in the enamel if it has been scratched by rough dental abrasives or by other causes. Various methods are used at present to alleviate or cure caries. One of the most common is the removal of the affected area and restoration with a chemical, plastic, or metallic material; this is performed with mechanical instruments at present. The permanence of such restorative work is dependent on the experience and the competence of the dental operator.

During the past several years, much work has been underway using a laser beam, which has been found to be quite effective in dental restorative application. The beam can drill holes in the carious tooth structure, cauterize or sterilize the cavity, or fuse the enamel portion of the tooth to cover the nondiseased but partially destroyed spots or areas. The results of the experiments have shown that "laser brushing" initially healthy enamel can prevent caries in the normal teeth. Laser beams from a ruby rod, neodymium-YAG, carbon dioxide, and others have been used with various degrees of success, at energy ratings of up to 2000 joules per square centimeter or at power ratings of up to 10^{10} watts per square centimeter in the Q-switched mode. Some of the problems involved and their solutions will be discussed in the sections that follow.

LASER-INDUCED INHIBITION OF CARIES

Extensive as well as intensive investigations have been conducted on teeth both in vivo and in vitro, using both ruby and carbon dioxide lasers.[3] The carbon dioxide laser beam has been found to be superior to the ruby laser because of the longer wavelength of the carbon dioxide laser beam. By using a laser density which is more than three times that of ruby, the invisible laser beam from carbon dioxide is readily absorbed by the tooth tissue. An added advantage is that the rise in tooth temperature is negligible with a carbon dioxide laser beam, thus making it more attractive for application in dental work.

The experiments on enamel have consisted of placing treated and untreated teeth in a demineralizing solution. The laser-brushed (treated) teeth have not developed cavities, while the teeth untreated with the laser beam have developed cavities. The laser density in the treatment is reported to be 25 to 50 J/cm^2, the higher density giving better results. In 1971, J. Vahl of Leipzig, Germany,[4] [5] indicated that the pulsed laser beam melts the enamel to a depth of 0.5 micrometer, or 5000 angstroms. The findings further indicate that cariogenic substances preferentially attack the prism borders of the enamel. It has been concluded that naturally occurring micropores in the enamel can be sealed, eliminating the invasion of cariogenic substances into the pores.

Further studies and experiments have been tried for fusing tooth-colored hard materials directly to the enamel. The researchers at the New York University and at the Eastman Kodak Park have achieved high success with their method. It can be postulated then that it should be possible to develop tooth-colored cement which would be placed into a tooth cavity and allowed to set chemically. The cement could then be glazed by laser brushing so that the cement-enamel interface is contiguous. Work has been started in this direction, using an inorganic salt solution to seal the cavity and subsequently to laser glaze the salt that has set on the enamel.[1]

DENTAL DRILLING AND CAUTERIZING

Work is also in progress on the drilling of holes in teeth where the carious process has begun to destroy the impaired enamel. While laser drilling of the enamel and part of the dentin (depending on the depth of the carious affection) can be performed successfully, the ultimate result is dependent on the skill of the operator of the laser system. In this point, the technique does not deviate from the present one using mechanical drills; that is, by going too far into the pulp cavity, the effect might be one of infection or destruction of the nerve endings, thus ending the life of that tooth. The laser beam must be controlled the same as the dentist's drill must be so that the drilling procedure can be arrested at any depth from the surface of the enamel. This requires a knowledge of the spectral characteristics of the laser beam utilized as well as an anatomical knowlege of the various elements of the particular tooth under instrumentation. The results obtained in tissue-laser interaction mechanisms offer great promise for the laser as a radiant tool in preventive dentistry.[1]

During drilling with a laser beam, the unintentional effects of the laser radiation upon the soft tissue surrounding the teeth, such as the mucus membranes, the contiguous gingiva, and the pulpal tissue cells, have also been considered.[3] The findings indicate that with or without preventive means to preclude the radiation from the soft tissue, the effect of the laser beam on the soft tissue is inconsequential. With properly designed equipment and accurately administered laser radiation to the work area, extreme precautionary measures would not be any more necessary than they are in a mechanical dental-drilling procedure.

The area in contact with the laser beam is immediately sterilized, owing to the rapid and extreme thermal conditions of the laser beam. However, because of the instantaneousness of the application of high heat from the laser, the surrounding tissues are not affected. When bleeding occurs during either a mechanical or a laser instrumentation of the dental area, the characteristic cauterizing property of the laser beam can be applied to arrest bleeding, as in medical work. In short, the laser beam offers a sophisticated, very effective means of drilling, glazing, cauterizing, and treating dental anomalies by selective application of the radiation.[1]

THE PROBLEMS INVOLVED IN POTENTIAL LASER APPLICATIONS IN DENTISTRY

A laser beam generally has the same characteristics as ordinary light. There are no mysterious emanations from it, contrary to the statements of early writers. The beam is a radiation of intense heat, capable of being concentrated at any conceivable point because of its monochromaticity, beam coherence, and ability to deliver extremely high energies in short pulse durations. The beam can be focused with lenses and manipulated with mirrors to any point selected on the work area. For instance, a 1-joule ruby laser beam projecting from a rod of ¼-inch diameter is harmless when it is incident on the palm of the hand. But, when this beam is converged with a lens to a 1-mil-diameter focus on the palm, the beam will instantly burn a hole in the palm tissue. When the laser energy is higher, such as 10 joules, the same hole-drilling effect will be observed but this time with a larger focus size. These effects follow optical principles known for centuries.

At present, it is sometimes necessary to use a tooth-colored cement or porcelain to temporarily fill tooth cavities for a period until the patient can return to the dental clinic for metal-filling the cavity. With a laser beam, the work can be made permanent by fusing and glazing the porcelain at the enamel. Not only will such a procedure be feasible, but the finished work on the tooth will look more natural. Carious destruction of the biting surfaces of the tooth will be eliminated.

The prosthetic aspects of the laser have been discussed earlier. At the present time, the most sophisticated laser welding equipment consists of a 4- × 6- × 24-inch laser head with a roomful of power supply. After numerous mechanical adjustments are made to stabilize the laser head and to direct the beam at a distance of up to 8 inches from the workpiece, the laser beam is focused through a microscope onto the work area in vitro. Potentially, laser welding of fixed prosthesis can be performed directly in the mouth to simplify restorative dentistry. However, it is not feasible at this time because of the bulkiness of the equipment and the lack of the flexibility in its use.

At present, there are many problems involved in carrying out this work. For instance, in the conventional method, the dentist presses his drill against the tooth and drills in any direction he deems necessary without any drawback. In the case of a laser beam from conventional laser equipment, the laser head has to be positioned by means of jigs and special fixtures to point the beam at the work area. The beam must first be focused by using a visible light through a microscope which the beam traverses. The light beam must then be turned off, and the laser beam must replace the light-beam path. All the while the operator is hoping that the laser focus will coincide with the position of the light-beam focus. For a second firing of the laser beam on another part of the tooth, the same procedure must be repeated. If the work has not been done properly during these firings of the laser beam, the whole process of focusing and firing has to be repeated.

All this work is bothersome, time consuming, and inflexible in procedure. The ultimate result, if satisfactory, cannot compensate for the time, cost, and inflexibility offered by the laser method versus the conventional mechanical method which is faster, lower in cost, and more flexible. Thus, the advantages gained by the laser-beam method are defeated by the many disadvantages of the laser equipment. Consequently, in order to utilize the useful characteristics of a laser-beam method, new and unique equipment should be designed and constructed so that it affords versatility, reduction of cost, permanency, and, above all, high-quality work that is superior to any method presently known to man. Anticipating these problems, the author has taken steps to design and patent a dental laser instrumentation system which uses a laser-beam manipulator of high versatility and flexibility of use to meet the requirements inherent in a dental instrumentation system.

LASERKINETICS DENTAL LASER INSTRUMENTATION SYSTEM

Two types of dental laser systems are being designed and developed by the Laserkinetics Corporation staff: (1) One type will be used on live human teeth for drilling holes and sterilizing the cavity.[1] It will also be used to restore the cavity with a chemical material, to glaze the tooth enamel, and to serve for therapeutic purposes. (2) The second type will be used for repairing fractures in bridgework.

Both of these systems will be relatively small in size and will be provided with a laser-beam conduit which can be employed to transmit the laser beam to any portion of the tooth under manipulation. These systems will allow the tooth to be worked on in the same manner as that used with conventional mechanical dental-drilling instruments. The laser beam can be manipulated in any direction toward the tooth and automatically focused to the spot or area to be worked on. Thus, both of these systems offer the ultimate in flexibility and ease of operation. The work should be fast, clean, and highly effective.

The first type of laser system is designated Model DL-102, and the second type is designated Model DL-202. They are shown in Figs. 6-2 and 6-3, respectively.

DESCRIPTION OF THE DENTAL LASER SYSTEM MODEL DL-102

The dental instrumentation laser system Model DL-102 is shown in Fig. 6-2. The diagram is only a typical representation of the system without detailed design and construction features. Principally the system comprises a dentist's chair A; laser control console B in association with the chair; a laser generator and a power supply enclosed within the seat of the chair; and laser-manipulation conduit C, which can be easily and conveniently directed to any area during dental instrumentation. A self-contained optical system, with an automatic focusing means, serves to focus the laser beam without the operator's attention whenever the operator adjusts the point of the laser conduit on the work area.

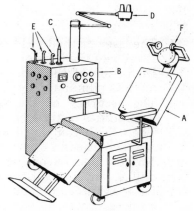

Fig. 6-2. Dental laser instrumentation system
Model DL-102.

Auxiliary binocular microscope D may be used when the work requires microscopic precision manipulation on the tooth. The microscope is provided with cool light which can be directed to the area under dental treatment. Certain auxiliary instruments required for routine manipulation are designated by provision E. Since the patient has to be immobilized in some cases of treatment, provision F is made at the back of the seat to immobilize the head in the position desired. The entire system is mobile and can be moved from one clinical office to another by releasing the permanently lubricated casters.

Note that the equipment is self-contained and does not require an additional dental chair for conducting routine dental work on the patient, although the choice is left to the dentist. With slight modification, any existing dental chair can be equipped with the Laserkinetics dental laser system. The flexible laser conduit can be directed to any part of the teeth for drilling, sterilizing drilled cavities, or cauterizing gingival tissue if bleeding occurs. Furthermore, certain types of fillings and bridgework repairs can be made in the mouth without inconvenience to the patient. The resulting work is rapid and clean.

LASER WELDER FOR DENTAL BRIDGEWORK

For many years, dental bridgework elements have been joined together by the use of gold or an alloy heated with a blow torch. This process wastes material, is time consuming, and the results obtained are inconsistent from one bridgework to another. The process is costly, and the cost invariably is passed on to the patient. Investigations conducted with laser-beam melting and welding of gold and other dental alloys have shown the following distinct advantages of the laser welder shown in Fig. 6-3 over the torch method.

1. The laser method yields superior joints and strength.
2. It reduces the time of fabrication 10 to 15 times.
3. Distortion of the finished product due to heat from the torch is eliminated by use of the laser beam.
4. The accuracy of the work approaches the theoretical possibilities of the laser.
5. The work is completed without an additional appointment for the patient.
6. No additional alloys are needed with the laser method, unlike conventional torch methods.
7. Laser-beam manipulation simplifies the operating procedures.

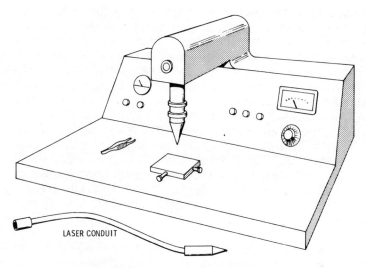

LASER CONDUIT

Fig. 6-3. Laserkinetics' laser welding system DL-202.

The laser instrumentation system for dental bridgework, Model DL-202, is compact and portable. It offers the same ultimate versatility as the Model DL-102 dental unit. The principal purpose of this system is in the dental laboratory for welding and drilling holes in a dental workpiece. The system can also repair numerous other articles and microelectronic devices used in aircraft and space applications. Accordingly, the use of the system is not limited to dental-laboratory work only but can also be used in the processing of industrial products. For instance, the equipment can weld, drill and cut microelectronic devices and materials; it can drill holes in thin- and thick-film circuits; it can scribe dielectric and ceramic materials, including certain plastics. The system can also solder and desolder circuit leads of microelectronic devices, such as transistors, diodes, capacitors, hybrids, etc.

The laser system Model DL-202 consists of a bench instrumentation unit with a switch in the foot treadle, which triggers the laser beam after the laser head contacts the workpiece. The driving of the laser head to the workpiece is also performed by the foot treadle. If the workpiece is too large to be accommodated under the laser head, the laser beam can be directed to the workpiece through a laser waveguide designed by the author for power loads up to 30 joules or 8 kW/cm^2. To use the laser conduit, the distal portion of the laser head is removed from the console, and the proximal end of the laser conduit, provided with an adaptor, is screwed onto the laser head; this operation can be performed within 30 seconds. The laser conduit then can be operated as easily and conveniently as a ballpoint pen. It is anticipated that in the future, when the application of the laser beam becomes prevalent in the dentist's office, the Model DL-202 will be used directly on the tooth to weld broken parts of fillings or denture inlays in the patient's mouth without removal of the parts.

A laser-welded dental bridge is shown in Fig. 6-4, which shows upper front incisor caps. The metal was cast and finished; then it was butt-welded in an area 0.2 inch long and 0.04 inch thick. A series of 8-millisecond, 16-joule pulses were used, and the pulse penetration was 4 mils. This work was performed by Thomas E. Gordon, Jr., D.D.S., head of the Laser Research Department, Orange Memorial Hospital in Orlando, Florida.

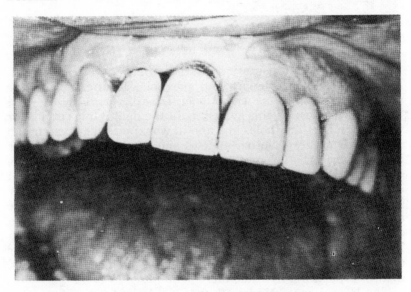

Fig. 6-4. A laser-welded dental bridge.

REFERENCES AND COMMENTS

The text on dental experiments and investigations contained in this chapter is based principally on the research and findings of Dr. Ralph H. Stern, School of Dentistry, University of California at Los Angeles. Since the discovery of solid-state lasers in 1960, Dr. Stern has spent many years in the investigation and study of teeth both in vitro and in vivo, using laser beams from solid-state and gaseous laser materials. His work has led to the discovery of laser-induced inhibition of caries, which means that for the first time the human tooth can be "laserbeam brushed" to prevent caries in the enamel. His latest investigations have been coupled with the work of his coinvestigators, Professor Reider F. Sognnaes, Professor Johanna Vahl, Dr. Harold F. Eastgate, and Dr. Donald Rounds.

1. General information gathered by the author from different sources conducting limited and specific investigations on dental tissues. This information should not be construed as having or not having the sanction of the investigators in (2), (3), and (4), since it is still in a premature state.
2. Stern, R. H.; Vahl, J.; and Sognnaes, R. F. "Lased Enamel: Ultrastructural Observations of Pulsed Carbon Dioxide Laser Effects." J. Dent. Res., 1972.
3. Stern, R. H. "Dentistry and the Laser." Report covering a decade of laser investigative work. School of Dentistry, University of California at Los Angeles, 1973.
4. Vahl, J. Dr. Stern's final report "Dentistry and the Laser" appeared in Item (2).
5. Vahl, J. "Gesunder und Pathologische Veranderter Zahnschmelz." Booklet 43 from the Meusser Collection. Leipzig, Germany: Johann Ambrosius Barth, 1971.

While the author does not believe that laser radiation is a panacea to all dental troubles and will supersede all mechanical dental work now being performed in a dental clinic, he strongly believes that with proper laser equipment and instrumentation techniques to ease and hasten the work of the dentist, the laser will eventually become an indispensable dental tool for both restorative and therapeutic dentistry.

CHAPTER 7

Metrological Laser Systems

INTRODUCTION

One of the most flourishing businesses in laser technology since 1960 has been the metrological applications of laser radiation in industry. Laser equipment using gas-laser generators has been used in laser gyroscopes and for aligning, surveying, range finding, target illuminating, and gauging of parts. Since the laser beam is monochromatic, intense, and unidirectional, measurements once considered to be impractical and impossible have become feasible with the laser beam. Precise systems for metrological applications have been constructed and are in use at the present time. The laser systems perform various metrological operations not only very accurately but also faster and more effectively, with fewer operators and at more-reasonable costs than conventional methods.

Some of the most common and important metrological laser instruments are those employed in tunnel digging, pipelaying, machine-tool aligning, surveying, range finding, and laser gauging of parts, and in guidance systems for earth moving and trenching.

LASER ALIGNMENT SYSTEMS

A laser alignment system consists of a continuous laser-beam generator, such as a helium-neon laser mounted on a platform or a sturdy tripod; a telescope to view the location of the laser-beam target or screen; and a remote detector or screen on which the laser beam is projected. The function of such a system is to determine straightness, flatness, squareness, levelness and accuracy.

The laser beam used in metrological work is first filtered and then expanded to about 10 diameters as it leaves the laser aperture of the unit. The expanded beam is collimated so that it is almost perfectly symmetrical and free from ghost fringes or birefringent effect. Ordinarily a 0.5-milliwatt laser beam is sufficient to accomplish the required operation. It is relatively safe for the operator to use the beam without wearing safety goggles (although it is recommended that the operator always avoid looking directly into the beam). Thus, an excellent compromise between high visibility and operating safety can be achieved.

In operation, the collimated pencil-thin laser beam is projected from the laser unit (which is supported at one starting point of the structure to be aligned) to a target which may be a specially prepared screen, an electronic detector, or a retroreflector. In pipelaying, the hub of the pipe may be marked on the screen and the laser beam focused on this point as a reference. This ensures that all structures to be aligned or all jigs to be erected for building the system are aligned accurately with respect to the laser beam. Since the laser beam does not sag as a string or wire reference line does, all parts built around the setting can be aligned to an accuracy of less than 1 millimeter, in structural lengths within 80 to 100 feet. Since the helium-neon laser beam has a divergence of approximately 0.2 arc second, for long distances up to 1000 feet the beam diverges slightly. However, the incident laser focus is so sharp that the center point of the beam can be readily determined visually and marked on the screen, or a detector can be centered at that point.

The advantage of using an electronic detector (photodetector) is that the X-Y axes can be accurately localized by an indicator built on the laser head, which is electrically connected to the photodetector through wires. Or, the indicator may be mounted on a unit containing the X-Y axes photodetector. An illustration for an alignment system in operation is given in Fig. 7-1.

Nearly a dozen laser manufacturers are producing alignment equipment. Among these manufacturers are: Hughes Aircraft Company, Perkin-Elmer Corporation, Electro-Optics Associates, Construction Supply Company, Spectra-Physics, and AGA Corporation. These firms are well known in industry as manufacturers of metrological laser equipment. (See Appendix I for their addresses.)

AGA Corporation claims its industrial laser dynamic testing unit has a capability of precision geometric measuring before the parts are made rather than measuring the results afterward. The system is used for quality control. Operation of the unit involves moving the unit, as if to actually cut metal, and recording the degree of geometric accuracy of the part. The results are claimed to be accurate, rapid, and reliable. Its application covers the measurement of large structural parts and the alignment of shafts, bearings, ships' propeller-shafts, turbines, etc.

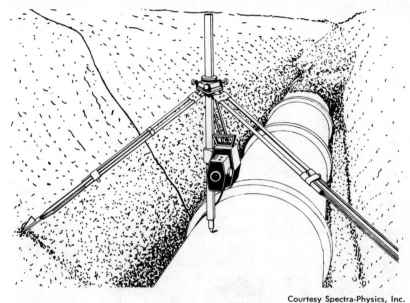

Courtesy Spectra-Physics, Inc.

Fig. 7-1. Illustration of an alignment system.

Another unique and portable laser alignment system, manufactured by Construction Supply Company, is the AccuBeam Model II. It provides a simple, accurate, and flexible measurement tool for line-of-sight alignment. The system can be mounted on a tripod or on a stage which permits clamping of the instrument on beams, rails, posts, or other sturdy supports in either a horizontal or a vertical position. It has solid-state electronic circuitry which operates on 12-volt, 1.5-ampere direct current, with a laser power output of 2 milliwatts at a 6328-angstrom wavelength.

According to the manufacturer, the laser beam retains its small diameter over long distances in both the horizontal and the vertical planes; and, by using an X-Y axis sensor, an exact beam center can be located to extremely close tolerances. Also by use of the X-Y axis sensor, alignment of crane rails, mine and tunnel borings, bridge references, machinery, and similar constructions becomes a simple and accurate procedure. The auxiliary equipment provides an automatic indicator with a red or a green light to indicate when the beam is accurately centered on the target. When an out-of-alignment condition occurs, an alarm sounds. The unit is shown in Fig. 7-2 with its accessories, comprising a utility target on which the beam is centered, an inverter to change ac to dc, and a mounting stage.

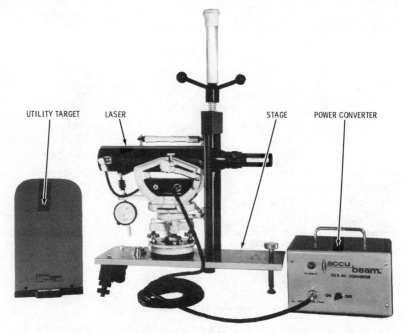

UTILITY TARGET   LASER   STAGE   POWER CONVERTER

Courtesy Construction Supply Company

Fig. 7-2. AccuBeam Model II shown with utility target, power converter, and mounting stage.

LASER RANGE FINDERS

Subsequent to the discovery of the ruby laser by the Hughes Research Laboratories, one of the first applications of the ruby laser beam was the development, by that company, of a laser ranging system dubbed COLIDAR (an acronym for *C*oherent *L*ight *D*etection *a*nd *R*anging). This system is operated by using a Q-switching technique. It provides pulses of several megawatts peak power, with durations in the nanosecond range. In operation, the Q-switched laser beam is projected on a retroreflector positioned at the remote end of the distance to be measured, and the counting of the pulses starts simultaneously with the triggering of the laser and continues until the beam returns to the system from the target. As the laser beam leaves the laser aperture, a small portion of the laser energy is sampled by a silicon photodetector which starts a megahertz pulse counter. The returning laser signal is detected by a photomultiplier, is amplified, and is then fed to the counter. When the signal reaches the counter, the counter stops. The distance is determined by the number of pulses, the pulse duration, and the speed of light. This can be expressed by a simplified equation:*

$$S_t = \frac{N_p \times T_p \times C}{2} \qquad \text{(Eq. 7-1)}$$

where,
S_t is the target distance in centimeters,
C is the speed of light taken as 3×10^{10} centimeters,
N_p is the number of pulses counted by the counter,
T_p is the time that it took the laser beam to travel to the target and back to the system.

Since this designates twice the distance between the target and the laser system, the resultant value is divided by two. A block diagram of a typical laser range finder is shown in Fig. 7-3.

The output laser beam is processed through a collimating telescope to obtain a parallel pencil beam. The beam returned

---

*The rise time is neglected in the equation.

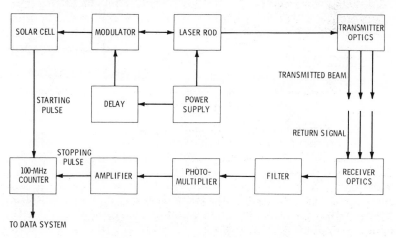

Fig. 7-3. Block diagram of a typical range-finder circuit.

from the target is gathered by a telescope, the noise is filtered from the signal, and the filtered signal is impressed on the photomultiplier where it goes to a counter through a signal amplifier. The present range finders employ helium-neon gas lasers which are less costly than other types, modulate relatively easily, and use less-cumbersome structural parts than conventional range finders.

Other improvements have been made by the same company and by other companies so that a laser range finder is now a reliable and accurate ranging tool. The equipment can be made compact and portable by using battery power from cadmium-sulfide cells or from nickel-cadmium rechargeable batteries. Some of them have been installed on military weapons and artillery. Some systems are made to track rockets, aircraft, and missiles. These systems can lock onto the moving target so that continuous intelligence is available with respect to the position and distance of the target. The laser beam is amplitude modulated to achieve better resolution than a Q-switched optical laser system. Also, the use of a telescope with a relatively large aperture makes the fine laser-processed signal resolution superior to microwave radar.

A very simple but accurate laser range finder developed in the author's laboratory utilizes a triangulation method for measuring target distances up to 600 feet. In operation, a laser beam is projected to a specific point on the target by accurately positioning the incident beam with a telescope mounted on the laser head, which is supported on a tripod. Then the system is moved a measured distance from the original point of measurement. The laser head is gradually rotated by means of a vernier protractor until the laser beam is again centered on the original target point. The angular rotation of the laser beam is read out directly from the protractor window and converted into linear distance by the use of the equation:

$$S_t = \text{Cot } \phi \times S_d \qquad \text{(Eq. 7-2)}$$

where,

S_t is the distance measured in centimeters,
S_d is the displacement in centimeters between the original tripod location and the final location,
ϕ is the angular rotation in degrees.

In moving the tripod to the second location, one must take special care to make the displacement at right angles to the laser beam that was projected to the target in the first operation.

Based on the range-finder principle, laser radars for detection of shorter distances at lower altitudes than what a microwave radar is capable of achieving have also been constructed and are in use very successfully. Both the transmitter and the receiver are built into one unit.

The Lincoln Laboratory at the Massachusetts Institute of Technology has developed a laser radar with an accuracy of 14 inches at a range of 50 miles. It is a well-known fact that microwave-radar information processing is dependent on the frequency of its broadcast beam. Since the laser radar has a frequency approximately 10,000 times that of the microwave radar, the laser radar is 10,000 times more accurate in both angular and doppler resolution. Thus, the distance of an object $3\frac{1}{2}$ miles away from the laser system can be determined within 1 inch. The system also can measure the velocity of a moving target to within $\frac{1}{4}$ mm/sec, as reported.

The Lincoln Laboratory laser radar uses a carbon dioxide laser generator operating with a 10-kHz frequency at a 5-microsecond pulse width. The returning laser beam from the target is detected by a mercury-cadmium telluride photodetector. The aerial attenuation of the system ranges from ratios of $\frac{1}{4}$ to 2 dB per kilometer, due to the carbon dioxide and water content of the atmosphere. In routine application and through cloudy atmosphere, the signal will be further attenuated; however, in combination with a microwave radar, the system can provide target acquisition as well as detailed information data. Because the backscatter signal characteristics from the target depend on properties different from that of microwave radar, an object visible by laser radar is not necessarily visible by microwave radar.

LASER GAUGE

Of the many laser-alignment manufacturers, at least two of them—Spectra-Physics, Inc. and Systems Research Laboratories—are apparently specializing in the manufacture of laser measuring devices for gauging and miking parts in quality control. The Spectra-Physics Model INF-1 Lasergage interferometer has been reported to be capable of providing fast and accurate linear measurements and displacement control. Its principal uses are the measurement of machines and ruling devices and the calibration and adjustment of linear-displacement devices. The unit, shown in Fig. 7-4, has a measuring range of 150 feet and a resolution of $\pm\frac{1}{2}$ wavelength. The firm manufactures other modifications of the Lasergage

Courtesy Spectra-Physics, Inc.

Fig. 7-4. Spectra-Physics Lasergage Model INF-1.

that can be employed in dozens of different metrological applications.

Systems Research Laboratories manufacture a LaserMike, Model 1150, which makes accurate and reproducible dimensional measurements—a requisite in quality control of parts that are manufactured to close tolerances. As Fig. 7-5 shows,

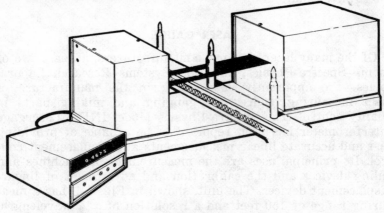

Fig. 7-5. A typical LaserMike in operation.

it is a gauging instrument for rapidly measuring the dimensions of parts without physically contacting them. The manufacturer claims that the instrument is ideally suited for on-line or off-line gauging and is capable of driving various computer and feedback control units. The device consists of a helium-neon laser beam collimated into a ribbon. Parts to be measured pass through the beam and their dimensional profiles are displayed on a digital readout at the rate of 10 readings per second. The range of the LaserMike is 0.015 inch to 1.75 inches and has an accuracy of ±0.15%. A large number of quality-assurance measurements can be made at very high rates. A slightly modified version of the LaserMike, (the Model 1150E) is particularly suitable for use in industrial production environments.

A QUALITATIVE HARDNESS TESTER

The laser beam has also been used in hardness testing of metals by comparing irregularities, such as pits, scratches, voids, and nicks in the surface profile of the inspected part with a previously inspected sound part. The laser beam scans the surface of the parts as they are conveyed over a conveying belt. A logic circuit incorporated in the inspection system decodes the information received from the part surface and rejects the part which does not meet the reference logic requirements. The system can be used in metal-fabrication industries that require accuracies within a few mils of deviation from the standard.

LASER GYROSCOPE

A laser gyroscope with no moving parts has been developed independently by several manufacturers. The system principally utilizes a three-axis inertial guidance system to provide a missile midcourse guidance and autopilot function to control the missile. The gyroscope uses two coherent laser beams traveling in opposite directions in a triangular path formed by mirrors. The mirrors guide the beam in the triangular ring that has a plane that is perpendicular to the input axis under measurement. The error signal or difference between the clockwise and the counter-clockwise frequencies of the two laser beams is a measure of the change of the missile attitude about the input axis. This signal is fed to the guidance control system to control the vehicle and to interface with the terminal-seeker head of the missile.

LASER VELOCIMETER

A velocimeter developed by Singer-General Precision, Inc. measures the speed and length of moving parts or materials with an accuracy of 0.1% of the velocity of the moving part. The system comprises a sensor head, a velocity indicator, and signal-processing electronic circuitry. A laser beam is projected on the moving material to illuminate its surface, and is then reflected to the sensor head which provides an output signal proportional to the speed of the material. This signal is processed in the electronic circuitry and converted to direct speed and length readings. The unit can read speeds from 2 feet per minute to 5000 feet per minute. Its applications include making length and velocity measurements and monitoring the automated processing of textiles, rubber, metals, plastics, and extruded products. It is claimed that the speeds of any moving object can be measured accurately, including rotating elements such as gears, rollers, bearings, etc.

LASER POLLUTION-MEASURING SYSTEMS

An infrared laser pollution-detection and -measurement system has been recently developed by the General Electric Company. The technique used consists of monitoring a long path through which the laser beam travels, integrating the pollution concentration along the entire path, and displaying the average pollution content at ambient conditions. The measurement is based on the spectral absorption of the laser beam, and the system uses relatively low and safe power levels over a range of several miles. Because of the long wavelengths used (in the infrared region), there is no radiation hazard to the eye. The transceiving optical system attenuates the laser power to less than 0.01 watt/cm^2.

The system comprises a laser scanner, a transceiver optical system, electronic circuitry for signal processing, and a retroreflector to aid in the integration of the pollutant particles along every point of the laser-beam path. The transmitter sends out a laser beam at varied wavelengths from a carbon dioxide laser to the retroreflector located at a remote point. The returned energy is integrated and compared with a reference laser output. An error signal is produced by the differences in the absorbed wavelengths, and this signal is converted into a direct readout of the pollutant concentration in the beam path. Since the carbon dioxide plasma is capable of giving off more than 50 wavelengths, the four wavelengths selected for pollution measurements are 95,050, 105,320, 106,750, and 107,190 angstroms to allow for a variety of weather conditions. Concentrations down to 14 ppb (parts per billion) of ethylene gas and 19 ppb of ammonia gas have been obtained. As an extension of the principle used in this system, a circular scanning system having multiple retroreflectors located at various points of the circled area has been advanced as a laser monitoring unit for urban areas.

A team of scientists at Bell Laboratories has devised a pollution-detection and -measurement laser system which is capable of identifying concentrations of pollutant gases as small as 1 part in 10 billion. Similar in some respects to that of the General Electric system, the Bell laser-computer unit utilizes the fact that different gases absorb laser light at different wavelengths. Since different gases exhibit specific absorption characteristics at different laser wavelengths, the amount of absorption by each wavelength indicates the amount of pollution in the atmosphere.

Air samples to be analyzed are held in an optoacoustic absorption cell to which the laser beam is directed. The energy of the laser absorbed by the air contained in the cell increases the temperature and pressure of the air sample in direct proportion to the amount of air. The pressure increase is sensed by a transducer or microphone in the cell and is converted into an electrical signal. The computer receives the electrical signal and then identifies the specific pollutant present by matching it with the gas-characteristic patterns stored in its memory. The computer can be programmed to process up to 20 different pollutant gases in this manner. The system is well suited to monitor and identify plant pollutants emanating from manufacturing processes.

One manufacturer has developed a portable laser densiometer for plant-pollutant monitoring and claims to meet the requirements of the Occupational Safety and Health Act (OSHA) and the Environmental Protection Agency (EPA). The laser densiometer consists of a 1-milliwatt helium-neon laser manufactured by Metrologic Instruments, Inc., and detects the amount of particulates in the plant atmosphere. A photocell in a separate unit detects the laser output as it emanates from the exit aperature, and this output is read as the initial particulate level. Any increase in the quantity of particulates in the air decreases the photocell current. This decrease in photocell current is translated directly into a density on an opacity scale, thus, determining the amount of particulates. The laser beam can be detected by the photocell when the cell is placed up to 50 feet away from the laser source. The device is not affected by ambient light conditions.

Several methods of pollution monitoring are shown in Fig. 7-6.

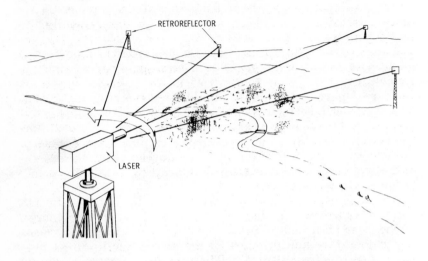

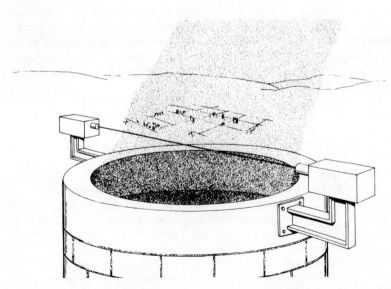

Fig. 7-6. Two schemes to monitor air pollution.

A GROCERY CHECKOUT SYSTEM

A new grocery checkout system developed by International Business Machines (IBM) is quite unique. It performs the grocery checkout by reading the Universal Product Code (UPC) on the merchandise, automatically decodes the symbols, and shows the name and price of the item on the terminal display panel. To operate the system, the checker places the UPC symbol face down and pulls the merchandise across the scanning window of the IBM machine. In addition to recording the price, the machine also prints the customer's receipt with the description and price of the item purchased. The IBM machine also maintains records on the supermarket activity and communicates the data to the central data-collector system. All scanning is accomplished by the use of a laser beam to light up the code at the scanning window. Errors are reduced, and all checkout calculations are performed speedily and accurately.

LASER PRINTING SYSTEM

A newspaper printing system using a carbon dioxide laser beam has been developed experimentally by Laser Graphic Systems, Inc. The system supplants the traditional stereotyping and engraving procedures, according to the developers. The pasted-up copies of a newspaper page are scanned by computer-controlled laser beams to produce a relief image on thin metal or plastic plates by vaporizing the scanned areas. This procedure eliminates the necessity of making photographic negatives or acid-etched plates, and the manufacturer claims that it cuts production time by one-half hour.

CHAPTER 8

Unique Laser System Innovations

The following laser-system innovations have been selected as some of the most promising products for market expansion of the laser field. Since they are unique in operation and performance, their applications in various other fields should be exploited to broaden their huge market potentials.

LASER SYSTEM FOR PERSONNEL VERIFICATION

A laser system that provides instant confirmation of fingerprints on identification cards has been developed by KMS Industries, Inc. The system scrambles the print to make substitution of unauthorized fingerprints almost impossible. To use the system, an ID card is prepared by using a laser beam to make a hologram of the identifying finger on a microdot in the usual ID card. The microdot is encapsulated together with the ID card in a plastic or metal substrate. The system is provided with two slots. The ID card is inserted into one slot, and the subject's matching finger is inserted into the other. The pattern on each image is scanned by a laser beam, and the two images are compared to automatically verify or deny the identification.

The elapsed time for the verification is 3 to 5 seconds. The system performs with an accuracy of 0.01%. The system is used in top-security clearance in industry and in government installations. A potential application would be the verification of credit cards to prevent the use and falsification of stolen cards. The operation of the system is illustrated in Fig. 8-1.

Fig. 8-1. KMS Industries' fingerprint identifying system, shown in operation.

FINGERPRINT IDENTIFIER

A laser-equipped fingerprint identifier, capable of identifying a fingerprint within one second, has been developed for the Federal Bureau of Investigation. The system employs a unit that preprocesses the fingerprints by optically scanning them and by using image enhancement techniques to identify the fingerprint patterns that are characteristic of each person. The processed information is relayed to a DEC PDP-15 section which compares and counterchecks the fingerprint data already on file. The system is expected to reduce the number of people now employed to manually check the 25,000 or more fingerprint inquiries received daily and to verify them against the 20 million prints on record. According to the manufacturer, the system takes less than one second to locate and identify a matching print among the 20 million prints on record.

SYSTEM FOR CHECKOUT OF TIRE-MOLD ROUNDNESS

Another innovation, first reported from Germany, is a laser system that checks and measures the roundness of tire molds. Developed by Siemens Aktiengesellschaft, the system uses a helium-neon laser with a 1-mW output at 1.6 kV, and checks by the triangulation method to reduce the length measurement to time measurement. The time gap between a reference plane and a working plane is translated to the error in roundness and is immediately displayed, thus giving the location and degree of the error. With this machine, the operator can measure parts of all kinds on lathes, milling machines, and presses. The complete equipment includes a laser probe; a photodiode which detects error; and a digital and an analog display, with a control unit. The system operates from a 110-V, 48- to 60-Hz current.

LASER MICROPHONE

A laser system has been developed in England that can "listen" to conversations carried out in a room. The system operates by projecting a laser beam onto a window, analyzing the beam vibration patterns on the window, and then decoding the patterns into speech. The window glass acts as a microphone and vibrates in accordance with the acoustic vibrations of the spoken words within the room. However, use of this system is restricted to a room having a glass window without a shade or a curtain, in order to prevent absorption or interference with the sound waves causing the vibration patterns on the glass.

CONTACT LENS DRILLING FOR COMFORT WEAR

Laser beams have also been used to drill very fine holes in plastic contact lenses to make them more comfortable for the wearer. The minute holes in the lens permit free circulation of the eye fluids; thus, the eye can breathe beneath the plastic lens. Not only does the laser drilling method save time but since the minute holes made by this method are clean-cut, it requires no repolishing of the lens, as in conventional mechanical methods. A 2-joule ruby laser with a 20-mm focal-length lens is used to drill 200 holes per minute in a single lens, compared with the 20 to 25 holes per minute that is possible with a mechanical drill. To perform drilling, the lens is positioned in the focus of the laser beam and holes are drilled by moving the lens under the laser head, which is cooled by a closed-circuit flow of water.

CATTLE AND SALMON BRANDING

When cattle and livestock are branded by using a heated iron, the cattle merchants claim that the animal loses from 20 to 30 pounds of its weight because of the suffering it undergoes and the after effect that the branding produces. Since branding with a laser beam is faster and since the animal does not suffer afterwards, a carbon dioxide laser system using 100 watts and up has been tried with favorable results. The beam scans a path of about 18 inches within one second and completes its work before the animal takes a second breath. The laser beam follows a continuous path designed in the branding template.

Hatchery biologists find that the laser-beam tagging of salmon and other edible fish is harmless to the fish. The radiation is directed to a template or a stencil and a mark is instantaneously made on the side of the fish for future identification. By controlling the frequency of the laser beam, only certain pigments are removed from the fish without harming the fish.

GYROSCOPE BALANCING WITH LASER BEAM

Rotating devices, such as gyroscopes or jet-engine turbine blades, must retain their balance almost perfectly at all times in order to effectively accomplish their jobs. In the past, gyroscopes have been balanced mechanically under very cumbersome and difficult situations, and this has been time consuming as well as costly. A laser pulse emanating from a laser welding or drilling machine can be used to conveniently balance a gyroscope in one-tenth the time originally required by mechanical methods. Another advantage is that the gyroscope can be balanced while it is rotating, which is the correct way to balance a gyroscope.

While the gyroscope is rotating, the laser beam removes a small amount of metal at the rate of a few micrograms to one milligram per pulse; by pulsing 20 to 30 times per minute, the beam can remove up to 30 milligrams of the metal per minute.

Different types of laser radiations may be used in the removal of metal in balancing the gyroscope. The commonly used lasers are: carbon dioxide TEA (transverse excited atmosphere), neodymium-YAG, neodymium-doped glass, and ruby lasers; used with or without Q-switching. However, since

Q-switched lasers pulse in nano-second pulse durations, they do have a drawback: the total laser energy is limited by the formation of high-density plasma which dissipates the energy by absorption when a certain energy level is reached. The amount of metal that is removed by each pulse is also limited because of low overall efficiency. For this reason, a TEA-type laser beam with a repetition of 20 to 30 pulses per minute and a removal rate of 20 to 30 milligrams of metal per minute has been preferred. All removed metal is separated from the gyroscope while it is spinning, thus avoiding any possible damage to the gyroscope.

In operation, the gyroscope is supported on a spinning shaft and is rotated at speeds of 10,000 to 40,000 rpm. The gyroscope is adjusted in front of the laser head, and its extent of unbalance is sensed by two detectors placed at right angles to each other on vertical and horizontal planes. When the sensors detect an unbalance, a laser beam of 40- to 100-microsecond pulsewidth is directed at the unbalance point. When a balanced point is attained, the gyroscope balancer automatically cuts off the laser beam from the workpiece.

ALGAE-MAPPING WITH LASER SYSTEM

A new algae-mapping laser instrument, known as a laser fluorosensor, has been developed by the National Aeronautics and Space Administration (NASA). It consists of a low repetition rate, pulsed, liquid rhodamine 6G dye laser. Mounted on the underside of a helicopter, it projects a 5900-angstrom laser beam onto the algae surface of water located about 30 meters below the craft. This causes irradiated algae to fluoresce and return a light beam, which is claimed to be 6850 angstroms. The intensity of the light beam is recorded on a linear analog-to-digital converter which indicates the amount of algae present in a given area.

LASER-EQUIPPED CANE FOR THE BLIND

A laser-equipped guidance cane for the blind is being manufactured by Bionic Instruments, Inc. under the sponsorship of the Veterans Administration. The cane contains a transmitter, near its crook end, with three gallium-arsenide laser diodes connected in series. The diodes emit 0.1-microsecond pulses at a 9000-angstrom wavelength at a rate of 40 pulses per second. The diodes form three light probes projecting forward, downward, and upward to warn the blind user of obstacles 3 to

12 feet ahead, above, or below, respectively. A receiver containing three photodiode sensors is located about 9 inches below the transmitter. The retroreflected signals are caught by the respective sensors located behind lenses. The sensors produce signal outputs which create a poking sensation in the blind person's fingers to warn him of obstacles lying ahead. The sensors also provide auditory sounds for objects located above or below the plane of the projected laser beam. The cane is about 50 inches long, and the guidance system is battery operated and has a laser output of 3 to 10 watts.

CHAPTER 9

Laser Communication Systems

The high coherence and directionality of laser beams have formed the basis for the development of laser communication systems capable of precise transmission of information data between several locations at the same time. The bandwidth of laser radiation is so wide—10^{13} to 10^{15} Hz—that 10^7 separate conversations can be carried on at one time, if necessary. The transmission beam is 10^4 times narrower than radio frequencies. The beam can be modulated by amplitude, intensity, phase, frequency, and polarization formats using analog, digital, or pulse transmission methods. In *amplitude* modulation, the *electric field* of the carrier beam is made proportional to the input-signal amplitude. In *intensity* modulation, the carrier *intensity* is made proportional to the input-signal amplitude. In *phase* modulation, the *phase angle* of the carrier beam is set by the amplitude of the input signal. In *polarization* modulation, the *polarization* of the carrier is made proportional to the input-signal amplitude, thus making the state of the art equivalent to microwave transmission characteristics. At laser-beam wavelengths, the frequencies are so high that beam divergence in milliradians or microradians can be achieved. Accurate pointing of the laser beam from the transmitter to the receiver is made possible by the directionality and the coherence of the radiation, thus minimizing the power requirements.

A laser beam traversing through space suffers some loss due to atmospheric carbon dioxide and water vapor, which absorb, refract, scatter, or otherwise attenuate the beam intensity. In spite of these limitations, a collimated laser beam can be transmitted to distances as far away as the horizon on a clear day, and to several miles away in hazy or contaminated atmospheric conditions. With some types of laser systems, the beam can be made to penetrate to a distance of 150 to 200 feet in sleet, rain, or snow. By using laser links or underground repeaters, transmission can be made to cover indefinitely long distances limited only by the number of links possible.

Other considerations enter into the application of laser beams for communication purposes. Aerial transmission of the beam requires that the beam energy be at low-hazard or at no-hazard levels. This means that a low-intensity beam must be used and that there will be a resultant limitation in the distance it can be projected. Also, the detector at the receiving end must be compatible with the beam characteristics in order to eliminate or alleviate the degradation effects of the beam. To reduce costs, the beam must not require cryogenic cooling, equipment elements, or operator attendance. The modulation speed of the beam determines the wavelength to be used. Since the best modulators operate in the visible spectral range, the power and efficiency of the laser are low, which makes the transmission distances proportionately low—only several miles. Among the laser candidates, carbon dioxide and neodymium-YAG furnish high power, but the carbon dioxide beam is difficult to modulate, which limits long-distance communication. Schemes for modulating helium-neon and semiconductor lasers have been developed but applications of the schemes are restricted to relatively short distances. Some applications are field use by the military or by surveyors, and person-to-person communications at large construction sites and in building installations.

Some of the principal advantages of the laser communication method over the radio communication method are:

1. The laser method allows communication to be kept absolutely private.
2. Because the laser system is passive, the signal can be picked up only by the party communicated with.
3. The laser beam can be locked onto the receiving system so that any movement by either party will not affect the conversation (for example, between two or more ships in movement, or between land and a moving target).
4. The laser communication range has an extremely wide bandwidth, 10^{13} to 10^{15} Hz.
5. The laser method makes efficient use of power in transmission.

6. The beam can handle 10^7 different channels at the same time.
7. The laser method is economical to use.
8. The communication can be carried out on land, in air, in outer space, and to a limited extent under water.
9. Conversation can be communicated from shore to ship, ship to ship, shore to target, ship to target, and moving target to shore or to ship, all at the same time.

A diagram showing how various communications can be conducted at the same time is illustrated in Fig. 9-1.

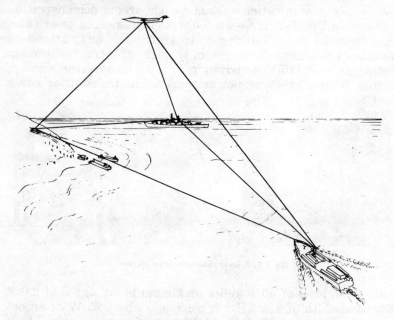

Fig. 9-1. Laser communications between stationary or moving stations.

For long-distance communication, optical transmission is used through light pipes, such as solid fiber optics or tubular fibers containing an organic, high refractive-index fluid. Repeaters at various points in the light pipes amplify the transmission signals. Bell Laboratories has tried a single-fiber quartz capillary tube, using tetrachloroethylene inside the tube to transmit the laser radiation. The tube has a minimum loss of 13.5 dB per kilometer in the near-infrared of 10,800-angstrom laser beam. Gallium-arsenide and neodymium-YAG lasers are also reported to be promising as optical oscillators. The outside diameter of the quartz fiber used is 95 microns, and its inside diameter is 65 microns. The index of refraction of the quartz fiber is 1.457 and that of the liquid tetrachloroethylene is 1.5, which fulfills the internal total reflection requirement for a laser beam. A report from Germany claims that a single quartz fiber with a laser transmission loss of 3 dB per kilometer has been developed; however, no details have been given regarding its surface coating or the diameter of the fiber.

HELIUM-NEON TRANSCEIVER

A laser communication system for classroom demonstration is shown in Fig. 9-2. It uses a 0.5-watt helium-neon laser tube, manufactured by Metrologic Instruments, and attendant auxiliary equipment. The system consists of a transmitter operating from a 115-V ac power source and a receiver also operating from a 115-V ac power source. The transmitter has a

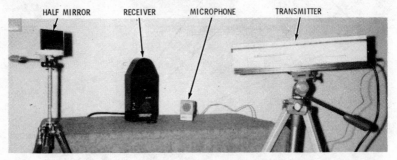

Fig. 9-2. A laser communication system.

modulation level of 50% and a maximum input signal of 2.0 V at a bandwidth of 125 kHz. It consumes about 25 W at an operating voltage of 2800 V dc. The receiver consumes about 4 W and has a bandwidth of up to 1 MHz.

In operation, an audio signal is fed to a VACO crystal microphone plugged into the transmitter. The transmitter amplitude modulates the voice signals, then amplifies them, and finally feeds the amplified signals into the laser tube which is biased at about 4.5 mA. The current passing through the tube is modulated by the input sound signals, and the laser beam projecting from the end of the unit is a modulated beam of red laser light. This beam is projected onto a photosensor located on the face of the receiver. The beam may be projected to the receiver either directly or after it has been reflected from one or more front-surface mirrors, depending on how many corners the beam is to be reflected from before it impinges on the receiver photodetector. A beam splitter may also be used so that two persons, each using a receiver, can hear the transmitted signal at different locations.

At the receiver, the photodetector (which is a phototransistor) demodulates the laser beam, which is then amplified and fed to a speaker incorporated into one side of the receiver. The audio signal of the laser beam can be transmitted up to three kilometers, if it is collimated, with only slight sacrifice in the sound volume. However, the sound volume can be improved by use of modified receiver circuitry. Fig. 9-3 is a block diagram of a laser communication system.

In principle, when the main switch is turned on, the power supply of the transmitter develops 5000 V dc which is impressed on the laser tube in order to ionize the helium-neon gas

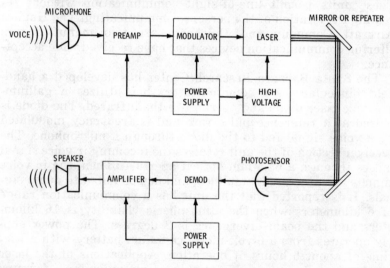

Fig. 9-3. Block diagram of a laser communication system.

sealed in the tube. When ionization occurs, the voltage drops to an operating level of 2800 V dc, the level necessary to sustain the operation of the laser tube. The modulator section controls the quiescent current by converting it into a modulated instantaneous signal current from the microphone. To avoid any influence of the line-voltage fluctuation upon the quiescent current through the laser tube, a zener diode is inserted in the circuit to regulate it.

At normal speech levels, the microphone output is about 0.2 V, which results in 5% modulation. Since voice or music signals have a wide dynamic range, the average modulation index is maintained at a low level. The crystal microphone provides a relatively high output level, close to 60 dB.

Higher-level modulations up to 100% with bandwidths up to 160 kHz are available from Metrologic Instruments, Inc. Their many years of experience in producing helium-neon tubes and their technological competence make this company one of the most successful laser-tube and laser kit manufacturers on this continent and abroad.

SEMICONDUCTOR LASER COMMUNICATION SYSTEMS

For short-range line-of-sight applications, semiconductor laser communication systems are becoming increasingly practical, especially for field use and military intelligence service. These units permit line-of-sight communication without revealing the location of the persons communicating. The Hughes Aircraft Company and Holobeam are two manufacturers offering communication devices that have received wide acceptance.

The Santa Barbara Research Center has developed a hand-held binocular laser communicator that utilizes a gallium-arsenide laser diode and operates in the infrared. The diode is pulsed at a reference pulse rate and is frequency modulated by a voice signal fed to the diode through a microphone. The receiver section of the unit receives the incoming ir voice signal pulses through a 63.5-mm optical aperture. Then, the ir voice signals are processed, amplified, and demodulated to audio signals. It is reported that the unit has a communication range of 6 kilometers when the atmospheric visibility is 16 kilometers and the beam divergence is 2 degrees. The power supply operates from a 6-volt nickel-cadmium battery with a lifetime of about 6 hours of operation. Applications of the laser communicator cover ship-to-ship communication, forestry service communication, and military field uses.

The Holobeam system employs a gallium-arsenide diode laser operating from a 28-volt power supply and having a beam divergence of 300 milliradians and a transmission capability of 75 meters. In operation, the laser beam is collimated to a 1-milliradian divergence, and the analog signal impressed on the microphone is converted into modulated signals in the transmitter. The modulated signals are projected to the receiver, which demodulates them. The unit uses a time-code modulation technique to transmit high-level digital data. This type of modulation is based on time synchronization, coding of time slots, and pulse-position technique by which a pulse can be transmitted in one microsecond. Since the operation of a gallium-arsenide laser is temperature dependent, Holobeam employs a thermal control loop consisting of a regulator, a modulator, and a thermistor which monitors the ambient temperature and controls the output level of the regulator.

Another brand of laser communication system is a binocular unit having a gallium-arsenide modulator built into the transmitter and using a photodiode as a detector in the receiver which is provided with a preamplifier and a demodulator. A dichroic beam splitter placed in the optical path separates the laser beam from the visible light. The beam splitter allows the laser beam to be visually observed through the binocular during signal transmission. A microphone, positioned underneath the binocular, feeds the voice signal to the transmitter. Adjacent to the microphone is an earphone jack for picking up the incoming message. The laser-beam divergence is 4 milliradians with a 10× collimator, and 2 milliradians with a 20× collimator. The transmitter operates from 60 volts dc, and the receiver operates from 9 volts dc. However, both the transmitter and the receiver are incorporated as one unit in the communication system.

It will now be apparent that all of these communication systems suffer from at least one common deficiency—the inability to scan and locate the target with which the communication will be carried out. None of the laser communicators developed thus far can locate a target. However, a unique method of scanning the aproximate area would be to use a divergent laser beam and, after locating the target, lock onto it. The beam could then be narrowed to the normal transmission beam diameter. It is now left for an innovator to incorporate such a scheme into the existing laser communication systems.

COLOR TELEVISION PROJECTION SYSTEM

The Japanese firm Hitachi has recently developed a laser television projection system that can project a color television picture composed of 1125 scanning lines per frame on a screen that can be from 10 to over 90 square feet. The three primary colors of the picture are obtained from ion laser beams: red from krypton-ion laser, green and blue from argon of tunable wavelengths. The system is said to have a polygon mirror driven by an 81,000-rpm motor which causes a horizontal resolution of 800 lines and a vertical resolution of 700 lines. A wideband video amplifier at 30 MHz is used.

VARIOUS LASER COMMUNICATION INSTRUMENTS

A laser communicator, transmitting 300 megabits per second by using a 200-milliwatt argon laser, has been developed by Lockheed Missiles & Space Division. Data have been transmitted to a distance of 1.2 miles in the atmosphere, and the developers believe that this distance can be increased in the future by further improvement of the system. The high transmision rate has been made possible by frequency-modulating the laser beam. The modulation is achieved by using a microwave transmitter to drive an optical device; this type of transmission, which uses both optical and microwave frequencies, makes the beam less susceptible to atmospheric disturbances than when the laser beam is amplitude modulated. By matching the 5100-angstrom wavelength radiation from the argon laser with the receiver silicon photodiode, the accuracy of the system has been greatly improved. The developers further believe that the laser communicator can be used as a substitute for cable television systems.

A laser communicator, manufactured by Laser Systems, Inc., generates 10-kHz pulses at 10 W to transmit 10-kilobit-per-second information to a distance of 25 miles in clear weather. It operates from 12 to 24 volts dc or 115 volts ac to drive a gallium-arsenide diode. The pulse rise time is 100 nanoseconds at a 9040-angstrom wavelength. The pulses are transmitted and received through telescopes using 10-power lenses. The telescopes are built side by side in the unit to provide a compact and portable laser communicator. Available beam divergence ranges from 1.3 to 10 milliradians with interchangeable lenses provided with the unit. It is claimed that it can detect signals as small as 0.58 nanowatt through a 50-millimeter aperture up to a 10-milliradian field of view.

LASER IMAGE TRANSMITTER

A laser system for sending wirephotos has been developed by the Massachusetts Institute of Technology. It uses a helium-neon laser beam of 1 milliwatt which is intensity modulated by a distant transmitter signal scan across a silver-emulsion photographic paper developed by the 3M Corporation. The paper records the varying signal intensities forming various shades of gray. The paper is then subjected to a thermal atmosphere to develop the image, with the result that high-gloss photographic quality is obtained. The prints are said to be suitable for storage for long periods of time without deterioration.

CHAPTER 10

Security Surveillance Laser Systems

Stealing, arson, prison escapes, illegal immigration at border areas from one country to another, and similar violations of the law are committed daily. Various contrivances have been devised, with some success, to deter lawbreakers, but the crime wave has not abated. For instance, mechanical traps have been devised to catch the culprit in person, television cameras have been planted to monitor the restricted areas 24 hours a day, and microwave devices and radio or radar equipment have been installed to detect trespassers. Although each has had some degree of success, none has been able to perform the function intended. Each device has been too bulky, too costly or too limited in scope. Some devices have been tripped by dogs, cats, rabbits, cows, or even birds. Accordingly, a more reliable and effective system that is less costly, smaller in size, wider in scope and easy to install has been needed for some time. It now appears that the problem has been solved with the use of laser equipment which has functions and capabilities superior to those of the earlier security systems or devices.

A security surveillance laser system is a combination of detection, acquisition, and alarm equipment designed to guard restricted areas and buildings against intruders or escapees. The laser system comprises a transmitter and a receiver, both of which are located strategically at a central station. One or more laser beams, preferably of infrared wavelengths, are projected by means of mirrors or repeaters so that they surround the area to be secured, forming a laser fence. When a human being breaks the beam by crossing it at any point, an alarm and a display immediately alert authorized personnel at a central station to take corrective measures.

When corrective action has been taken, the alarm system is manually stopped by resetting the laser system for the next event. A simplified diagram of the security laser system is illustrated in Fig. 10-1.

Variations of laser security systems are many. For instance, one system uses a single laser beam on the perimeter of the secured ground and reflects the beam from one mirror to another at corner junctions until the beam reaches a receiver located adjacent to the transmitter. When the laser beam is

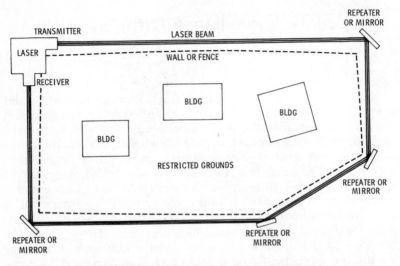

Fig. 10-1. A security surveillance laser system installation.

interrupted by a person crossing it, an alarm system is actuated. However, this type of system places everyone in confusion because no one knows where the intrusion has occurred; thus this system is not any better than the old burglar alarms which use a visible light beam.

Another type of laser system projects a laser beam through several isolated detectors and ends at a control station, where the location of the intrusion event is determined from the frequency of the beam. Still another system has a number of sensors located in the path of the laser beam, and the location of the intrusion is determined by the particular sensor that has been actuated. One other laser system, which possibly transcends all others, projects laser beams at various sections of a wall or fence. This system can determine whether the person is entering or escaping from the grounds and can give the exact location of the beam interruption. Also, this latter system actuates a "talking alarm" which audibly informs personnel that an intrusion or an escape is in progress.

INTRUSION-DETECTION LASER SYSTEM

In the patented segment-locating intrusion alarm system of Fig. 10-2, a laser beam from a master transmitter located at

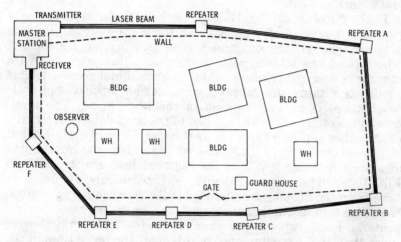

Fig. 10-2. A diagram of an intrusion alarm system for protecting a typical facility.

a central station is directed around the perimeter of the protected area by means of repeaters located at various points. When a laser beam between two repeaters is intercepted by a person crossing it, the repeater closest to the central station produces a logic signal characteristic of that repeater. This signal passes through the other repeaters without transformation and is received at the central station. The receiver at the central station decodes the signal, indicates which segment has been intercepted, and then actuates a continuous alarm to alert authorized personnel. When the event is over, the system is reset to a quiescent operational state.

The repeater consists of a receiver transducer which receives a laser signal either from the main transmitter at the central station or from the preceding repeater during the quiescent operational state of the system (i.e., when there is no beam interruption). The transducer output is partially coupled to an

OR gate logic circuit and partially coupled to a ramp generator. The OR gate feeds its output to a transmitter transducer (in the repeater) containing a gallium-arsenide laser diode, which emits a pulse of laser radiation. The ramp generator output is coupled to a signal-level detection circuit in which the signal from the ramp generator is compared to a preset reference dc voltage. When the ramp (reset) signal is equal to the reference voltage, an output pulse is produced which is coupled to a pulse shaper. The output from the pulse shaper is connected to the second input side of the OR gate. The resultant output of the OR gate is coupled to the transmitter transducer, as illustrated in Fig. 10-3.

In the diagram of Fig. 10-3, when the receiver transducer of repeater A in Fig. 10-2 receives an input laser signal, it feeds a pulse through the OR gate to the transmitter transducer, which produces a laser pulse from the gallium arsenide with minimum delay in relation to the OR gate signal received. This condition retains the repeater at a normal operational state when there is no interruption in the laser beam. The level-detection voltages that are applied to the level-detection circuits of the other repeaters from B to E become successively higher. A "signature" pulse is produced when the beam is interrupted at a segment (for instance, the segment between A and B of Fig. 10-2). This signature pulse is increasingly displaced in time from the missing transmitted pulse. For the next repeater, the pulse time is further increased, and so on for the other repeaters. Each repeater produces a characteristically longer pulse than the preceding one. In this way, the pulse time in the segment at which the intrusion has occurred can be decoded by the master receiver. The master receiver then indicates the precise segment area where the intrusion occurred. One princi-

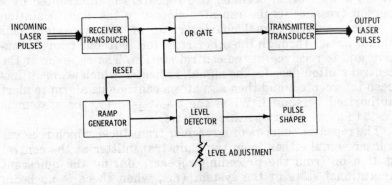

Fig. 10-3. Block diagram of a repeater system.

pal disadvantage of this system is that it cannot indicate whether the person is escaping from the facility or entering it.

FACILITY-MONITORING LASER SYSTEM

A unique security surveillance laser system, developed and patented by the Laserkinetics Corporation, secures a restricted facility by projecting four laser beams over the top and sides of the walls or fence surrounding the guarded area. In this system, the interruption of any one of the four laser beams initiates visual displays in the central station where the laser transmitter and receiver are located. At the same time, the system verbally informs security personnel whether the person is escaping from or entering the grounds. A block diagram of the entire system is shown in Fig. 10-4.

The system, consisting of a laser transmitter, a receiver, and a display panel, is located at a central station. The laser beam from the transmitter is collimated and split by half mirrors into four laser beams of equal intensity. Two of the beams are transmitted on each side on the upper part of the wall or fence, and the other two are transmitted a foot or so from the ground on each side of the wall. The four laser beams are projected along the entire perimeter of the secured ground by using either mirrors or repeaters at the points where it is necessary to bend the beam. The beams reach the master receiver at the central station and are sensed by four photodetectors. The outputs of each amplifier is coupled to a spring-biased latching relay which retains the relay at an open-circuit state during continuous photodetection of the laser beam.

When one of the laser beams—for instance, top outer beam A—is interrupted by a person crossing (entering) it, photodetector 1 fails to receive any photosignal and no photocurrent is produced in amplifier 5. As a result, the spring-biased latching relay in channel 9 closes a circuit which feeds current to indicator 13 and to alarm-signal amplifier 17. Amplifier 17 energizes the acoustic system to broadcast the alarm. Acoustic system 21 has four sound tracks, one for each channel. Since the laser signal was received from the laser beam covering the outer top section of the wall, the signal indication on the wall panel will be ENTER and every two seconds the acoustic channel will play the words "he is entering," in order to alert personnel. Had the laser-beam signal come from the inside section of the wall, the acoustic system would have played "he is escaping." In this case, the signal would have been processed through photodetector 2, amplifier 6, relay channel 10, and amplifier 18

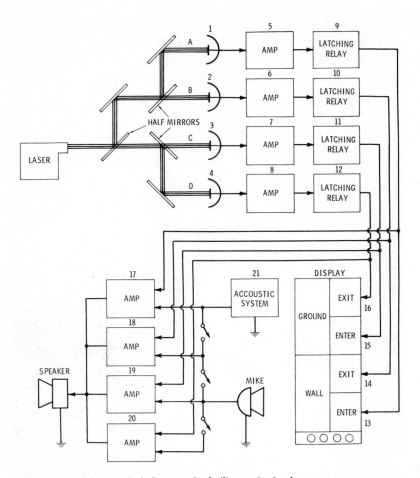

Fig. 10-4. Block diagram of a facility-monitoring laser system.

before it energized the second track of the system. The display panel would indicate EXIT at point 14.

PORTABLE LASER FENCE

A portable security surveillance laser system has been developed by the Mitre Corporation and Air Force Systems Command, Electronic Systems Division, Hanscom Field, Maine. The system, called Intrusion Detection and Identification System (IDIS), detects and identifies the location of an intruder in the restricted area where aircraft and military weapons are kept. The equipment, shown in Fig. 10-5, resembles six vertically mounted traffic-light tubes attached to a 6-foot post. Each

Fig. 10-5. The Air Force portable laser system.

tube is provided with a horizontally mounted laser generator, and the tubes are positioned 1 foot apart, starting 6 inches from the ground. Each laser generator is a gallium-arsenide diode, operating at 9050 angstroms, in a transmitter with a focusing lens. A companion post, provided with matching tubes, contains the receiver electronics and a lens in each tube. This post can be located at distances up to 500 feet from the transmitter.

In operation, the six pulse-coded laser beams are transmitted to their respective receivers at the 500-foot distance. Each pulse of ½ watt laser energy is projected at a repetition rate of 1000 pulses per second. When an intruder crosses one or more of the beams at the same time, some of the pulses from each of the laser transmitters are interrupted. The detector located in each receiver detects the missing counts. These missing counts are decoded in the receiver, and the location of the intruder is immediately determined by the reading of the receiver counter. The system operates from either a set of batteries or a local ac source.

LASER SYSTEM AS CONTINENTAL BORDER SENTRY

An extension of the Laserkinetics security surveillance laser system, now under development, is a system that provides continuous monitoring and detection along borders between two countries, such as Mexico and the United States. The projected development program consists of laser detectors placed 15 miles apart, along the entire border separating one country from the other. The detectors monitor the activity of the traffic day and night. The intelligence signals coming from various segments of the laser fence are decoded and displayed on a huge display panel. The time and the location of the intrusion are constantly recorded on monitoring tapes. The location of the intrusion is automatically determined on a chart which records the results of the surveillance for each event separately.

The system consists of laser transmitters, receivers, pulse counters, decoders, and information-charting equipment coupled together to form a central intelligence system. The central intelligence system can receive a maze of signals from the approximately 1500 miles of border land. The circuitry rejects incorrect messages, such as those produced by moving animals, birds, wind-blown objects, and the like. The intrusion signal is picked up by a processor, which discriminates between human and nonhuman bodies, and which triggers a sensor transmitter. The sensor transmitter sends a coded infrared signal to the central station either directly or through a repeater. The receiver signal is either immediately processed or stored for complete-event occurrence.

The decoded and processed signal is printed out, showing the transmitter identification code, the segment code, the time of occurrence, and the character of the event. A panel chart indicates by a lighted map display the area and the point of intrusion. If this action is progressive, the map shows a continuous extension of the light path over the intruded area. The system is complemented by an alarm system which is activated in emergency cases in order to alert patrol stations along the border.

LASER FIRE-ALARM SYSTEM

The principle of a laser fire alarm is generally similar to that of a range finder, with the exception that the fire-alarm system is much simpler in construction. Instead of having a counter to measure the time of laser travel, the system contains a photodetector which is continuously fed with a reference laser signal. When the return signal (from the area where the fire or smoke has started) reaches the photodetector, a signal difference is created. This signal difference is amplified and fed to an alarm system. The signal difference may be used to turn on sprinklers at the area where the fire is first detected. An illustration of the fire-detection system is shown in Fig. 10-6.

Using the same principle, RCA has developed an intrusion alarm to protect anything from bank vaults to missile sites. The system employs infrared laser beams projected back and

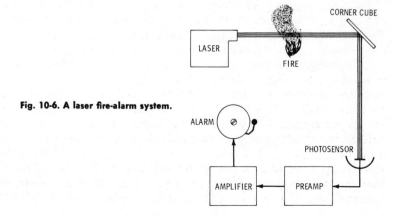

Fig. 10-6. A laser fire-alarm system.

forth with mirrors. An interruption in the laser beam actuates an alarm to alert security personnel.

SWIMMING-POOL MONITORING LASER SYSTEM

A swimming-pool monitoring laser system consisting of a transmitter and a receiver has been developed by the author's staff. By monitoring the perimeter of a swimming pool, the system will detect any person or animal that accidentally falls into the pool. In principle, a single laser beam from the transmitter is split into two beams and projected from corner to corner around the perimeter of the pool. One beam is 6 inches above the ground, and the other is 10 inches above the first beam. After circling the pool, the laser beams become incident on two photodetectors in the receiver. The photodetectors are located at the same heights from the ground as the laser beams. As long as no beam is interrupted, the system operates in a quiescent state. When one or both of the beams are interrupted, the receiver energizes a latching relay. The latching relay turns on an alarm system having two alarm devices. One is located outside the house, and the other is located inside the house. The device operates from 115-volt household current and uses a gallium-arsenide laser generator. When the event is over, the device may be reset manually. In the presence of a group of people around or in the pool, the system may be turned off and turned on later when no one is in the pool. The system can be adapted for use for protection of a house from vandals, burglars, and other criminals.

CHAPTER 11

Laser Systems for the Garment Industry

The rapidly advancing laser application field has become a very important factor in everyday economy. New applications of the laser have been responsible for increasing man's production of consumer products.

One of these applications was developed by the Hughes Aircraft Company in 1971 for the garment-cutting industry. As a unique application of the laser beam, this development revolutionized garment cutting. The first laser garment cutter was installed by Genesco, Inc., one of the largest garment-cutting plants in the United States. The laser system, programmed by a computer, cuts garments one at a time at lightning speed. It has reduced the garment-cutting time to one-fifth the time necessary with conventional mechanical cutters. The benefits claimed by the laser cutter are: low cost, fast delivery of the garment to the consumer, quick response to fashion changes, reduction of inventories, and a tolerance of the width of a single thread of the garment. The system can also be used to cut shoe leather, plastics, and rubber sheets of all types and shapes.

Since a laser can cut cloth, plastics, paper, and similar products, it is not improbable for it to be capable of sewing garments and bonding plastic and paper materials; we shall soon learn how this innovation has been achieved.

LASER GARMENT CUTTER

The garment-cutter laser system developed by Hughes Aircraft Company is equipped with a carbon dioxide laser made by Coherent Radiation Corporation. The movement of the laser is controlled by a programmed computer which directs the beam by means of programmed instructions to cut any pattern in mixed batches. By merely pressing a button for the selection, the system can be programmed to cut any pattern selected from a number of patterns in the computer memory. The clothing material rolls off from a bolt and is moved by a large conveyor belt toward the laser head. Although the garments are cut in a single layer, the speed of the laser cutting method more than compensates for this disadvantage; fifteen to twenty suits can be cut per hour. A photograph of the laser cutting system is shown in Fig. 11-1.

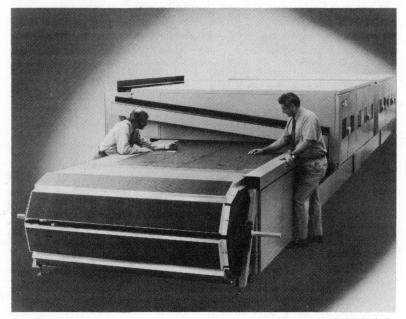

Courtesy Hughes Aircraft Co.

Fig. 11-1. Hughes' garment-cutting laser system.

The laser cutting system uses silicon mirrors in a pentaprism arrangement to direct the carbon dioxide laser beam on the clothing. The laser head gyrates as it follows the outline of the computer-selected pattern. The laser beam is focused on the clothing by means of gold-plated aluminum mirrors. The cut is made by burning through the material, and the kerf is claimed to be narrow, sharp, and clean. The temperature of the cutting area is controlled by a cooling system.

Several laser firms have been considering the development of small laser garment cutters suitable for use by small-business garment-cutting firms. So far, the high cost of the laser cutter would not make it affordable by small garment cutting plants nor would the cost be competitive with the presently used mechanical garment cutters.

LASER SEWING MACHINES

A laser sewing machine has been designed by the author for use by garment-fabrication firms. The system makes use of the melting and bonding capabilities of the laser radiation combined with the chemical and thermal properties exerted at the interface of the bond. The laser beam is transmitted through a quartz optical element which directs the laser beam through an achromatic optical system to the point of material contact and fuses the two layers of the material together. As in a mechanical sewing machine, the material is conveyed auto-

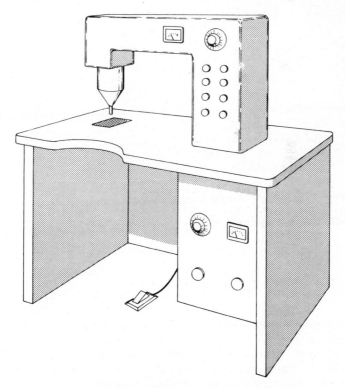

Fig. 11-2. A laser sewing machine.

matically toward the laser head. The sewn path is variable in pattern, from a seam-bond, as in metals, to a zigzag, as in stretch fabrics. Provision is also made so that separate bonds in the form of broken lines, spaced from 1 mil to 20 mils apart can be programmed by the laser-system memory unit. Depending on the type of material to be sewed, the speed of sewing varies from a fraction of an inch to several inches per second. An illustration of the laser sewing machine is shown in Fig. 11-2.

The system employs a neodymium-YAG laser generator which operates in the pulsing mode and uses a closed-circuit refrigerated deionized water system for cooling. The buttons on the left-hand side of the instrument panel are for selection of the sewing pattern, and those on the right-hand side are for the selection of the sewing speed. The system is intended to sew synthetic garment materials, plastic furniture materials, rubber goods, and other textiles.

CHAPTER 12

Stenographic Laser Erasers

As explained earlier in the chapters on industrial applications of laser radiation, a focused laser beam can vaporize metals, ceramics, plastics, and other materials. The extent of vaporization depends on the energy level of the beam and on the density and optical characteristics of the material. The same principle is employed in erasing errors from typewritten matter and from drawings without damaging the substrate on which the matter is printed. This is possible due to the absorption properties of a controlled-energy laser beam; it is absorbed by dark, black, and colored surfaces and is reflected by white and shiny surfaces.

The principal advantages of a laser eraser are: it is easy to use, it does not damage the paper on which the character is written, and it instantaneously erases the mistake. Another characteristic of the present eraser is that it employs a defocused divergent laser beam (unlike the focused laser beam used in welding and drilling metals) to afford coverage of a larger area. Since the energy content of the defocused laser beam is much smaller per square area than that of a focused beam, it is easier to control—another advantage. For instance, a laser beam of 1-joule energy focused to a point of 5 mils on a written character will drill a 5-mil hole in the character. However, when the beam is defocused and expanded to a 1-mm square area and then directed to a 1-mm square character, the character will disappear instantly due to the oxidation of the ink of the character.

DESCRIPTION OF LASER ERASERS

Version 1

One of the laser erasers developed and patented by Laserkinetics Corporation consists of a hand-held erasing stylus suitable for use on a typewriter. It has a small power-supply unit which can be readily attached to the side of the typewriter. The stylus has a cone-shaped (coniform) erasing head with an aperture at its tip for ejecting a laser beam from the stylus onto the character to be erased. The laser generator consists of an array of semiconductor laser diodes energized from a pulsing circuit in the power-supply unit. A beam-integrating element, positioned adjacent to the laser diodes, integrates the laser radiation from the array with the radiation reflected from a parabolic reflector enclosing the diode array. The integrated radiation is directed onto a converging lens. The laser beam emerging from the lens is focused within the coniform section of the stylus and then exits from the aperture of the stylus tip as a divergent beam. When a thumb button on the stylus is depressed the laser beam is triggered.

The divergent laser beam becomes attenuated in intensity as it radiates from the tip of the stylus. Since it will be difficult for the user to determine what part of the beam should be used for erasing, the lens is adjusted within the coniform section so that the energy of the emergent laser beam at the exit port of the tip is just sufficient to vaporize the character to be erased, when the tip is placed in contact with the character. Thus, for most erasures, the diameter of the emergent beam at the exit port is adjusted to a 2-mm diameter using a 1-joule laser energy. For higher energies, which will be required to erase larger-size characters, the laser energy from the power-supply unit is increased and the diameter of the laser beam at the exit port is adjusted so that the incident beam will cover the entire character. Since the laser-beam energizing current is pulsing, a single pulse is all that is necessary to erase the character. The diameter (d) of the emergent beam cone at the exit port can be determined by the relation:

$$d = \frac{D \times s}{S} \qquad \text{(Eq. 12-1)}$$

where,

D is the diameter of the lens optical plane,
s is the distance between the laser-beam focus in the coniform section and the tip of the stylus.
S is the distance between the optical plane of the lens and the laser-beam focus.

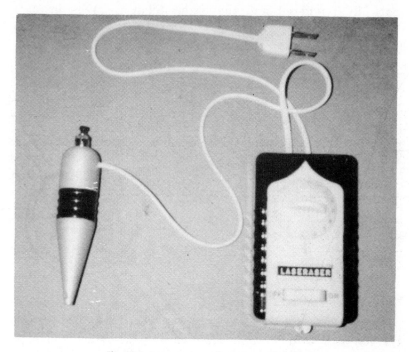

Fig. 12-1. Laser eraser and power-supply unit.

The diameter can be adjusted by internally adjusting the lens within the coniform section. Markings are printed for various diameters of focus sizes. A photograph of the laser eraser and the power-supply unit is shown in Fig. 12-1.

Provision has also been made in the power-supply unit to convert a 120-volt ac current (received from any household current source) to a low-level operating voltage, as desired. A pulse-forming circuit raises the frequency to 1000 Hz or more, as desired, for the operation of the laser generator. In another model of the device, provision is made so that the device can operate with direct current, using rechargeable batteries.

Operator safety has been the prime requirement in this device so that neither an electric shock nor any laser radiation can harm the operator or any persons in the immediate vicinity. The maintenance cost of the device is insignificant, since the device uses current only when it is in operation, and that is only a fraction of a second.

In a modified version of the device, no external switch is used. Its operation is automatic when the tip of the stylus is placed on the letter and pressed against it; the laser is automatically triggered and the letter (character) is instantly erased.

Version 2

This laser eraser is a modified form of Version 1. The laser head is miniaturized so that it can be permanently attached to the typing lever of the typewriter. The power-supply unit is incorporated within the typewriter housing, and the eraser head is mounted on a key lever controlled by a red key on the right side. The laser-triggering switch is installed under the key. When the key is depressed, the typewriter carriage moves back one space and simultaneously the laser eraser moves to the printing area where the error character is located. As the laser-head tip contacts the character to be erased, the key simultaneously contacts the trigger switch. The trigger switch then triggers the laser generator, vaporizing the error character. When the key is released, the eraser head moves back to its original position. A typewriter with a built-in laser eraser is shown in Fig. 12-2.

Laser Eraser and Microwelder

This device is a laser eraser as well as a microwelder, and outwardly resembles the laser eraser shown in Fig. 12-1. The

Fig. 12-2. Key-mounted laser eraser typewriter.

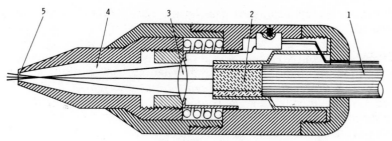

Fig. 12-3. Cross sectional view of the stylus of the laser eraser and microwelder (magnified 1.25×).

system consists of a power-supply unit connected to a stylus through a fiber-optic conduit; a cross-sectional view is shown as 1 in Fig. 12-3. The conduit receives laser radiation at the power-supply unit and transmits it to the stylus. The fiber distal end contains a ruby rod (2) surrounded by a sapphire tube to conserve radiation. The outer face of the ruby rod is made partially reflective by depositing a multilayer dielectric to form a resonant cavity between the ruby, the lasing fiber optics, and the lasing element (such as ruby, neodymium-YAG, or glass) of the laser generator located in the housing of the power supply. Either a continuous-wave or a pulsed laser radiation can be obtained from the power-supply circuit. The pulse-network circuit furnishes a 1-millisecond pulse during each trigger; this pulse is used for erasing or for single spot welds. In the continuous mode, the beam is used for welding fine wires, thin films, small components, watch parts, and jewelry, and for erasing long lines in diagrams. The device can also drill fine holes—one mil to several mils in diameter in metals and in ceramic wafers used in semiconductor fabrication.

The laser radiation from fiber-optic conduit 1 passes through ruby rod 2 and becomes incident on lens 3, which focuses the laser beam within coniform chamber 4 of the stylus. The beam diverges from the focus as it leaves exit aperture 5 at the tip of the stylus. When the tip of the stylus is placed on an error character and is pressed against it the laser is triggered and the character receives the divergent beam at point 5 and instantly becomes vaporized. For microwelding, the lens is internally adjusted to move the focus of the beam to the plane of the stylus tip. Thus, when the tip is placed on the work to be welded, the beam is exactly focused on the material being welded. When it is necessary to focus the laser beam farther into the material, the lens can be readjusted to the exact depth desired.

Other modifications of the laser eraser are also available, one of which resembles a ball-point pen and can be carried in a pocket. The laser generator has a pulse-forming circuit operating from a rechargeable battery. The laser element is an array of semiconductors which furnish the radiant energy within a variable energy level; this energy is adjustable within the device. Triggering of the device can occur only when the stylus is perpendicularly positioned on the error character and pressed against it. This feature, which is also found in the other eraser devices decribed in the preceding sections, makes the laser eraser safe to use; the user can never see the laser radiation or its reflections.

CHARACTERISTIC FEATURES OF LASING ELEMENTS IN THE ERASERS

Laser erasers are provided with special lasing elements and optics. For instance, ordinarily the laser rods used in commercial laser equipment are solid, one-piece elements. However, in the laser erasers, the lasing rod is a two-piece circular rod. The two pieces are cemented together with a balsam which also acts as a thermal reflector from the center to the periphery of the rod. Another modification contains a central bore in the rod to dissipate the heat effect as well as the optical-lens effect that occurs when the rod temperature is elevated during operation. As stated in an earlier section, thermal effects and lens effects within the lasing element reduce the efficiency of the element as a laser generator and may even cause the destruction of the element by cracking. Furthermore, the combination of a lasing rod and a plurality of lasing glass plates arranged axially in a 45° format to the laser rod amplifies the laser output of the device. This means cooling requirements of the instrument become almost negligible, and that is why no cooling system has been included in the laser erasers discussed. However, one type of laser eraser, which has a high degree of usage and uses semimconductors as the pumping element, has a Peltier-effect cooling system surrounding the optical pump.

CHAPTER 13

Laser Waveguides

Laser waveguides are light pipes which transmit laser radiation from a laser source to a destination. Laser waveguides are ordinarily made of fibers of glass, plastic, or quartz. The diameter of each fiber varies from 2 microns up to 250 microns, depending on the type of material and the type of service for which it is intended. Usually, the fibers are gathered into a bundle and enclosed in a polyvinyl chloride sheath. Then the ends are bonded together with an epoxy material and polished. The light pipe is also known as a fiber-optic bundle.

It has long been known that as light travels through any transparent medium, there is a loss of brightness due to several factors. These are: the angle at which the light enters the fiber conduit, the length of the fiber, the absorption characteristics of the fiber, the reflection loss at the end face, and the index of refraction of the fiber core. The fiber, similar to an optical lens, has a numerical aperture which determines the light-gathering property of the fiber surface. Also, the numerical aperture for a straight fiber is slightly different from that for a curved fiber; however, because of the very small diameter (in microns) of the fiber used for laser transmission, this difference is not significant.

There are two general types of fiber-optic conduits: coherent and noncoherent. In the coherent type, the fibers along the entire bundle are arranged so that their relative positions at both ends are the same. This type of fiber-optic bundle is used as an image conduit because the image formed on the face of one end is transmitted unchanged to the other face. This type is used extensively in medical diagnostic applications. In the noncoherent type, the fibers are randomly grouped together but have relatively the same light-transmission efficiencies as the coherent type. Fiber-optic laser conduits have many uses in industrial, medical, dental, and military applications; each will be discussed presently.

Since the discovery of fiber-optic materials, many improvements have been made to increase the efficiency of transmission by improving the purity of the material, the density, the transparency, and the refractive index of the fiber. One of these improvements is the coating or cladding of the fiber-optic strand with a glass of lower refractive index in order to increase the transmission by total internal reflection. This improvement takes advantage of the reflection of light from one surface of the wall to another during its travel through the fiber. Any impurity or contaminant within the core or the surface of the fiber affects its transmission efficiency. Even fingerprints on the fiber surface affect laser transmission. If the surface is painted with some material having a relatively high refractive index or absorption property, total extinction of the laser light through the fiber occurs; this effect is known as light frustration.

The spectral transmission of the fiber optic includes ultraviolet, visible, and infrared regions, and there are specific fibers for transmitting the particular wavelength of radiation desired. For instance, quartz fiber can transmit ultraviolet as well as visible wavelengths; germanate and lanthanate glass and germanium fibers can transmit infrared wavelengths.

CHARACTERISTICS OF FIBER OPTICS

Numerical Aperture

Since all the fiber optics presented in this book are the coated type, the solid angle of the light cone incident on the surface of the fiber depends on the indexes of refraction of the core material and the coating material. The numerical aperture (NA) is the maximum light-admitting measure of the fiber and is numerically equal to the product of the refractive index, N_a, of the medium (air, $N_a = 1$) and the sine of angle ϕ, which is the angle between the normal to the fiber end surface and the light-beam direction. The relation may be expressed as:

$$NA = N_a \sin \phi = (N_1{}^2 - N_2{}^2)^{1/2} \qquad \text{(Eq. 13-1)}$$

where,

N_a is the refractive index of the external medium, such as air,
N_1 is the refractive index of the fiber core,
N_2 is the refractive index of the coating of the core.

In order that the greatest efficiency of laser transmission will occur through the coated fiber, the refractive index, N_1, of the core must be greater than the refractive index, N_2, of the coating, C.

As stated previously, a ray of laser light travels through a fiber optic by total reflection. This occurs when the laser ray, for instance R in Fig. 13-1, becomes incident on the end surface of the fiber core having a higher refraction index, N_1, than that of cladding N_2 and when the laser ray is within the critical angle. The ray, then, makes multiple reflections from the interface between the cladding and the core until it reaches the opposite end, where it projects out at the same angle of incidence, ϕ. If the ray is incident on the fiber surface at a greater angle than ϕ, the ray will be lost by reflection from the surface as well as at the interface, since no total reflection will occur. Although the reflected rays considered in a straight fiber (Fig. 13-1A) will behave in accordance with Equation 13-1, for curved fibers (Fig. 13-1B) the relation will change. But for very fine-diameter fibers, within the range of 40 microns, the relation becomes insignificant. The fibers used for laser transmission will be confined to this diameter thickness.

The core refractive index of a glass fiber is typically 1.65, and the cladding index is 1.53. This proportion changes with different types and qualities of fiber and cladding materials; this change in proportion may vary the numerical aperture. For plastics, the indexes of refraction of the core and the cladding are lower than these figures. The fiber-bundle diameter for applications discussed in this book varies from a millimeter up to one-half inch. Numerical apertures may

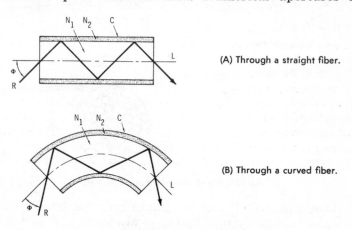

(A) Through a straight fiber.

(B) Through a curved fiber.

Fig. 13-1. Laser-ray transmission

typically range from 0.2 to 1.0 (greater or smaller values are possible). By judicious combination of various core and cladding materials, it is possible to vary the numerical aperture, the thermal properties, and the transmission characteristic of the fiber.

Packing Density

The packing density of a fiber-optic bundle is the ratio of the area of total number of fibers in the bundle to the area of the bundle. This can be explained by using the illustration in Fig. 13-2A, in which d is the diameter of the core and D is the diameter of the fiber with its cladding. If there are N number of fibers in a bundle (Fig. 13-2B), then the total area of the fiber core (A_c) will be:

$$A_c = \frac{N\pi(d)^2}{4} \qquad \text{(Eq. 13-2)}$$

And the area of the bundle (A_b) will be:

$$A_b = \frac{N\pi(D)^2}{4} \qquad \text{(Eq.13-3)}$$

The packing density (P_d) of the fiber-optic bundle will then be given as:

$$P_d = \frac{A_c}{A_b}$$
$$= \frac{d^2}{D^2} \qquad \text{(Eq. 13-4)}$$

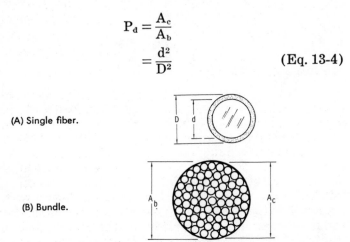

(A) Single fiber.

(B) Bundle.

Fig. 13-2. Round fibers in a round format.

Percent utilization (P_u) of the total fiber-optic bundle will be the total core area divided by the total bundle area and multiplied by 100, as shown in Equation (13-5).

$$P_u = \frac{d^2}{D^2} \times 100 \qquad \text{(Eq. 13-5)}$$

Let us assume that a certain fiber-optic bundle has 400 fibers, each fiber having a diameter of 60 microns and a cladding thickness of 5 microns. What will be the packing density of the bundle? What will be the percent utilization of the fiber-optic bundle?

From Equation 13-4, the packing density will be:

$$P_d = \frac{d^2}{D^2}$$

$$= \frac{(60)^2}{(70)^2} = \frac{3600}{4900}$$

$$= \frac{36}{49} = 0.73$$

And the percent utilization will be:

$$P_u = 0.73 \times 100 = 73\%$$

From these relations it is readily apparent that the larger the diameter of the fiber, the greater the utilization percentage. However, other optical factors enter into the utilization of these equations in laser waveguides. For instance, the numerical apertures will change and the resolution will suffer when coherence is the prime requirement as in medical work. Also, to achieve flexibility, the fiber diameter would be decreased and the number of fibers would be increased.

Types of Fiber Optics

There are a number of different types of fiber optics or light pipes: plastic cores with plastic cladding, lead-glass cores with soda-lime glass cladding, quartz cores with glass cladding, and tubular fibers with liquid or polymer fillings. Also, there are small-diameter single-fiber laser conduits which have found extensive application in medical diagnosis, surgical work, and dental restorative work. These are: gastroscopes, 8 to 10 millimeters in diameter, using coherent fibers with a high degree of flexibility for the exploration of the alimentary canal; sigmoidoscopes for examination of the rectum and the colon; urethroscopes for urinary-tract diagnosis; bronchoscopes for examining the bronchial region; nasopharyngoscopes for the examination of nose and pharynx regions; hypodermic probes of a single fiber for tissue examination under the skin; and many others. Some of these instruments contain rigid fibers of the coherent type. Fiber optics for dental restorative work have also been devised; the enamel of the tooth is "brushed" with an unfocused laser beam to form a thin microscopic layer of the enamel over the tooth for prevention of caries. In both dental and medical surgery, laser-waveguide fibers are used for incision and cauterization of various cancerous tissues and gingival infections, and for the removal of superficial skin blemishes.

For industry and the consumer, a variety of fiber optics, mostly plastic, of varying diameters and sizes are being produced for many uses: lighting, illumination, inspection of sites inaccessible by conventional methods, reading print, reading computer cards, communication with light or laser beams, cathode-ray tube faces, imagescopes connected to television cameras or motion-picture cameras in order to take pictures around corners, and borescopes for quality control of welded tubular structures.

For applications in the laser systems discussed in this text, only those fiber optics that are flexible, compatible with laser wavelengths, and made of durable glass or quartz materials with relatively low solarization properties will be discussed. In the industrial applications involving lasers, fiber-optic bundles of diameters up to 1.5 inches and with cooling jackets that conduct active and inert gases will be discussed. Tubular fiber optics containing organic liquids to increase the transmission efficiency of the waveguide will be taken up with systems used for both the medical and the communication fields. Single-fiber laser waveguides will be discussed in connection with communication systems because of the low transmission losses in these types of fibers.

FIBER-OPTIC APPLICATIONS

Fiber Optics for Industrial Laser Welders

To date, all industrial welding with a laser unit has been accomplished with a laser head that is integrally built onto a console. This has limited the uses of the laser welder because any material that cannot be inserted under the laser head cannot be welded, drilled, scribed, or cut. However, with the improvements already made in laser waveguides, this limitation will soon be overcome. The improved laser system will be able to transmit the laser beam to areas remote from the console through the use of flexible, laser-compatible, and durable tubular or solid waveguide. The waveguide will be capable of conducting laser energy in kilojoules or gigawatt pulses. This conduction will be made possible by the use of cooling fluids flowing through the waveguide jacket. Both lead-glass and quartz fibers will be employed. The waveguide may also be provided with special optical lenses with central holes, or it may have plano-conical (axicon) lenses for seam welding of heavy metals, or welding of light plastics using reduced laser energy.

For the microelectronics industry, a three-foot long fiber-optic waveguide may facilitate welding or bonding of thin and thick films in hybrid microcircuits, lead bonding of integrated circuits and transistors on printed-circuit boards, and scribing lines on ceramic wafers. The fiber waveguide also should reduce the processing time and cost considerably. Repairing of miniature parts, links, fasteners, and cables will be easily accomplished and the laser beam will not produce any heat-affected zone or cracks at the bond interface because of the rapidity with which the bonding or welding is achieved.

Laser Waveguides for Medical Surgery

Another unique laser waveguide developed and patented by the author consists of a flexible laser conduit with an instrumentation stylus at its distal termination. Thumb controls are provided for administering local anesthesia to the patient prior to laser surgical incision. As the anesthetic fluid passes through the waveguide, it travels on the periphery of the optical conduit, which is enclosed in a jacket. In doing so, the anesthetic fluid temperature-conditions the conduit so that the transmission losses due to thermal effects are reduced practically to zero. Provision is made at the proximal end of the waveguide for connection to an external source of inert, sterile gas. During surgery this gas is used to cool the areas contiguous to the incision and to cool the blood vessels that have been cauterized by the laser beam. This laser waveguide is especially useful during surgery on the bleeding organs—the liver, spleen, stomach, and the kidneys. They can be operated upon conveniently and almost bloodlessly with the use of this instrument. Cancerous structures in the viscera, the brain, the nasopharyngeal tract, the larynx, and the external ear canal are readily accessible for precise surgical treatment and manipulation with this instrument. Externally, tattoos, warts, skin cancer, and other dermal blemishes can be removed easily and permanently. Since in surgical work the point of the laser stylus does not touch the tissues, it may not be necessary to sterilize the stylus. However, if sterilization is necessary, the stylus (including the entire waveguide) may be sterilized by soaking it in a cold solution of Zephiran chloride.

As stated in an earlier chapter, various tissues in the body are selectively susceptible to laser wavelengths. For that reason, the waveguide material that is used has to be compatible with the particular wavelength of laser radiation that is administered to the patient. For example, the radiation from an argon-laser generator is highly absorbed by hemoglobin in the blood; therefore, it is preferred for photocoagulation. Also, argon-laser wavelengths are compatible with optical fibers that are commonly available.

Carbon dioxide furnishes a considerable amount of laser energy and is highly absorbed by body tissues; thus, it is an excellent laser scapel. Since the laser wavelengths from carbon dioxide are in the infrared region, they are easily aborbed by ordinary optical elements. They also are incompatible with the optical fibers that are compatible with argon-laser wavelengths. Therefore, fibers made of germanium, lanthanate glass, or arsenic sulfide must be used. Of course, this compatability requirement includes the optical lenses that focus the carbon dioxide laser beam on the tissues.

Neodymium-YAG has the advantages of compatibility with optical fibers and suitability for surgical work, but its incising power is not equal to that of carbon dioxide laser radiation. When laser waveguide is selected, careful thought should be given to the optical fibers and lens materials that are used in it.

Laser Waveguides for Dental Work

With the use of the laser waveguide just discussed, dentists will be able to administer restorative treatment to the teeth in vivo and in vitro. One principal application of the laser waveguide that deserves special reference is its ability to drill and sterilize the teeth cavities, cauterizing the tissues that have been diseased, such as in gingivitis or trench mouth. By defocusing the laser beam, the laser beam can be diverged to any usable diameter, limited only by the laser energy. It can then be applied to the enamel of the tooth for strengthening and protecting it against caries. The divergent beam can also be used to sterilize exposed patches of dental tissue prior to filling or crowning with metal or plastic. Any gingival suppuration (pus discharge) can also be punctured and vaporized by the laser beam and the remaining tissues can be cauterized. An abscess at the root of the tooth can be removed, and the remaining tissue can be safely sterilized by cauterizing. The same problems of waveguide transmission losses and wavelength compatibility of laser beams found in medical work are also found in dental instrumentation work.

Automatic Laser Focusing and Triggering System

In order to eliminate human errors from the operation of a laser system, the equipment should be provided with means for automatically focusing and adjusting the focus size relative to the thickness of the material to be worked upon. In addition to these conditions, the system should trigger the laser beam without the operator's attention. Accordingly, the localization of the work area, adjustment of the focus size and of its position with respect to the workpiece, and triggering of the laser beam should be performed in exact sequence in order to obtain uniform laser results. Such means have been developed, although they are not in general use at present. Fig. 13-3 shows an illustration of the device. The device is adaptable for both console operation and fiber-optic laser-transmitting conduits.

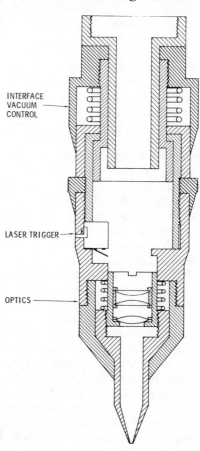

INTERFACE
VACUUM
CONTROL

LASER TRIGGER

OPTICS

Fig. 13-3. Automatic laser-focusing and triggering system head.

Laser Waveguides in Military Applications

Laser fiber-optic guides are gradually replacing the conventional electric cables in the military communication field where weight and cost is of specific concern. The Navy is the first to use fiber-optics in aircraft, in ships, and for underwater applications. One of the principal reasons for the replacement of metallic cables is that no electromagnetic interference exists in fiber-optic light transmitters. Other reasons are: the lightweight quality of the material, the smaller space it occupies, and the lower cost as compared to its copper- or aluminum-cable counterparts. For the A-7 Attack Aircraft, the use of fiber-optic cables reduces the total number of metallic wires used to one-sixth of the previous number and also reduces the weight of the cables by the same order of magnitude. The cost of the new installation will also be decreased to approximately one-fourth, making the replacement very attractive both in effectiveness and in economy.

Earlier, it was not economically practical to replace metallic wires with fiber-optic cables because the light attenuation losses in the fibers were several hundred decibels (dB) per kilometer of transmission. At present, fiber-optic materials have been produced with attenuation losses of 3 dB per kilometer for commercial applications. This figure is even lower on laboratory or pilot-plant scale when gallium-arsenide diodes or He-Ne laser tubes of 0.5- to 1.0-milliwatt output are used. Communication in this manner can be conducted up to distances of 30,000 feet without the use of optical links or repeaters.

Apparently, the Navy is even satisfied with higher losses at present, since it is reported that fiber-optics with attenuation losses greater than 4 dB per kilometer are being tested by the Navy department. It is also reported that the present closed-circuit television cables used on shipboard will eventually be replaced by fiber-optic light guides. In the Marine Corps communication systems, fiber-optic cables will be used to transmit messages and other tactical data.

Character transmission is also being conducted by the use of coherent optical fibers. Such fibers were used at the Apollo launch pad to study the behavior of liquid oxygen in the first stage, where environmental extremes would not permit direct acquisition of physical data. The monitoring fiber-optic cable furnished visual information through the fiber-optic bundle to a series of lenses; the lenses transmitted the image to a camera which monitored the information on a continuous film. High resolution was obtained from fiber-optic bundles having fiber diameters down to 10 microns, with field flatteners of 8 microns. The American Optical Company deserves much credit for this achievement, as well as for its contribution to fiber-optics technology in medical applications.

Special Fiber-Optic Laser Waveguide

A single, hollow quartz fiber of capillary diameter, filled with a liquid of higher refractive index than quartz, has been developed by Bell Laboratories. This fiber is said to have an attenuation loss of less than 3 dB per kilometer, and this rate is said to be improving so that the loss will be reduced to about 1 dB per kilometer. Such an achievement may provide a bandwidth capability over 10 GHz per kilometer of transmission.

FIBER OPTICS FOR TELEPHONE COMMUNICATION

One of the leading glass fiber-optics manufacturers is Corning Glass Works, Corning, New York. This company has been involved in fiber-optic developing, testing, and manufacturing since the inception of the material. The aim of this company is to produce fiber optics with a 2.1-dB loss per kilometer, which is said to be close to the theoretical limit of 2 dB. Their present production-fiber losses are 10 dB per kilometer, which they consider to be amply suited to long-distance data and voice communication. At present they are involved in the military application of their fiber-optic material, but it is reported that this will be followed by applications for telephone communications.

The ITT Electro-Optical Products Division, Roanoke, Virginia, has been conducting research and development in fiber-optic communication systems. The company now produces and markets fiber-optic systems primarily to the military, but it expects to expand its operations to civilian voice transmission, facsimile transmission, and video transmission using fiber-optic cable. Some of the present wire communication systems will soon be converted into wideband fiber-optic communication systems to relieve the presently overburdened communications systems.

CHAPTER 14

Needed Laser Developments

The ideas and problems presented in this section have been selected for the reader who has gained a basic understanding of laser principles and is capable of putting his knowledge into practice. In suggesting the ideas, the author has attempted to present a plan of approach to the problem and has given any background history necessary for solving the problem.

Identification Friend or Foe (IFF)—The present radar, microwave, or infrared IFF devices do not seem to be effective and rapid. A reliable infrared-ultraviolet system, using an argon or dye laser in the ultraviolet region and using neodymium-YAG in the infrared region, is needed. The system should be capable of projecting two beams to the underside of the aircraft to be identified. In the unidentified aircraft, the system should have sensors which will automatically return coded signals identifying the aircraft.

Auto Proximity Indicator—There is a blind area in the rear of each automobile; a car in the rear at close range to the driver cannot be seen through the driver's mirror. An abrupt movement by the driver to change lanes may result in an accident. A low-cost laser device, using a gallium-arsenide diode to scan the rear of the car, would alert the driver and would be welcomed by auto owners.

Aircraft-Collision Preventer—Various aircraft-collision devices have been developed experimentally for this purpose, but not one is sufficiently practical to be installed on any commercial or private plane at low cost. Infrared or ultraviolet laser beams, which would be projected to the incoming aircraft and retroreflected to photosensors, could be developed. Gyrocontrolled synchros would automatically maneuver the aircraft upward and to the right. Corresponding tactics must be provided on both aircraft.

Ship-Collision Preventer—Every year damages worth millions of dollars are caused when ships collide in the dark. These collisions could be prevented by a laser beam capable of penetrating and scanning an area 2000 yards in radius, 360° horizontally and 15° vertically, and warning the captain to maneuver the ship to the right or the left. The maneuvers do not have to be cooperative between the ships if one is equipped with sensors and the other is not.

Target Search and Acquisition System—Present radar-activated systems are not precise and cannot acquire low-level target information. A system using a laser beam diverged to 10 milliradians and projected up to 20,000 feet above ground is needed. The ground system would lock onto the target by retroactive acquisition. After locking onto the target, the system would reduce the beam diameter to that of a pencil beam and then would acquire data on the speed, the direction, and the character of the target.

Home-Security Sentinel—Present infrared, microwave, or acoustic home-security equipment is too large and costly. An effective means of protection for the home and family, such as an alarm system that alerts the residents as well as the neighbors, is needed. One solution to this problem might be an invisible laser fence that surrounds homes and that can be made at reasonably low cost.

Portable Intrusion Alarm for Campers—A portable, invisible laser fence, which could be easily erected around a cabin or a tent, would be ideal for campers. Sensors would alert campers to intruding animals and persons at night. A low-cost gallium-arsenide device with an alarm could be made in a compact package with rechargeable batteries.

Auto Theft Alarm—A laser-beam fence surrounding the car would continuously monitor the car. Any activity would trip the beam, sounding an alarm. The system would be activated when the car owner left his car and locked it. This system could be set automatically or manually as the driver leaves the car.

Circuit-Board Plating Thickness Monitor—A liquid-tight laser beam and sensor could be installed in the plating tank so that a retroreflective action would be possible on the sensor. Normal turbulence of the plating solution would be adjusted to zero reference. Any change in the interferometric condition between the plating and the sensor would be recorded on the chart of a recorder connected to the sensor output. A calibrated reading would indicate thickness down to microns.

TV Station and Sound Changer—With an infrared laser beam from a gallium-arsenide diode projected on a detector with a servo, it would be possible to change stations with every logic-clocked pulse. The sound volume of the station should be changed at the rate of 1 dB per second with continuous laser illumination.

Laser Propellant for Space Vehicle—When a nominal-power laser beam is focused on an object, it reacts explosively, creating a pressure or thrust of several million pounds per square inch. Utilizing this thrust, a space vehicle could be propelled in space where vacuum conditions exist. The system could have enormous potentialities.

Aircraft Fuel-Contaminant Monitor—Aircraft fuel systems are vulnerable to contaminants in the fuel; the contaminant plugs up the delicate fuel lines and valves. A laser monitoring device installed near the fuel system to monitor the flow of fuel during fueling would alert the attendant if the contaminant content exceeded 15 to 20 milligrams per liter of fuel.

Automobile Counter—In order to determine whether or not a signal light is needed at an intersection, the highway transportation department needs a precise instrument that can count automobiles passing across a specific road and can discriminate against other objects. The present infrared or pneumatic devices for counting automobiles are said to be only approximate in their count.

Missile Velocimeter—At missile test ranges, the velocity of the missile at altitudes less than 1000 feet cannot be accurately measured by radar. A laser system is needed that could measure altitudes of only several feet above ground. The proposed system would measure the velocity of the missile by computer translation of the target position with respect to its time at clocked intervals.

X-Ray Laser System—X-rays propagate divergently in all directions and cannot be focused to a point. A laser-incited X-ray beam would enable the X-ray beam to be converged and focused to the work area. This would increase the X-ray intensity at the focus over a million times and largely eliminate the danger of affecting the normal tissue contiguous to that under medical therapy. Radiographs produced by a focusable X-ray beam would have high diagnostic definition.

Atomic-Fusion Initiator—Much experimental work is now being done in the application of atomic power to daily living. One application might be the development of a small, high-powered laser device which would produce a single pulse to "ignite" an atomic fuel.

Thermal Imaging System—At present, medical thermal imaging methods use either an infrared device or a spray of liquid crystal dispersed in a liquid vehicle. However, the colors produced in imaging are changeable in rapid progression as the patient's nervous condition changes. A thermal imaging system having a high sensitivity and using a compatible laser beam in the 10,000- to 100,000-angstrom wavelengths would give improved imaging performance, which would make medical diagnostic work more reliable. A television screen used with this system would aid in more accurate diagnosis of superficial skin-disease and carcinomatous breast images.

Depth Indicator—There are many depth indicators on the market; they vary from a crude line with a weight at its end to an electronically controlled acoustic sounding device. Each has a disadvantage—size, cost, or reliability. A laser device based on the clocked time-code mechanism of the range-finder principle would give highly precise indications of depths up to 150 feet. With this device, boatmen and fishermen could accurately sound the ocean for obstructions, schools of fish, sunken treasure, etc. (use green laser beam).

Laser-Beam Scanner With Control—The scanner could consist of a laser-beam source with a beam-deflection control for scanning and for rapidly positioning the beam spatially. A possible technique might be the use of a prism effect to control the index of refraction of the source material.

Flash Laser Beam—A compact, hand-carried laser generator to produce a high-intensity flash is needed. One approach would be to Q-switch the laser beam, but, at present, Q-switching equipment is bulky and costly. However, a technique similar to Q-switching yet simpler and less expensive would have wide industrial and military (photographic, holographic, and tactical work) applications.

Overpressure Detector—It is a well-known physical fact that when the atmospheric pressure changes, certain meteorological changes occur including the density of the atmosphere. A laser-beam device to detect overpressure or rarefaction of 0.01 to 10 dynes/cm^2 above a reference pressure would be welcome by meteorological manufacturers and users. Since laser beams are sensitive to pressure changes, one should be able to develop this device by using some of the principles discussed in previous chapters.

Meteorological Sounding System—A meteorological sounding system for shipboard application would be welcome by various military agencies because present telemetering methods cannot be used under emission-control conditions. The system should have unlimited altitude capabilities, should use a completely passive means to obtain data, and should operate reliably in all climatic conditions and at all temperatures. The laser beam, being highly directional and insensitive to jamming, would be an admirable candidate for this purpose.

Atmospheric Water-Vapor Indicator—Current meteorological instruments measure all types of parameters and telemeter them to weather stations. However, they are not suitable for sensing humidity precisely. There is a need for a humidity sensor that would operate at ambient temperatures from 0°C to 60°C and would measure dew points from −10°C to 30°C with high accuracy. The laser radio-diffusion principle might be used to develop this sensor.

Visual Acquisition of Downed Airman in Water—A laser system could be used to locate an airman downed in water. The proposed system would be installed on an aircraft and would scan a minimum area of two square miles, from an altitude of 600 to 1000 feet. A television-tube-type scanner with a laser beam, using an electronic locking mechanism on the object, would be needed to achieve this development. A high visual contrast is needed between the target and the water, both during daytime and nighttime. Use ir and uv laser beams selectively.

Laser-Beam Door Opener—Searching for a key and a keyhole in the dark sometimes becomes a nuisance. Besides being a nuisance at times, the present lock system is vulnerable to master keys or other methods employed by thieves and vandals. An infrared laser-beam door opener could eliminate this problem. A laser beam would be continuously projected from a door which could be operated *only* by means of a photosensor. This photosensor would be the shape and size of a quarter dollar and would be held in front of the beam to unlock the door. This device would not only be burglar-proof but would be a quick and easy way to unlock a door at night. It should work any time of the day or night.

New Fiber-Optic Material—A new fiber-optic material that is compatible with a 106,000-angstrom carbon dioxide laser is needed for optical communication and for medical surgery. The material should combine spectroscopic properties with physical properties such as hardness, coefficient of expansion, high thermal conductivity, and flexibility. The material could possibly be selected from rare-earth ions contained in a durable host material. The fiber diameter should be approximately two millimeters. The transmission loss should be one dB or less per kilometer.

Laser Timer—The general-type mechanical timers and electronic timers presently in use are not stable and are affected by environmental conditions. A timing device with an accuracy of less than 0.1% is needed. This timer could be useful in underwater missile applications.

CHAPTER 15

Laser Systems for the Military

The military applications of laser beams are varied and numerous. Only a few of the applications of general technological interest to the reader will be discussed here. They are confined to both nondestructive and destructive aspects of the systems. In the nondestructive applications, laser beams are being used to guide missiles, aircraft, drones, and other moving projectiles to their targets with high precision. The beam is also employed in battleground training of soldiers who, instead of using blank ammunitions, project laser beams at each other from rifle-configured devices. The rifle housing the laser generator fires a pencil beam of laser light up to a range of 1000 feet. Upon receiving the beam, sensors in the helmet, body area, and extremities of each soldier activate an electronic antenna erected in the helmet of each soldier. This transmits a signal to a computer in the central station. The signal informs the computer memory center whether the soldier was hit in the head, body, or limb so that he can be eliminated from the field.

For the development of battlefield maneuvers with laser beams, the government has assigned 175,000 acres of land for various military experimental operations using laser-beam "weapons," soldiers, and electronic instruments.

Ruby-laser range finders are being employed on M-60 forward air controllers for artillery range finding, and on AH-56A Cheyenne hellicopters as part of the navigation system. Battery-powered laser scanning devices are also being employed by the military, and more recently by the police in many states of the country. These devices can detect light invisible to the naked eye and amplify it 45,000 times so that the enemy can be seen in the dark.

In the destructive applications of the laser beam, high-power laser energy is directed in a pencil beam at targets. The laser beam then destroys strategic points on the targets or drills holes in fuel tanks to explode the targets. In the battlefield, with a forward air controller or a ground observer maintaining a laser beam on a coordinate, a missile from a single fighter bomber can home in on the target with no trouble. Laser-guided bombs have already proven to be most effective counter-weapons against 130-mm guns. It has been stated in a number of publications that a devastating laser-beam weapon, which will make nuclear weapons obsolete, may be in the developmental stage. There are also reports that sufficiently high-powered laser beams have been developed to destroy nuclear warheads in moving missiles. Materials for lasing high-energy laser radiations have been developed to a point that soon they might be used for triggering the explosion of nuclear warheads or for initiating controlled nuclear fission for peacetime atomic energy utilization.

While several different methods have been employed with laser rifles to simulate the firing of actual weapons one unique method is the use of a time-code modulation technique based on time synchronization, pulse position, and coding time slots. The laser employed in this technique is a gallium-arsenide diode, which is sensitive to temperature conditions during operation. The diode threshold current decreases at low temperatures and increases at elevated temperatures. When excessive lasing occurs below room temperature, failure results from current limitation. Above room temperature, excessive current density of the diode causes the failure. Accordingly, close control over the temperature is achieved by the provision of a thermal control loop comprising a modulator, a thermistor, and a regulator. The regulator controls the dc current to the modulator in order to generate a supply voltage proportional to current for lasing. The laser beam collimated in the transmitter has a beam divergence of one milliradian and uses a simple lens of three-inch focal length.

A battery-powered scanning telescope using photosensors has been developed. This telescope amplifies the light from the moon as it shines on land up to 45,000 times and makes the terrain visible at night to soldiers or to helicopters flying at altitudes of 2000 feet above ground in a hostile environment. The night scene can also be magnified and projected on a screen. Those viewing the screen can acquire intelligence information from moving objects or persons on the ground. Police cruising in patrol cars after dark can also utilize the system to detect vandalism and theft, thus making arrests more rapid and effective.

LASER WEAPON SYSTEMS

Directed-Beam Laser Rifle

A directed-beam laser rifle, patented by Arthur M. Muncheryan, the chief physicist of Laserkinetics Corporation, consists of a portable laser system built into a rifle configuration with a self-charging power supply. The device consists of a number of solid-state laser rods interfaced with coniform fiber-optic amplifiers. The laser rods are individually activated by flashlamps which receive high-voltage pulsed current from a bank of capacitors contained in the stock of the rifle configuration. The capacitors are energized by a self-charging battery network. This battery network obtains its energy from a radioactively excited battery of cells and from silicon solar cells illuminated by the flashlamps during operation of the laser system. To reduce the size, weight, and the cost of the system, a vibrator mechanism is used. The vibrator mechanism converts the low-voltage direct current to a pulsing high-voltage current for energizing the flashlamps.

Fig. 15-1 illustrates a sectional side view of the forward half of the laser rifle in which the laser generator is located. The generator consists of three ruby or neodymium-YAG rods designated by 1, 2, and 3 and disposed alternately between fiber-optic cones 4, 5, and 6. The fiber-optic cones amplify the laser beam by condensing the beam before transmitting it to the next lasing rod. The laser rods are excited to emission by flashlamps 7, 8, 9, and 10. Between the flashlamps and the

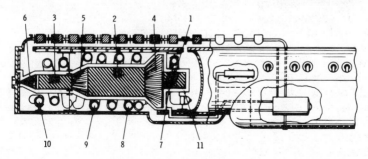

Fig. 15-1. Directed-beam laser rifle.

laser rods separated by the fiber-optic cones, there is glass envelope 11 through which a cooling fluid circulates to cool the lasing elements. When the laser-triggering mechanism is actuated, this fluid is supplied from a compressed-fluid reservoir within the system. For emergency action the batteries may be recharged from an external source of 115-V alternating current.

The system can furnish a low-power laser beam for battle-field maneuvers as discussed previously, or it can provide a high-power laser beam for drilling holes in objects or for destroying the delicate working mechanisms of a target system located at distances of 100 to 200 meters, or more, depending on the power supply provided within the laser system or isolated from it. Because of its high-power capability, the device may be used to dig holes in concrete, metal-ore mines, and granite. Also, the device may be employed as a portable welding system that can weld aircraft-fuselage skin and structural parts in the field without disassembling them from the craft.

Directed-Beam Laser Handgun

The directed-beam pistol-like laser device shown in Fig. 15-2 is a self-contained laser generator developed by the patentee of the laser rifle. While it serves the same purpose as the rifle-configured laser system, its power is limited to smaller work projects, such as drilling or welding fine micro-electronic devices and sheet materials. Similarly to its larger

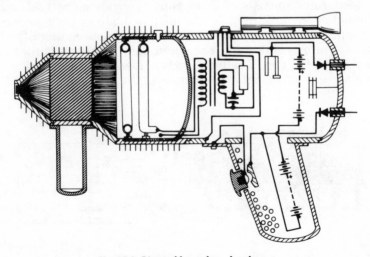

Fig. 15-2. Directed-beam laser handgun.

counterpart, the device includes a ruby or neodymium-doped glass rod optically pumped by a flashlamp energized from a battery of rechargeable cells. Voltage amplification is accomplished by an oscillation mechanism, which converts the dc voltage to a pulsating unidirection current and then magnifies and feeds the high voltage to the flashlamp when the trigger mechanism is actuated.

HIGH-POWER LASER EQUIPMENT

Other high-power laser equipment for military use could be developed by increasing the size of the lasing element, which is optically pumped by continuous flashlamps from a mercury arc or a carbon arc, similar to those used in aerial advertising and in military searches for flying aircraft. Such a system would be capable of producing megajoules of laser-energy pulses. When the beam is concentrated to a one-centimeter diameter and directed to hostile targets, it can instantly cut large areas of metal or drill holes through strategic mechanisms to deactivate or destroy the mechanisms. The laser beam could be first produced in exit aperatures of several feet, collimated, and then concentrated to suitable diameter beams and directed to a point of interest. The resulting concentrated laser energy could be made equivalent to fissioned atomic energy at the point of contact. The system could be made to trigger a H-bomb without an A-bomb as detonator.

Safety Precautions

Two types of safety precautions should be taken in handling laser equipment: precautions against electrical shock and precautions against laser radiations. The first type involves disconnecting all the electrical sources furnishing current to the laser system. This should be done before an attempt is made to repair or modify any part of the electronic circuitry because the voltages present are dangerously high and can be lethal in some cases. The second precautionary measure is concerned with preventing exposure to a laser beam by looking directly at it or at its reflections.

ELECTRICAL PRECAUTIONS

Almost all laser systems operate at voltages of dangerous levels (in kilovolts). Therefore, the following should be observed before anyone attempts to work on the circuitry:

1. No one should work on the system unless he is familiar with the circuitry and the proper safety precautions.
2. The main switch should be turned off before anyone handles the circuit connections.
3. A jumper with an insulated handle should be used to discharge the capacitors before any work is done on the circuits.
4. A bare wire should never be contacted while the circuit is on.
5. The circuitry should be covered up when no one is working with it.

6. For maximum safety, all laser systems should have grounded outlets.
7. The safety interlocks should be in good operating condition; if they are not, they should be immediately repaired.
8. The laser tube may implode if damaged or cracked by rough handling.

RADIATION PRECAUTIONS

As stated in a previous chapter, laser beams are 10,000 times brighter than the sun's rays, and much more hazardous. When a beam of laser radiation is absorbed by living tissue, the extent of damage caused is dependent on several things: the energy level of the radiation, the type of tissue irradiated, the wavelength of the laser radiation, and the time of exposure to the radiation.

A beam of laser radiation is hazardous to the body when the energy level of the radiation is sufficiently high to cause interaction with the body tissue. Or, in other words, when intense laser-beam energy is absorbed by the body, it is converted into heat. This heat coagulates the protein in the body's tissues (just as boiling water coagulates egg albumin) and destroys the cells.

For a given level of laser energy, certain tissues in the body will be more vulnerable to laser radiation than others. For example, the human eye is the most vulnerable tissue to all types of laser radiation because it is not "clothed" as most of the other parts of the body are; therefore, high-intensity radiation is easily absorbed by the eye. The tissue in the retina (the "screen" at the back of the eyeball that receives the light or image) is particularly susceptible to damage because the lens of the eyeball concentrates and focuses the laser beam on the retina.

Different laser wavelengths interact differently with the body tissue. For instance, retina tissue is affected in lessening intensity by ruby, helium-neon, and argon laser beams, in that order. The cross-sectional view of the eyeball shown in Fig. 16-1 illustrates the interaction of a laser beam with eyeball tissue.

As the laser beam impinges on the eyeball, part of the beam is prevented from entering the eye by the iris, a colored disc behind the cornea. The iris acts like an automatic photographic shutter and constricts when high-intensity light impinges on the eye. The shutter action keeps part of the light from reach-

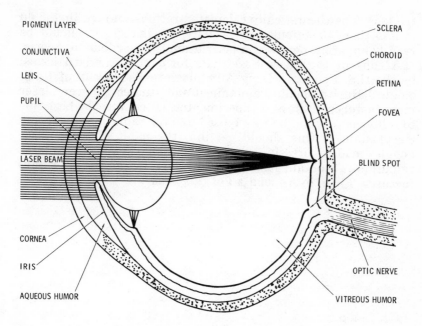

PIGMENT LAYER
CONJUNCTIVA
LENS
PUPIL
LASER BEAM
CORNEA
IRIS
AQUEOUS HUMOR

SCLERA
CHOROID
RETINA
FOVEA
BLIND SPOT
OPTIC NERVE
VITREOUS HUMOR

Fig. 16-1. Cross-sectional view of the eyeball.

ing the retina, where the image patterns are formed, and from injuring the retinal tissue. The retina is surrounded by a thin, dark-brown choroid membrane containing arteries, veins, and pigment cells. Since this membrane is dark colored and would easily absorb radiation, it must be protected.

The retina is sensitive to all color wavelengths, from the 3800- to 9000-angstrom spectral range. It is also sensitive to some degree to infrared wavelengths beyond 9000 angstroms. Although the infrared or ultraviolet rays are not visible, they still affect the eye. In fact, the invisible ultraviolet rays are more dangerous to the eye than the visible rays because of the absorption of the ultraviolet rays by the cornea and the conjunctiva of the eyeball. If the eyes are exposed to extreme amounts of ultraviolet rays, cataracts may form over the lenses of the eyes. The sun's rays and welding arcs contain large amounts of ultraviolet rays.

Fig. 16-1 shows that part of the laser beam is absorbed by the corneal and conjunctival tissues. The laser beam is converged and focused on the fovea of the retina by the lens. From laser-welding principles we know that the focus is the hottest point. The laser-energy density at the fovea is about 10^4 to 10^6 times more concentrated than that received by the cornea and the lens. The theoretically calculated retinal-damage threshold is less than 10^{-6} joules per square centimeter. It should be readily apparent now why a laser beam is hazardous to the eye. A copy of the Laser Safety Performance Standard issued by the U.S. Food and Drug Administration's Bureau of Radiological Health should be obtained and studied by every laser manufacturer, user, and experimenter. Of course, the best rule to follow is to avoid being exposed to laser radiation under any circumstances. One should get into the habit of using laser goggles made expressly for the prevention of exposure to laser radiation. To obtain laser goggles, refer to the list of manufacturers given in Appendix I of this book.

Laser Related Manufacturers List

1. American Optical Corporation General Manager: C. Gilbert Young
   14 Mechanic Street Marketing Manager:
   Southbridge, MA 01550 David A. Belforte
   Phone: (617) 765-9711
   Mfg: Laser rods; fiber optics; laser systems; safety products.

2. Apollo Lasers, Inc. President: Dr. Fred P. Burns
   6357 Arizona Circle Marketing Manager:
   Los Angeles, CA 90045 Robert W. Weiner
   Phone: (213) 776-3343
   Mfg: Laser systems, trimmers, scribers, and accessories.

3. Broomer Research Corporation President: Cyril J. Broomer
   23 Sheer Plaza Sales Manager: Seymour Slochower
   Plainview, NY 11803 Phone: (516) 249-1544
   Mfg: Precision optics, beam splitters, reflectors, coatings.

4. Capacitor Specialists, Inc. President: Bruce R. Hayworth
   PO Box 2052 Marketing Manager:
   Escandido, CA 92025 Wayne C. Steinberge
   Phone: (714) 747-4000
   Mfg. Laser capacitors.

5. Chromatix, Inc. President: Dr. Robert Rempel
   1145 Terra Bella Avenue Marketing Manager:
   Mountain View, CA 94040 Wayne C. Lockhart
   Phone: (415) 969-1070
   Mfg. Ne:YAG lasers, tunable dye lasers, precision controls.

6. Coherent Radiation, Inc. President: Dr. James L. Robart
   3210 Porter Drive Marketing Manager:
   Palo Alto, CA 94304 George A. Stephen
   Phone: (415) 493-2111
   Mfg: Pulsed and Q-switched CO, YAG, dye, and ion lasers; collimators.

7. Corning Glass Works   Vice President: Allen W. Dawson
   Houghton Park   Marketing Manager:
   Corning, NY 14830   S. L. Arbertolli
                          Phone: (607) 962-4444
   Mfg: Capacitors; optical filters, fiber optics; laser rods and tubes.

8. Crystal Optics Research, Inc.   President: James C. Smith
   3680 South State Street   Marketing Manager: C. E. Creps
   Ann Arbor, MI 48104   Phone: (313) 761-1083
   Mfg: Optical crystals; Ne:YAG, ruby, sapphire; delay lines.

9. Ealing Corporation   President: Paul Grindle
   2225 Massachusetts Avenue   Marketing Manager:
   Cambridge, MA 02140   Rudolph W. Lindich
                          Phone: (617) 491-5870
   Mfg: Attenuators, beam directors, filters, polarizers, prisms, etc.

10. Eastman Kodak Company   President: Walter A. Fallon
    343 State Street   Marketing Manager:
    Rochester, NY 14640   Van B. Phillips
                           Phone: (716) 325-2000
    Mfg: Q-switch solutions, organic dyes, chelates, dye lasers.

11. Ferranti Ltd.   Manager: A. C. Bustable
    Dunsinane Avenue   Sales Manager: J. M. Lowe
    Dundee, DD23PN, Scotland   Phone: 0382-89321
    Mfg: He-Ne, argon, and CO_2 lasers; power meters.

12. Karl Feuer Optical Associates   President: Karl Feuer
    PO Box 862   Marketing Manager: William Feuer
    Montclair, NJ 07043   Phone: (201) 783-7294
    Mfg: Coatings, etalons, beams splitters, lenses, mirrors, polarizers.

13. General Electric Company   General Manager: W. J. Kuehl
    570 Lexington Avenue   Marketing Manager: A. W. Howard
    New York, NY 10022   Phone: (607) 729-2511
    Mfg: Ruby and YAG lasers; range finders; target designators; LEDs.

14. GTF 3ylvania, Inc.   General Manager: D. O. Kiser
    PO Box 188   Marketing Manager: G. Hammel
    Mountain View, CA 94040   Phone: (415) 966-2312
    Mfg: YAG, CO_2 lasers; beam expanders; Q-switches; coolers.

15. Hadron, Inc   President: Dr. S. Donald Sims
    800 Shames Drive   Marketing Manager: T. Lefler
    Westbury, NY 11590   Phone: (516) 334-4402
    Mfg: Laser systems, accessories, holography, communications.

16. Holobeam, Inc.   President: Dr. Melvin Cook
    560 Winters Avenue   Marketing Manager: R. Pressley
    Paramus, NJ 07652   Phone: (201) 265-5335
    Mfg: Glass, ruby, YAG lasers; Q-switches; beam expanders; detectors.

17. Hughes Aircraft Company   Division Manager: J. T. Mendel
    3100 West Lomita Boulevard Sales Manager: Richard P. Roemer
    Torrance, CA 90509   Phone: (213) 534-2121
    Mfg: Ar, He-Ne, Xe, Kr lasers; rangers, surveying lasers.

18. ILC Technology, Inc.   President: G. Sorenson
    164 Commercial Street   Marketing Manager: J. Moffet
    Sunnyvale, CA 94086   Phone: (408) 738-9244
    Mfg: Xenon and krypton flashlamps; triggers; inductors; sapphire.

19. International Holographics, Inc. President: John Munchower
    PO Box 586   Director: T. H. Jeong
    Lake Forest, IL 60045   Phone: (312) 362-4750
    Mfg: Holographic cameras, film processors, films, plates, solutions.

20. KMS Industries, Inc.   President: Dr. Joseph Farber
    18551 Von Karman Avenue   Marketing Manager:
    Irvine, CA 92664   John F. Towson
                                Phone: (714) 833-3570
    Mfg. Holography; fingerprint identifiers; optical mounts; radar.

21. Korad, Division of Hadron, Inc. General Manager:
    2520 Colorado Avenue   William C. Thurber
    Santa Monica, CA 90406   Operations Manager:
                                Bernie Newman
                                Phone: (213) 829-3377
    Mfg: Ruby, glass, YAG, and CO_2 lasers; scribers; trimmers; holography.

22. Laser Diode Laboratories, Inc. President: Howard W. Bertram
    205 Forrest Street   Marketing Manager:
    Metuchen, NJ 60618   Peter J. Schneider
                                Phone: (201) 549-7700
    Mfg: Gallium-arsenide diodes, arrays, laser illuminators, power supplies.

23. Laserkinetics Corporation   President: Hrand M. Muncheryan
    1735 N. Morningside Street   Public Relations: George Kaiser
    Orange, CA 92667   Phone: (714) 637-4683
    Mfg: Laser erasers; medical and dental systems; laser security systems; welders.

24. Metrologic Instruments, Inc. President: C. Harry Knowles
    143 Harding Avenue   Marketing Manager:
    Bellmawr, NJ 08030   Joseph J. O'Donnell
                                Phone: (609) 933-0100
    Mfg: He-Ne, He-Cd, and uv lasers; power supplies; holography kits.

25. Optical Industries, Inc.   President: Richard P. Griot
    1218 East Pomona Street   General Manager: Jan A. Melles
    Santa Ana, CA 92707   Phone: (714) 547-4159
    Mfg: Lenses, prisms, mirrors, polarizers, dichroic filters, gratings.

26. Power Technology, Inc.　　President: Thomas H. Burgess
    Box 4403　　　　　　　　　Marketing Manager: J. L. Robinson
    Little Rock, AR 72204　　Phone: (501) 565-1750
    Mfg: Flashlamp power supplies; gas- and diode-laser power supplies.

27. Quantronix Corporation　　Vice President: C. E. Burnett
    225 Engineers Road　　　　Marketing Manager: P. Vokrot
    Smithtown, NY 11787　　　Phone: (717) 397-7661
    Mfg: Laser scribers; YAG lasers; electro- and acousto-optics; welders.

28. RCA Corporation　　　　　President: Herbert M. Dwight, Jr.
    Lancaster, PA 17604　　　Marketing Manager:
    　　　　　　　　　　　　　　James O. Steele
    　　　　　　　　　　　　　　Phone: (415) 961-2550
    Mfg. He-Ne and He-Cd lasers; GaAs diodes and arrays; photodetectors.

29. Spectra-Physics, Inc.　　General Manager: George Olson
    1250 West Middlefield Road　Marketing Manager:
    Mountain View, CA 94040　　Rodney L. Waters
    　　　　　　　　　　　　　　Phone: (213) 322-2086
    Mfg: All types gas lasers; filters; windows; expanders; alignment.

30. TRW Instruments, Inc.　　President: Dr. Richard T. Daly
    (Quantrad)　　　　　　　　Marketing Manager: Ted Brandt
    139 Illinois Street　　　Phone: (516) 273-6900
    El Segundo, CA 90245
    Mfg. Gas and solid lasers; trimmers; lenses, mirrors; holography.

Metric and British Units

Table II-1. Conversions

Angstroms	Microns	Milli-meters	Centimeters	Inches	Meters
1	10^{-4}	10^{-7}	10^{-8}	2.5×10^{-8}	10^{-10}
10^4	1	10^{-3}	10^{-4}	2.5×10^{-4}	10^{-6}
10^7	10^3	1	10^{-1}	0.04	10^{-3}
10^8	10^4	10	1	0.4	10^{-2}
2.54×10^8	2.54×10^4	25.4	2.54	1	0.025
10^{10}	10^6	10^3	10^2	39.4	1

LENGTH UNITS

1 light year $= 5.9 \times 10^{12}$ miles $= 9.5 \times 10^{12}$ kilometers
1 mile $= 1760$ yards $= 5280$ feet $= 63,360$ inches
1 kilometer $= 10^3$ meters $= 10^5$ centimeters $= 10^6$ millimeters
1 yard $= 3$ feet $= 36$ inches $= 0.9144$ meter
1 foot $= 12$ inches $= 0.3048$ meter
1 inch $= 2.54$ centimeters
1 meter $= 1.093$ yards $= 3.279$ feet $= 39.37$ inches

ANGULAR UNITS

1 circumference $= 360$ degrees $= 2\pi$ radians $= 2\pi r$ ($r =$ radius and $\pi = 3.1416$)
¼ circumference $= 90$ degrees $= \pi/2$ radians
1 degree $= 60$ minutes $= 3600$ seconds $= 0.01745$ radian
1 minute $= 60$ seconds
1 radian $= 1000$ milliradians $= 57$ degrees 17 minutes 44.8 seconds $= 57.2958$ degrees

Laser-Related Terms

Brightness—The power emitted per square centimeter per steradian; equivalent to radiance.

Calorie—The amount of heat required to raise the temperature of 1 gram of water 1 degree Celsius (centigrade).

Coulomb—Coulomb (Q) = CV
where,
 C is in farads,
 V is in volts.

Dye Laser—A liquid laser in which the lasing material is organic dye, which may continuously flow through the system or may be sealed in. rare-earth chelate; trimetal ion in benzoylacetonate may also be used.

Hertz—Frequency, or number of cycles per second.

Ion Laser—Gas laser; molecular laser; laser radiation that is produced by excited molecular gases, such as CO_2, CO, krypton, argon, etc.

Kerr Cell—An electro-optic cell filled with nitrobenzene, with an index of refraction that changes with the square of the electric field.

Laser Efficiency—Laser-emission efficiency equal to laser output times 100 divided by power input on the flashlamp.

NEP—The noise-equivalent power in photosensors and the minimum-detectable noise power given in watts.

Planck's Constant—6.625×10^{-27} erg-second; used in relation to photonic energy, $h\nu$, (h is Planck's constant and ν is frequency).

Refractive Index—The ratio of the sine of the angle of incidence in a substance to the sine of the angle of refraction.

Specific Heat—The number of calories required to raise the temperature of 1 gram of a substance 1 degree Celsius (cal/gm/°C).

TEA Laser—Transverse excited atmosphere, in which the lasing gas flows at right angles to the excitation field.

Thermal Capacity—The specific heat multiplied by the weight of the substance in grams.

Thermal Conductivity—The ability of a substance to conduct heat; calories per square centimeter per second for a gradient of 1°C/cm.

YAG—Yttrium-aluminum-garnet host, usually with neodymium dope.

Theory of Laser Radiation

In order to understand the mechanism of laser emission from atoms, we shall assume the Bohr model of orbital quanta and discuss the behavior of atoms under various energy conditions. According to the Bohr concept, all atoms in the normal state exist at their lowest energy levels, which are variously known as stationary states, ground states, lowest-quantum states, and at-rest states. In the stationary state, there is no energy change in the atom, since no energy is received or given off by the atom. For emission of laser radiation (or any electromagnetic radiation), an energy transition must occur in the quantum states. The energy can be imparted to the atom in several ways. For example, if the atom is a gas, the gas can be confined in an electron discharge tube to which a voltage has been applied. The voltage energy is transferred to the atom, which then becomes excited or ionized. Another method of energy transfer is to irradiate the atom by some electromagnetic radiation or by optical pumping. Before the atom can radiate, it must be excited or ionized, and the energy required to excite or ionize the atom is expended in the form of a radiation when the atom returns to the ground state.

An atom consists of an equal number of positive charges (protons) and negative charges (electrons). An atom at rest, then, is electrically neutral. All positive charges are in the nucleus; the electrons occupy orbital positions around the nucleus. All orbital electrons are assigned to definite orbits known as quantum states. A loss of one or more electrons from the orbits causes the atom to become ionized with a positive charge. All laser radiations occur in the extranuclear quantum states; this involves the energy states of the orbital electrons and their transitional behavior within the quantum states.

An atom at ground state, with its orbital electrons revolving in their normal, privileged orbits, possesses the lowest energy. When an atom receives energy from an external source, it becomes excited and the electrons move farther away from the nucleus and revolve in higher quantum levels, or orbits. The process of transition from a lower energy state to a higher energy state is known as *excitation*. The minimum voltage needed to raise a normal atom to an excited state is called the *excitation voltage*. When the atom is intensely excited and one or more of its orbital

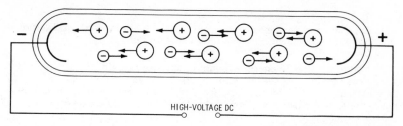

Fig. IV-1. An electron discharge tube containing neon gas with a high voltage applied.

electrons become completely removed from the orbits, it is ionized. This process is called *ionization* because the nucleus then contains the same number of positive charges as the number of electrons removed. The atom then becomes a positive ion, and the electron or electrons that have been disrupted from the quantum orbits become free negative ions. Such a process is ideally produced in an electron discharge tube impressed by a relatively high voltage, as shown in Fig. IV-1.

In Fig. IV-1, when a high voltage is applied across the discharge tube, the orbital electrons move farther from the nucleus. When the electrons are out of the influence of the nuclear electrostatic force, the atoms that have lost electrons become ionized. The positive ions move to the negative electrode, called the cathode, and the electrons move to the positive electrode, called the anode. This process continues as long as the voltage is sustained across the discharge tube. During the operation of the tube, the neon gas in the tube glows with a characteristic red color.

It should now be noted that an excited, or ionized, atom is in an unstable energy state. Such an atom has a strong affinity to regain its original energy state when the applied energy is removed. In order to revert to its normal energy state, the atom must regain this energy by the return of the excited electron to the vacant low-energy quantum level. During this transition, the electron radiates and gives off a photon of energy equal to the energy difference between the quantum position of the excited electron and the orbit to which it returns.

In the case of a neon atom, the radiation occurs with an emission of red light. This is because the frequency ν of the photon energy $h\nu$ happens to be in the visible spectrum at the red wavelength region, which is 6328 angstroms. If the atom were argon, it would have a higher frequency and a shorter wavelength; therefore, the radiation would have a higher energy with a wavelength of about 4800 angstroms. The radiation color would then be confined to the blue region of the spectrum. Thus, the higher the frequency of the photon, the shorter the wavelength; and at high frequencies, the radiation will occur in the blue or ultraviolet region of the spectrum. Conversely, the lower the frequency, the longer the wavelength; and at low frequencies, the radiation will occur in the red or infrared region of the spectrum. The radiations occurring between the two extremes will be in the visible spectral range. An equation expressing this relation may be given as:

$$h\nu = \frac{Ve}{300} = \tfrac{1}{2}mv^2 \text{ ergs} \qquad \text{(Eq. IV-1)}$$

where,

h is Planck's constant (6.625×10^{-27} erg-second),
ν is the frequency of the photon,

V is the voltage applied to the tube in volts,
e is the charge of the electron equal to 4.8×10^{-8} esu (electrostatic unit),
m is the mass of the electron equal to 9.0×10^{-28} gram,
v is the velocity of the electron in cm/sec.

It must be noted that these three equal quantities ($h\nu$, Ve/300, and $\frac{1}{2}mV^2$) in the order given, are the photonic energy, the voltage energy applied to the electron, and the kinetic energy gained by the electron in the discharge tube, or medium. We may now write the photonic energy in terms of its wavelength:

$$h\nu = \frac{hc}{\lambda}$$ (Eq. IV-2)

where,
c is the velocity of light in cm/sec,
λ is the wavelength of the photon in cm.

Now, let us assume that a single neon atom (shown in Fig. IV-2) in an electric field is excited by the collision of electron A from the cathode expelling electron B from the at-rest quantum state 1 (Fig. IV-2A) to quantum state 2 (Fig. IV-2B). As a result of the collision, electron B moves to the higher quantum state, gaining energy equal to or greater than the energy required to move the electron. The quantum state in which electron B is now revolving has a higher energy than the original quantum state.

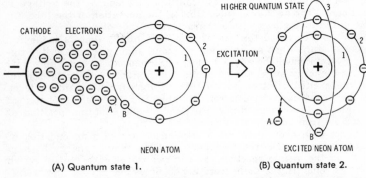

(A) Quantum state 1.   (B) Quantum state 2.

Fig. IV-2. Electron transition from a lower to a higher quantum state.

The neon atom has thus made a transition from a normal state to an excited state. As we know, an atom in an excited state is unstable and must regain its original normal, or at-rest, state. To achieve the normal state, the electron must fall back into the first quantum state to complete the orbit. During a transition from the orbi of a higher quantum state to one of a lower quantum state, the electron radiates, giving off a quantum of light, or a photon. This type of atomic encounter with an electron is known as an *inelastic collision*. However, when the electron collision cannot raise the atom to at least the first excited state, no transfer of energy to the atom occurs and, therefore, no radiation can occur. This type of electron-atom reaction is called *elastic collision*. If an electron of energy Ve/300 collides with another electron in the discharge tube, the second electron in the encounter gains kinetic energy ($\frac{1}{2}mv^2$) from the colliding electron and moves toward the anode, where it is electrostatically attracted. When the second electron reaches the anode, it expends its energy in the form of heat.

GAS LASER GENERATORS

A gas laser generator is constructed like a neon discharge tube, except that the anode and the cathode are usually the ring type instead of the cup type (which encloses the ends of the tube internally). Also, the neon gas is mixed with helium in a proportion as high as 7 to 1, respectively. The helium atoms have long metastable lives and help increase the gain of the laser. For laser emission to occur, the gaseous atoms must be excited to higher quantum states, just as they must be in the neon tube already discussed. However, in addition to excitation (or ionization) of atoms, oscillation of the emitted photons must occur within the discharge tube in order to cause photonic amplification (Fig. IV-3).

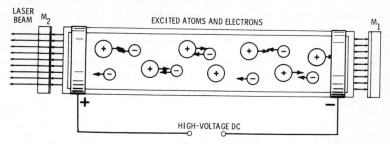

Fig. IV-3. Diagram of a helium-neon laser.

In discussing the mechanism of laser radiation, we shall combine the classical theory with the quantum theory. According to the classical theory, interatomic energy transfer occurs by resonance of the colliding atoms. And in the quantum theory, the radiation is emitted as a result of energy ($h\nu$) transfer. Resonance excitation must occur between the excited atom and the photon during encounter to produce a coherent, homogeneous laser radiation of 6328 angstroms. To achieve this interaction, the discharge tube must have a reflector or mirror at each end. During their travel across the tube, the emitted photons oscillate between the mirrors and collide with excited atoms to stimulate them to photon emission. The result of the collision is a net cumulative photonic energy of high gain and of much greater intensity than the energy in the ordinary neon discharge tube commercially used for decorations and window signs.

As stated earlier, mirrors M_1 and M_2 act as quantum feedback for the stimulated laser emission. To conduct the amplified emission to the exterior of the resonant cavity formed by the discharge medium and the mirrors, one of the mirrors, M_2, is a Fresnel type, partially reflective and partially transmissive; the other mirror, M_1, has a thick mirror coating, making it 100% reflective. The high voltage must be unidirectional to reduce recombination effect which acts to diminish the dominance of excited atoms. Two other harmonic laser emissions of different wavelengths are also produced, but the most dominant wavelength is 6328 angstroms.

SOLID-STATE LASERS

Solid-state lasers are those producing radiation from ruby, neodymium-YAG, neodymium glass, and other synthetic glass rods. These are ion-doped crystalline or glass rods and *do not* include semiconductor diode lasers. All solid-state laser rods are optically pumped, i.e., they receive their excitation energy from the illumination of a high-intensity flashlamp. Therefore, the energy transition is accomplished by the optical coupling of the photons produced from the flashlamp illumination with the ions of the dopes of the host materials, such as aluminum oxide (sapphire), calcium tungstate, lead glass, and other optically suitable materials. The dopant content of these hosts is from 1 to 3%.

The flashlamp consists of a quartz tube containing xenon gas and having stainless steel, aluminum, or cadmium electrodes. The flashlamp should be either helical or linear in configuration and its length should be equal to or slightly greater than the laser rod in order to completely cover the rod. A few turns of high-voltage triggering wire are sometimes looped around the flashlamp to start the electrical discharge. Once the discharge occurs, the high voltage from the power supply sustains the potential across the tube. The flashlamp radiation may be a continuous or a pulsing type. The flashlamp usually starts with a higher voltage and settles down to a sustained lower voltage. This is because the internal resistance of the tube stabilizes after the first discharge. Interelectrode resistance R across the tube is directly proportional to electrical-discharge length L and is inversely proportional to cross-sectional area A of the discharge column. Thus:

$$R \approx \frac{L}{A} \qquad \text{(Eq. IV-3)}$$

In a solid-state laser rod, the ionization occurs in the dopant rather than in the host material. In the ruby, the dopant, or the active element, consists of chromium ions; in the neodymium-YAG, the dopant is the neodymium; and in lanthanate glass, the dopant is lanthanum ions. The flashlamp photons have high energy and are capable of transferring energy to the dopant atom equal to or greater than that required for excitation of the atom, whether chromium or neodymium. After the excitation takes place, the dopant ions behave in the same manner as the gaseous ions in a helium-neon discharge tube. The excited atoms are raised to a higher quantum state after which, with the emission of photons, they spontaneously return to the ground state. When the energy transition from the flashlamp photons to the dopant atoms is not sufficient to raise the atoms to an excited state, no radiation is emitted from the atoms; the energy in transition may dissipate in the form of heat from the laser rod. This type of heat, together with the direct radiated heat from the flashlamp, elevates the temperature of the laser rod. The increase in temperature causes loss in efficiency of emission. Therefore, the laser rod has to be cooled by circulation of air or by circulation of pure deionized water for high-power laser generators.

Most of this heat is concentrated in the central axis of a circular rod where it acts as multiple lenses, decreasing the intensity of the radiation that reaches the exterior of the rod. For this reason, the author has tried cylindrical laser rods with a central bore and found that the thermal stresses within the rod are alleviated and that cracking is thus prevented. Of course, the resultant laser beam is tubular. However, for practical purposes, this configuration does not seem to have any influence on the ultimate incident laser energy on the workpiece. The author has also used two flat-sided quadrangular bars cemented together. The cement behaves as a reflector of heat from the flashlamp. Both of these two methods will reduce the thermal effect of a flashlamp and a laser rod, and both will retain the normal efficiency of the rod for intermittent pulsing without an external cooling means.

It should now be easy to understand why a laser beam is said to be spatially coherent; that is, any two selected photonic waves describing a harmonic, unidirectional motion in the resonant cavity are of the same phase, frequency, amplitude, and direction. This is because the lasing photons are produced by equal-energy photons. And since any increase or decrease of this energy transition will correspondingly increase or decrease the frequency and, hence, photon energy $h\nu$, the resulting radiation will be of different wavelengths. Such a radiation wave lacks the capability of being in phase and thereby ceases to be coherent. While perfect coherence has not yet been obtained, laser radiation is closest to perfection. When waves of equal frequency and amplitude are not in phase, an interference phenomenon takes place in which the waves cancel each other; no photonic light is produced and darkness occurs. In an interferometer these will occur as dark lines, which are of special interest in the spectrographic analysis of various metals or nonmetals.

SEMICONDUCTOR LASERS

A semiconductor laser is a diode having a pn junction that is utilized as an electronic discharge tube. The most common of the semiconductor diode lasers is the gallium-arsenide laser, which radiates in the infrared spectrum at 8500 angstroms. The MIT Lincoln Laboratory has developed a PbSnTe heterojunction laser by using a low-temperature vacuum-deposition technique to deposit an n-type PbTe film on a p-type PbSnTe substrate. The diode has a low-threshold current density and operates in the pulsed mode. It emits at 10.6 microns when cooled to 4.2 K and emits at 8.9 microns when the temperature is increased to 77 K.

There are other semiconductor diodes that emit electroluminescence, but they are not lasers. Such diodes are indium arsenide luminescing at 3500 angstroms, gallium antimonide at 16,000 angstroms, indium antimonide at 5200 angstroms, etc. Our interest is particularly centered on the behavior of the gallium-arsenide laser and its characteristics.

As in semiconductor rectifying diodes, the preparation of gallium arsenide consists of cleaving a semiconductor wafer, depositing a p-type active material on the surface of one wafer and an n-type active material on the surface of the other, and then positioning the two active surfaces with a tiny gap between them so that a pn junction is formed. When a current is sent through this junction, the wafer emits a laser radiation with a power varying from several watts to several-hundred watts per square centimeter. In terms of joules, its energy is equivalent to less than a millijoule per diode. The diode operates at rates as high as 1000 pulses per second.

The current flow in a semiconductor diode is from the n-type active layers to the p-type active layer. The n-type layer consists of electron donors and the p-type consists of electron acceptors. The p-type layer has the electron acceptor because it contains holes that are positively charged entities. As in a gaseous discharge, the semiconductor atom must receive an energy equal to its threshold before an electron is discharged from it, and above this threshold the material will radiate. This threshold current is about 100 milliamperes at room temperature. A current below the threshold will cause the diode to radiate with an incoherent light. For example, the p-type material has a hole concentration of 10^{19} holes per cubic centimeter, and the n-type material has a carrier concentration of

10^{18} carriers per cubic centimeter. When the surfaces of the two active layers are placed together, the gap between them is a fraction of a micron. A typical diode has a length of about 10 mils, a width of 5 mils, a height of 4 mils, and a pn junction of less than 1 micron. The external surfaces of the diode wafers are plated or electrodeposited with a metallic layer, such as gold over nickel, and the anode and cathode leads are connected to this deposit.

The p- and n-type materials are prepared as follows: the p-type layer is a mixture of about 8 grams of gallium metal, 1.8 grams of gallium arsenide, and 0.5 gram of zinc metal. All three materials are heated to form a molten state at about 930°C. This mixture is deposited on the semiconductor wafer to a thickness of 4 mils. The n-type material is a mixture of 8 grams of gallium metal, 1.2 grams of gallium arsenide, and 0.004 gram of tellurium. This mixture is heated to about 900°C to mix the molten materials together. The mixture is then epitaxially grown on the wafer to the same thickness as the p-type layer and is placed against the n-type surface so that a pn junction is sandwiched between them, the p-doped side acting as the positive electrode and the n-doped side acting as the negative electrode.

When the current flow is in the forward direction, an emission of photons occurs through the pn junction. As compared to incoherent visible light, a diode laser is less efficient in photon production. But, as compared to other laser materials, the diode laser is much more efficient. Its efficiency can be determined by measuring the number of photons produced at the pn junction and dividing the result by the number of electrons that pass the junction. For example, the number of photons, N_q (number of quanta), may be given as:

$$N_q = \frac{P_t}{hc/\lambda}$$ (Eq. IV-4)

where,
P_t is the total power emitted,
h is Planck's constant,
c is the velocity of light,
λ is the wavelength of the photon.

The number of electrons (N_e) that pass the pn junction per second may be given as:

$$N_e = \frac{I}{e}$$ (Eq. IV-5)

where,
N_e is the number of electrons crossing the pn junction,
I is the current in amperes,
e is the charge of the electron equal to 4.8×10^{-10} esu (electrostatic units).

The external quantum efficiency (U) of the diode will be the ratio of the number of photons produced to the number of electrons that have passed the pn junction. Thus:

$$U = \frac{N_q}{N_e} = \frac{P_t \times e \times \lambda}{hc \times I}$$

$$= \frac{P_t e \lambda}{hcI}$$ (Eq. IV-6)

where,
U is the external efficiency of the quantum emission at the junction.

As discussed earlier, some of the applications of semiconductor diodes are range finders, communication systems, repeaters, night telescopes, fire detectors, burglar-alarm devices, pollution detectors, laser illuminators, laser rifles for training soldiers in the field, and credit-card readers.

LIQUID OR DYE LASERS

Liquid or dye lasers are of great interest to scientists for several reasons. One is their potential applicability in physics, biomedicine, and chemistry. Another reason is that dye lasers are tunable from ultraviolet to the visible spectrum with wavelengths in the range of 2500 to 6500 angstroms. This means that a single dye-laser system can accomplish the work of several solid-state lasers operating at low energy levels. Dye lasers can be produced diffraction limited and optically pumped by an argon laser, a nitrogen laser, or a neodymium-YAG laser. The dyes are organic materials, such as xanthene, oxazine, rhodamine B, fluorescein, rhodamine 6G, pyronine B and Y, and others. The output of the dye laser can be frequency-doubled by using crystals of ammonium dihydrogen phosphate (ADP), potassium dihydrogen phosphate (KDP), lithium niobate ($LiNbO_3$), etc. Since the output can be frequency-doubled, the laser can be operated at the ultraviolet range, which is especially useful in biomedical work. It is reported that Dr. S .E. Harris of Stanford University has tripled the frequency of 10.6-nm Nd-YAG and 6943-angstrom ruby laser radiations in mixtures of xenon gas with lithium or sodium vapor. The laser-emission mechanism of these materials is similar to that of gas or solid-state radiation materials.

Although liquid or dye lasers do not have the power necessary to weld, cut, drill, and scribe materials, they nevertheless have many other applications. Some of their more important applications are: optical pumping of atoms and molecules, spectroscopic studies, photoconductivity studies, selective excitation of chemical bonds, excitation of vibrational and rotational transitions in physics studies, holographic data storage, television primary colors, initiators of chemical reactions, dissociation of chemical bonds, ultraviolet sources for the medical treatment of dermal diseases, and optical communication.

As stated earlier, our discussion in this book is confined primarily to solid-state, semiconductor, and gas lasers because of their importance in industrial, medical, dental, and military applications. The reader may refer to many excellent books written on the subject of liquid dyes and lasers. This section is intended only to acquaint the reader with various usable properties of dye lasers and to give him an appreciation of the many applications of dye lasers in scientific and educational endeavors.

Index